THE
CLASSIC
1000
BABY NAMES

THE CLASSIC 1000 BABY NAMES

foulsham

LONDON · NEW YORK · TORONTO · CAPE TOWN · SYDNEY

foulsham

Yeovil Road, Slough, Berkshire SL1 4JH

ISBN 0–572–01838–X

Copyright © 1993 W. Foulsham & Co. Ltd.

Printed in Slovakia.

Girls

Abbey See **Abigail**

Aberah See **Avera**

Abigail [Hebrew]
'Father rejoiced'. Also the
18th century name for a
maidservant.
*(Ab, Abbey, Abbie, Abby,
Gael, Gail, Gale, Gayl)*

Abra [Hebrew]
'Mother of multitudes'.

Acacia [Greek]
The symbol of
immortality and
resurrection.

Acantha [Greek]
'Thorny'.

Ada [Teutonic]
'Prosperous and joyful'.
A popular name in
Victorian times.
*(Adda, Addie, Addy, Aida,
Eda)*

Adabela See **Adabelle**

Adabelle [Combination
Ada/Belle]
'Joyous and beautiful'.
(Adabel, Adabela, Adabella)

Adah [Hebrew]
'The crown's
adornment'. One who
gives added lustre to the
most eminent position.

Adalia [Teutonic]
An early Saxon tribal
name, the origin of which
is not known.

Adaline See **Adelaide**

Adamina [Latin]
'From the red earth'.
Fem. of Adam.
(Addie, Addy, Mina)

Adar [Hebrew]
'Fire'. Name sometimes
given to Jewish daughters
born in the sixth month of
the Jewish year which is
known by the same name.

Adara [Greek]
'Beauty'.

Addie See **Adamina**

Adela See **Adelaide**

Adelaide [Teutonic]
'Noble and kind'. A
gracious lady of noble
birth. A name popular in
Britain in the early 19th
century, in compliment to
Queen Adelaide of Saxe
Meiningen, Consort to
King William IV.
*(Adaline, Adela, Adele,
Adelia, Adelina, Adelind,
Adeline, Adila, Dela, Della,
Edeline, Edelina)*

Adele See **Adelaide**

Adelia See **Adelaide**

Adelina See **Adelaide**

Adelind See **Adelaide**

Adeline See **Adelaide**

Adelphia [Greek]
'Sisterly'. The eternal
friend and sister to
mankind.
(Adelfia, Adelpha)

Aderyn [Welsh]
'Bird'.

Adina [Hebrew]
'Voluptuous'. One of
ripe, mature charm.
(Adena)

Adolfina See **Adolpha**

Adolpha [Teutonic]
'The noble she-wolf'
Fem. of Adolf. The noble
matriarch who will
sacrifice everything,
including life, for her
young.
*(Adolfa, Adolfina,
Adolphina)*

Adonia [Greek]
'Beautiful goddess of the
resurrection'. The eternal
renewal of youth.

Adora [Latin]
'Adored and beloved gift'

Adorabella [Combination
Adora/Bella]
'Beautiful gift'.

Adorna [Latin]
'Adorned with jewels'.

Adria See **Adrienne**

Adriana See **Adrienne**

Adrienne [Latin]
'Dark lady from the sea'.
Fem. of Adrian. A dark,
mysterious lady.
*(Adria, Adriana, Adriane,
Adrianna, Adrianne,
Hadria)*

Aelda See **Aldora**

Aeldra See **Aldora**

Aerona [Welsh]
'Like a berry'.
(Aeronwen)

Aeronwen See **Aerona**

Africa [Celtic]
'Pleasant'. Twelfth-
century queen of the Isle
of Man.
*(Afrika, Africah, Afrikah,
Affrica)*

Afton [Old English]
'One from Afton'.

Agata See **Agatha**

Agatha [Greek]
'Good'. One of
impeccable virtue.
*(Ag, Agata, Agathe, Agathy,
Aggie, Aggy)*

Agathe See **Agatha**

Agathy See **Agatha**

Agave [Greek]
'Illustrious and noble'.

Aggie See **Agatha**

Aglaia [Greek]
'Splendour'.

Agna See **Agnes**

Agnella See **Agnes**

Agnes [Greek]
'Pure, chaste, lamblike'.
The untouchable virgin.
*(Aggie, Agna, Agnella,
Annais, Annis, Ines, Inez,
Nessa, Nessie, Nessi, Nesta,
Neysa, Ina, Ynes, Ynez)*

Ahuda [Hebrew]
'Praise; sympathetic'.

Aidan [Gaelic]
'Little fire'. A girl with
bright red hair.

Aiden See **Edana**

Aileen [Greek]
A derivative of 'Helen',
q.v.
*(Aleen, Alene, Aline, Eileen,
Elene, Ilene, Iline, Illene,
Illona, Illeana, Ilona, Isleen)*

Ailsa [Old German]
'Girl of cheer'.
(Aillsa, Ailssa, Ilsa)

Ainsley [Gaelic]
'From one's own
meadow'.

Aisha [African]
'Life'.
(Asha, Ashia, Asia)

Aisleen [Gaelic]
'The vision'.

Akili [Tanzanian]
'Wisdom'.
(Akela, Akeyla, Akeylah)

Alain See **Alana**

Alameda [Spanish]
'Poplar tree'.

Alana [Celtic]
'Bright, fair one'. A term
of endearment used by
the Irish.
*(Alain, Alanna, Alayne,
Alina, Allene, Allyn, Lana,
Lane)*

Alarica See **Alarice**

Alarice [Teutonic]
'Ruler of all'. Fem. of
Alaric.
(Alarica, Alarise)

Alberta [Teutonic]
'Noble and brilliant'.
Fem. of Albert. A nobly
born and highly
intelligent girl. Popular
name in Victorian times
in compliment to the

Prince Consort.
*(Albertina, Albertine, Allie,
Berta, Berte, Bertie, Elberta,
Elbertine)*

Albertina See **Alberta**

Albertine See **Alberta**

Albina [Latin]
'White Lady'. One whose
hair and colouring is of
the very fairest.
*(Albinia, Alvina, Aubina,
Aubine)*

Albinia See **Elvira**

Alcina [Greek]
'Strong minded one'. The
legendary Grecian lady
who could produce gold
from stardust; one who
knows her own mind.
(Alciana, Alcinette)

Alcinette See **Alcina**

Alda [Teutonic]
'Wise and rich'.
(Eada, Elda)

Aldora [Anglo-Saxon]
'Of noble rank'.
(Aelda, Aeldra)

Aleria [Latin]
'Eagle like'.

Aleta See **Alida**

Aletha See **Alice**

Alethea See **Alice**

Alexa See **Alexandra**

Alexandra [Greek]
'The helper of mankind'.
Popular name in early
20th century in
compliment to Queen
Alexandra.
*(Alex, Alexa, Alexine,
Alexis, Alix, Lexie, Lexine,
Sandy, Sandra, Zandra)*

Alexine See **Alexandra**

Alexis See **Alexandra**

Alfie See **Alfreda**

Alfonsine [Teutonic]
'Noble and ready'. Fem.
of Alphonse.
*(Alphonsina, Alphonsine,
Alonza)*

Alfreda [Teutonic]
'Wise Counsellor'. Fem.
of Alfred. A name
popular in Anglo-Saxon
times, but one which died
out after the conquest.
(Alfie, Allie, Elfreda,

Elfreida, Elfrieda, Elfrida,
Elva, Elga, Freda)

Alice [Greek]
'Truth'. A name
popularised in the mid
19th century, when it was
much used by the Royal
Family.
(Alicia, Alicea, Aletha,
Alethea, Aliss, Alithia,
Allys, Alyce, Alys, Alisa,
Alissa, Allis, Aleece, Alla,
Allie, Ally, Elissa, Elisa,
Elke)

Alicia See **Alice**

Alida [Latin]
'Little winged one'. A girl
who is as small and lithe
as the woodlark.
(Aleda, Aleta, Alita, Leda,
Lita)

Alima [Arabic]
'Learned in music and
dancing'.

Alina See **Alana**

Alison [Combination
Alice/Louise]
'Truthful warrior maid'.
(Alie, Allie, Allison, Allson,
Lissie, Lisy)

Aliss See **Alice**

Alix See **Alexandra**

Alla See **Alice**

Allegra [Latin]
'Cheerful'. As blithe as a
bird.

Allson See **Allison**

Alma [Latin]
'Cherishing spirit'. Name
popularly given to girls
after the battle of Alma,
in the Crimean War.

Almeda [Latin]
'Pressing toward the
goal'.

Almira [Arabic]
(Elma)
'Truth without question'.
(Almeira, Almeria, Elmira)

Aloha [Hawaiian]
'Greetings'. A romantic
name from the Hawaiian
Islands.

Aloisa See **Louise**

Alonza See **Alphonsine**

Alpha [Greek]
'First one'. A suitable

name for the first baby, if she is a girl.

Alphonsina See **Alfonsine**

Alta [Latin]
'Tall in spirit'.

Althea [Greek]
'The healer'.
(Aletha, Alethea, Altheta, Althee, Thea)

Althee See **Althea**

Altheta See **Althea**

Alula [Latin/Arabic]
'Winged one' (Latin).
'The first' (Arabic).
(Alloula, Allula, Aloula)

Alura [Anglo-Saxon]
'Divine Counsellor'.

Alva [Latin]
'White Lady'.

Alvina [Teutonic]
'Beloved and noble friend'.
(Alvine, Vina)

Alvina See **Albina**

Alvine See **Alvina**

Alyssa [Greek]
'Sane one'. The small white flower Alyssum derives from this name.

Alzena [Arabic]
'The woman'. The embodiment of all feminine charm and virtue.

Ama [African]
'Born on Saturday'.

Amabel [Latin]
'Sweet, lovable one'. A tender, loving, loyal daughter.
(Amabella, Amabelle)

Amabella See **Amabel**

Amadea [Latin]
'The beloved of God'.

Amalie See **Amelia**

Amanda [Latin]
'Worthy of being loved'.
(Manda, Mandie, Mandy)

Amarantha [Greek]
'Unfading'.

Amaris [Hebrew]
'God has promised'.

Amaryllis [Greek]
'Fresh, new'.
(Amarillis, Marilla)

Amber [Arabic]
'Jewel'. This name had a
surge of popularity in
America and Britain in
the 1940's, following the
publication of the novel
Forever Amber.

Ambrosia See **Ambrosine**

Ambrosina See
Ambrosine

Ambrosine [Greek]
'Divine, immortal one'.
Fem. of Ambrose.
(Ambrosia, Ambrosina)

Amelia [Teutonic]
'Industrious and
striving'.
*(Amalia, Amalie, Amealia,
Amelea, Ameline, Amelita,
Amelie, Emelina, Emeline,
Emilia, Emily, Emmeline,
Emelie, Mell, Mellie,
Milicia, Mill, Millie)*

Amelinda [Spanish]
'Beloved and pretty'.
(Amalinda, Amelinde)

Amelinde See **Amelinda**

Ameline See **Amelia**

Amelita See **Amelia**

Amena [Celtic]
'Honest'. One of
incorruptible truth.
(Amina, Amine)

Amethyst [Greek]
The name of the semi-
precious stone which has
(it is alleged) the power
to ward off intoxication.

Amine See **Amena**

Aminta [Greek]
'Protector'. The name of
a shepherdess in Greek
mythology.
(Amintha, Aminthe)

Amintha See **Aminta**

Amity [Old French]
'Friendship'.

Amorette [Latin]
'Darling'.
(Amarette, Morette)

Amy [French]
'Beloved friend'.
(Aim-ee, Ami, Amie)

Ana See **Anastasia**

Anastasia [Greek]
'She who will rise again'.
The very apt name of the
Grand Duchess who was
officially killed during the
Russian revolution, but
who was alleged to be still
living until a few years
ago.
*(Ana, Anstice, Stacey,
Stacia, Stacie, Stacy)*

Anatola [Greek]
'Woman of the East'.
Fem. of Anatole.
(Anatolia, Anatholia)

Anatolia See **Anatola**

Ancelin [Latin]
'Fairest handmaid'.
(Celine)

Anchoret [Welsh]
'Much loved'.

Andre See **Andrea**

Andrea [Latin]
'Womanly'. The epitome
of feminine charm and
beauty.
*(Andreana, Aindrea, Andria,
Andriana, Andre, Andree)*

Andrea See **Edrea**

Andreana See **Andrea**

Aneira [Welsh]
'Honourable'.

Anemone [Greek]
'Windflower'. The
nymph of Greek
mythology who, when
pursued by the wind,
turned into the flower,
anemone.

Angela [Greek]
'Heavenly messenger'.
The bringer of good
tidings.
*(Angelina, Angeline,
Angelita, Angel, Angie)*

Angelica [Latin]
'Angelic one'. A name
often used by Medieval
writers to typify the
perfect woman.
(Angelique)

Angharad [Welsh]
'Free from shame'

Angwen [Welsh]
'Very handsome'.

Anita [Hebrew]
'Grace'. A form of Anne,
q.v. (for continuity).
(Anitra)

Anna See **Anne**

Annabelle [Combination
Anna/Belle]
*(Annabel, Anabel,
Annabella, Annie, Annabla,
Belle, Bella)*

Annais See **Agnes**

Anne [Hebrew]
'Full of Grace'. One of
the most popular
feminine names. The
name of several British
Queens Consort and a
Queen Regnant.
*(Ann, Anna, Annetta,
Annette, Annie, Annika,
Annora, Anita, Ana, Nan,
Nana, Nanna, Nancy,
Nanette, Nanetta, Nanete,
Nanine, Nanon, Nina,
Ninette, Ninon, Hannah,
Hanna)*

Annetta See **Anne**

Annette See **Anne**

Annika See **Anne**

Annis See **Agnes**

Annora See **Anne**

Annunciata [Latin]
'Bearer of news'. A
suitable name for a girl
born in March,
particularly 24th March,
as it derives from the
'Annunciation' — the
announcement of the
Virgin's conception.

Annunciata See **Nunciata**

Anona [Latin]
'Yearly crops'. The
Roman Goddess of the
Crops.
(Annona, Nonnie, Nona)

Anora [English]
'Light and graceful'.

Anselma [Norse]
'Divinely protected'.
(Anselme, Selma, Zelma)

Anselme See **Anselma**

Anstice See **Anastasia**

Anthea [Greek]
'Flowerlike'. One of
delicate, fragile beauty.
*(Anthia, Bluma, Thea,
Thia)*

Antoinette See **Antonia**

Antoinietta See **Antonia**

Antoni See **Antonia**

Antonia [Latin]
'Beyond price, excellent'.
Fem. of Anthony. A jewel
beyond compare.
*(Anthonia, Antoinette,
Antoni, Antonina,
Antoinietta, Antonietta,
Toinette, Toni, Netta, Nettie,
Netty)*

Antonina See **Antonia**

Anya [Hebrew]
'Grace; mercy'.
(Annia)

Aphra [Hebrew]
'Female deer'.
(Afra)

Appoline [Greek]
'Sun'.
(Apollene)

April [Latin]
'The beginning of
Spring'. The name of the
first month of the Roman
calendar and the fourth
month of the Julian
Calendar.

Ara [Greek]
'Spirit of revenge'. The
Grecian Goddess of
vengeance and
destruction.

Arabella [Latin]
'Beautiful altar'.
*(Arabelle, Arabela, Aralia,
Arbelie, Arbelia, Arbel, Bel,
Bella, Belle)*

Arabelle See **Arabella**

Aralia See **Arabella**

Aramanta [Hebrew]
'Elegant lady'.
(Araminta, Aramenta)

Aramenta See **Aramanta**

Araminta [Greek]
'Beautiful, sweet smelling
flower'.

Araminta See **Aramanta**

Arbel See **Arabella**

Arbelia See **Arabella**

Arbelie See **Arabella**

Arda See **Ardelle**

Ardath [Hebrew]
'Field of flowers'.
(Aridatha, Ardatha)

Ardatha See **Ardath**

Ardelis See **Ardelle**

Ardella See **Ardelle**

Ardelle [Latin]
'Enthusiasm, warmth'.
*(Arda, Ardella, Ardere,
Ardis, Ardine, Ardene,
Ardeen, Ardella, Ardelis,
Ardra)*

Arden [Old English]
'Eagle valley'.

Ardere See **Ardelle**

Ardine See **Ardelle**

Ardis See **Ardelle**

Ardra See **Ardelle**

Areta [Greek]
'Of excellent virtue'.
One of untarnished
reputation.
*(Arete, Aretha, Aretta,
Arette)*

Arete See **Areta**

Aretha See **Areta**

Aretta See **Areta**

Argenta [Latin]
'Silvery one'.
(Argentia, Argente)

Argente See **Argenta**

Argentia See **Argenta**

Aria [Latin]
'Beautiful melody'.

Ariadna See **Ariadne**

Ariadne [Greek]
'Holy one'. The
mythological maiden who
rescued Theseus from his
labyrinth.
(Arlana, Ariane, Ariadna)

Ariane See **Ariadne**

Aridatha See **Ardath**

Ariel See **Ariella**

Ariella [Hebrew]
'God's lioness'.
(Ariel, Ariella, Arielle)

Arlana See **Ariadne**

Arleas See **Arlene**

Arlen See **Arlene**

Arlena See **Arlene**

Arlene [Celtic]
'A pledge'.
*(Airleas, Arlana, Arleen,
Arlen, Arlena, Arlette,
Arletta, Arlina, Arline,
Arlyne, Herleva)*

Arletta See **Arlene**

Arlette See **Arlene**

Armida [Latin]
'Small warrior'.

Armilla [Latin]
'Bracelet'.

Armina [Teutonic]
'Warrior maid'.
*(Armine, Arminia, Erminie,
Erminia)*

Armine See **Armina**

Arminia See **Armina**

Arnalda [Teutonic]
'Eagle-like ruler'. Fem. of
Arnold.

Arselma [Norse]
'Divine protective
helmet'.

Arva [Latin]
'Pastureland, seashore'.

Ashley [Old English]
'From the ash tree
meadow'.

Aspasia [Greek]
'Welcome'.

Asphodel [Greek]
The wild lily of Greece.

Assunta [Italian]
'From the Assumption
(of Mary)'.

Asta [Greek]
'Starlike'.
(Astra)

Astra See **Asta**

Astrid [Norse]
'Divine strength'.
(Astra)

Atalanta [Greek]
'Might bearer'. The
legendary Greek
huntress.
(Atlanta, Atalante)

Atalante See **Atalanta**

Atalia See **Athalia**

Atalya [Spanish]
'Guardian'. One who
protects hearth and
home.

Athalia [Hebrew]
'God is exalted'.
*(Atalia, Athalea, Athalie,
Athie, Attie)*

Athalie See **Athalia**

Athena [Greek]
The Greek Goddess.
(Athene, Athenee)

Athene See **Athena**

Athenee See **Athena**

Athie See **Athalia**

Attie See **Athalia**

Aubina See **Albina**

Aubine See **Albina**

Audie See **Audrey**

Audrey [Anglo-Saxon]
'Strong and noble'.
Derives from the Anglo-
Saxon Aethelthryth.
(Audrie, Audry, Audie, Dee)

Augusta [Latin]
'Sacred and majestic'.
Popular name in Royal
and Noble families in
18th and early 19th
century.
(Auguste, Augustina,

*Augustine, Austine, Gussie,
Gusta, Tina)*

Auguste See **Augusta**

Augustina See **Augusta**

Augustine See **Augusta**

Aura [Latin]
'Gentle breeze'. A name
said to endow its owner
with gentility.
(Aure, Aurea, Auria)

Aura See **Aurelia**

Aurea See **Aurelia**

Aurel See **Aurelia**

Aurelia [Latin]
'Golden'. The girl of the
dawn.
*(Aura, Aurea, Auristela,
Aurora, Aurelie, Aurel,
Aurie, Ora, Oralia, Oralie,
Oriel, Oriole)*

Aurie See **Aurelia**

Auristela See **Aurelia**

Aurora See **Aurelia**

Aurore See **Aurora**

Ava See **Avis**

Aveline See **Hazel**

Avena [Latin]
'Oatfield'. A girl with
rich, golden hair.
(Avene)

Avene See **Avena**

Avenida [Chilean]
'An avenue'.

Avera [Hebrew]
'Transgressor'.
(Aberah)

Averil [Old English]
'Slayer of the Boar'.
(Avril, Averyl, Avyril)

Avery [Old French]
'To confirm'.
(Averi)

Avi See **Avis**

Avice [French]
'Warlike'.
(Avisa, Hadwisa)

Avicia [German]
'Refuge in war'.

Avis [Latin]
'A bird'.
(Ava, Avi)

Avisa See **Avice**

Avishag [Hebrew]
'Father's delight'.

Avital [Hebrew]
'God protects'.

Aviva [Hebrew]
'Springtime'.

Awena [Welsh]
'Poetry; prophecy'.

Aylwen [Welsh]
'Fair brow'.

Azalee See **Azaliea**

Azaliea [Latin]
'Dry earth'. From the
flower of the same name.
(Azalia, Azalee)

Azaria [Hebrew]
'Blessed by God'.
(Azeria, Zaria)

Azura [French]
'The blue sky'. One
whose eyes are sky blue.

Aaron [Hebrew]
'Exalted'. The brother of
Moses. *(Aron, Haroun)*

Abbe See **Abbott**

Abbott [Anglo-Saxon]
'Father of the abbey'.
(Abbot, Abott, Abbe)

Abdiel [Hebrew]
'Servant of God'.

Abdul [Arabic]
'Son of'.

Abe See **Abraham**

Abel [Hebrew]
'Breath'. The first
recorded murder victim.

Abelard [Teutonic]
'Nobly resolute'.

Abner [Hebrew]
'Father of light'.

Abraham [Hebrew]
'Father of multitudes'.
The original patriarch.
*(Abram, Abe, Abie, Bram,
Ibrahim)*

Abram See **Abraham**

Absalom [Hebrew]
'Father of peace'.
(Absolom)

Ace [Latin]
'Unity'.
(Acey)

Acey See **Ace**

Achilles [Greek]
'Swift'.

Ackerley [Anglo-Saxon]
'From the acre meadow'.

Ackley [Anglo-Saxon]
'From the oak tree
meadow'.

Adair [Gaelic]
'From the oak tree near
the ford'.

Adalard [Teutonic]
'Noble and brave'.
(Adelard, Adhelard)

Adalwine See **Audwin**

Adam [Hebrew]
'Of the red earth'. The
first man, according to
the Bible.

Adan See **Adin**

Adar [Hebrew]
'Fiery'.

Addison [Anglo-Saxon]
'Adam's son'.

Adelbert See **Albert**

Adelpho [Greek]
'Brother'.

Adin [Hebrew]
'Sensual'.
(Adan)

Adlai [Hebrew]
'My witness, my
ornament'.

Adler [Teutonic]
'Eagle'. One of keen
perception.

Adley [Hebrew]
'The fair-minded'.

Adney [Anglo-Saxon]
'Dweller on the island'.

Adolph [Teutonic]
'Noble wolf'.
*(Adolphe, Adolphus, Adolf,
Adolfus, Ad, Dolf, Dolph)*

Adolphe See **Adolph**

Adolphus See **Adolph**

Adon [Hebrew]
'Lord'. The sacred
Hebrew word for God.

Adrian [Latin]
'Dark one' or 'Man from
the sea'.
(Adrien, Hadrian)

Adriel [Hebrew]
'From God's
congregation'.

Aelhaearn [Welsh]
'Iron brow'.

Aeneas [Greek]
'The much praised one'.
The defender of Troy.
(Eneas)

Aethelard See **Allard**

Agamemnon [Greek]
'Resolute'.

Agilard [Teutonic]
'Formidably bright'.

Aherin See **Ahern**

Ahern [Gaelic]
'Horse lord' or 'Horse
owner'.
*(Aherne, Aherin, Ahearn,
Hearne, Hearn)*

Ahmed [Arabic]
'Most highly praised'.

Ahren [Teutonic]
'The Eagle'.

Aidan [Gaelic]
'Little fiery one'.
(Adan, Eden)

Aiken [Anglo-Saxon]
'Little Adam'.
(Aikin, Aickin)

Ailean See **Alan**

Ainsley [Anglo-Saxon]
'Meadow of the
respected one'.

Airleas See **Arlen**

Ajax [Greek]
'Eagle'.

Alabhaois See **Aloysius**

Aladdin [Arabic]
'Servant of Allah'.

Alair [Gaelic]
'Cheerful'.

Alan [Gaelic]
'Cheerful harmony'.
*(Alain, Allan, Allen, Allyn,
Aland, Ailean, Ailin)*

Aland See **Alan**

Alard [German]
'Noble ruler'.

Alaric [Teutonic]
'Ruler of all'.
*(Alarick, Ulric, Ulrich,
Ulrick, Rich, Richie, Ricy,
Rick, Rickie, Ricky)*

Alastair See **Alexander**

Alban [Latin]
'White complexion'. A
man of outstandingly fair
colouring.
(Alben, Albin, Aubin, Alva)

Albern [Anglo-Saxon]
'Noble warrior'.

Albert [Teutonic]
'Noble and illustrious'.
Name which became
popular in Britain after
the marriage of Queen
Victoria to Prince Albert
of Saxe-Coborg-Gotha.

*(Aldabert, Adelbert, Delbert,
Elbert, Ailbert, Aubert)*

Albin See **Alban**

Alcott [Anglo-Saxon]
'Dweller at the old
cottage'.

Aldabert See **Albert**

Alden [Anglo-Saxon]
'Old, wise friend'. One on
whom friends could rely.
*(Aldin, Aldwin, Aldwyn,
Elden, Eldin)*

Alder [Anglo-Saxon]
'At the alder-tree'.

Aldin See **Alden**

Aldis [Anglo-Saxon]
'From the old house'.
(Aldous, Aldus)

Aldo [Teutonic]
'Old, wise and rich'.

Aldrich [Anglo-Saxon]
'Old, wise ruler'.
(Alric, Eldrich, Eldric)

Aldus See **Aldis**

Aldwin See **Alden**, **Alvin**
or **Audwin**

Aleron [Latin]
'The eagle'.

Alexander [Greek]
'Helper and protector of
mankind'.
*(Alastair, Allister, Alec,
Alex, Aleck, Alexis, Alick,
Alsandair, Alister, Alasdair,
Sandie, Sandy, Sander,
Saunders, Sasha)*

Alexis See **Alexander**

Alf See **Alfred**

Alfie See **Alfred**

Alfonso See **Alphonse**

Alford [Anglo-Saxon]
'The old ford'.

Alfred [Anglo-Saxon]
'The wise counsel of the
elf'.
*(Aelfred, Ailfrid, Alf, Alfie,
Alfy, Al)*

Alger [Teutonic]
'Noble spearman'.
(Algar)

Algernon [French]
'The whiskered one'. The
man with a moustache or
beard.
(Al, Algie, Algy)

Algie See **Algernon**

Ali [Arabic]
'Greatest'.

Alison [Anglo-Saxon]
'Son of a nobleman', or
'Alice's son'.
(Allison, Al, Allie)

Allan/Allen See **Alan**

Allard [Anglo-Saxon]
'Noble and brave'.
*(Alard, Aethelard,
Aethelhard, Athelhard,
Ethelard)*

Allister See **Alexander**

Almo [Anglo-Saxon]
'Noble and famous'.

Alonso See **Alphonso**

Alonzo See **Alphonso**

Aloys See **Aloysius**

Aloysius [Latin]
'Famous warrior'.
*(Aloys, Lewis, Louis,
Ludwig, Alabhaois)*

Alpheus [Greek]
'God of the river'.

Alphonse See **Alphonso**

Alphonso [Teutonic]
'Noble and ready'.
*(Alfonso, Alphonse, Alfonse,
Alphonsus, Alonso, Alonzo)*

Alphonsus See **Alphonso**

Alpin [Early Scottish]
'Blond one'. Name borne
by the descendants of the
earliest Scottish Clan —
McAlpin.

Alric See **Aldrich**

Alric See **Ulric**

Alroy [Gaelic]
'Red-haired boy'.

Alsandair See **Alexander**

Alston [Anglo-Saxon]
'From the old village'.

Altman [Teutonic]
'Old, wise man'.

Alton [Anglo-Saxon]
'Dweller in the old town'.

Alva See **Alban**

Alvah [Hebrew]
'The exalted one'.
(Alvar)

Alvan See **Alvin**

Alvin [Teutonic]
'Friend of all' or 'Noble
friend'.
*(Alwin, Aldwin, Alwyn,
Alvan)*

Alwin See **Alvin**

Amadeo [Spanish]
'Beloved of God'.

Amandus [Latin]
'Worthy of love'.

Amasa [Hebrew]
'Burden bearer'.

Ambert [Teutonic]
'Shining, bright light'.

Ambler [English]
'Stable-keeper'.

Ambros See **Ambrose**

Ambrose [Latin]
'Belonging to the divine
immortals'.
*(Ambrosius, Ambroise,
Ambros, Emrys)*

Ambrosius See **Ambrose**

Amerigo See **Emery**

Amery See **Amory**

Amhlaoibh See **Olaf**

Amirov [Hebrew]
'My people are great'.

Ammon [Egyptian]
'The hidden'.

Amnon [Hebrew]
'Faithful'.

Amon [Hebrew]
'Trustworthy'.

Amory [Teutonic]
'Famous ruler'.
(Amery)

Amos [Hebrew]
'A burden'. One used to
tackling difficult
problems.

Amund [Scandinavian]
'Divine protection'.

Ananias [Hebrew]
'Grace of the Lord'.

Anarawd [Welsh]
'Eloquent'.

Anastasius [Greek]
'One who shall rise
again'.

Anatole [Greek]
'From the East'.
(Anatol)

Ancel [German]
'Godlike'.

Anders See **Andrew**

Andre See **Andrew**

Andreas See **Andrew**

Andrew [Greek]
'Strong and manly'. The
Patron Saint of Scotland,
St. Andrew.
*(Andreas, Andre, Aindreas,
Anders, Andrien, Andie,
Andy)*

Andrien See **Andrew**

Androcles [Greek]
'Man-glory'.

Aneurin [Celtic]
'Truly golden'.
(Nye)

Angelo [Italian]
'Saintly messenger'.

Angus [Celtic]
'Outstanding and
exceptional man'. One of
unparalleled strength.

Angwyn [Welsh]
'Very handsome'.

Annan [Celtic]
'From the stream'.

Anscom [Anglo-Saxon]
'Dweller in the secret
valley'. An awe-inspiring,
solitary man.
(Anscomb)

Anse See **Anselm**

Ansel [French]
'Nobleman's follower'.
(Ansell)

Ansel See **Anselm**

Anselm [Teutonic]
'Divine helmet'.
*(Anse, Ansel, Anselme,
Anshelm)*

Ansley [Anglo-Saxon]
'From Ann's meadow'.

Anson [Anglo-Saxon]
'Ann's son'.

Anstice [Greek]
'The resurrected'. One
who returns to life after
death.
(Anstiss)

Anthony [Latin]
'Of inestimable worth'. A
man without peer.
*(Antony, Antoine, Anton,
Anntoin, Antonio, Tony)*

Antinous [Greek]
'Contradictory'.

Anton See **Anthony**

Antonio See **Anthony**

Anwell [Celtic]
'Beloved one'.
(Anwyl, Anwyll)

Anwyl See **Anwell**

Anyon [Celtic]
'The anvil'. One on
whom all the finest
characteristics have been
forged.

Aodh [Celtic]
'Fire'.

Aodh See **Hubert**

Apollo [Greek]
'Beautiful man'.

Aquila [Latin]
'Eagle'.

Archard [Teutonic]
'Sacred and powerful'.
(Archerd)

Archer [Anglo-Saxon]
'The bowman'.

Archer See **Archibald**

Archibald [Teutonic]
'Noble and truly bold'. A
brave and sacred warrior.
*(Archimbald, Gilleasbuig,
Arch, Archie, Archer, Archy)*

Archimbald See
Archibald

Archimedes [Greek]
'Master mind'.

Arden [Latin]
'Ardent, fiery, fervent,
sincere'. One of intensely
loyal nature.
(Ardin)

Ardley [Anglo-Saxon]
'From the domestic
meadow'.

Ardolph [Anglo-Saxon]
'The home loving wolf'.
The roamer who longs
only for home.
(Ardolf)

Argus [Greek]
'The watchful one'. The
giant with a hundred
eyes, who saw everything
at once.

Argyle [Gaelic]
'From the land of the
Gaels'.

Aric [Anglo-Saxon]
'Sacred ruler'.
(Rick, Rickie, Ricky)

Ariel [Hebrew]
'Lion of God'.

Aries [Latin]
'A ram'. One born in
April, from the sign of the
Zodiac — Aries.

Aristotle [Greek]
'Best thinker'.

Arledge [Anglo-Saxon]
'Dweller by the lake
where the rabbit dances'.

Arlen [Gaelic]
'Pledge'.
(Airleas)

Arlie [Anglo-Saxon]
'From the rabbit
meadow'.
(Arley, Arly, Harley, Harly)

Arlo [Spanish]
'The barberry'.

Armand [Teutonic]
'Man of the army'. The
military man personified.
(Armin, Armond)

Armand See **Herman**

Armin See **Armand**

Armond See **Armand** or
Herman

Armstrong [Anglo-Saxon]
'Strong arm'. The tough
warrior who could wield
a battle axe.

Arnall [Teutonic]
'Gracious eagle'. The
nobleman who is also a
gentleman.

Arnatt See **Arnett**

Arnett [French]
'Little eagle'.
(Arnatt, Arnott)

Arney [Teutonic]
'The eagle'.
(Arnie, Arne)

Arnie See **Arney**

Arno See **Arnold**

Arnold [Teutonic]
'Strong as an eagle'.
*(Arnald, Arnaud, Arne,
Arnie, Arno)*

Arnott See **Arnett**

Arpad See **Arvad**

Artair See **Arthur**

Artemis [Greek]
'Gift of Artemis'.
(Artemas)

Arthfael [Welsh]
'Bear strength'.

Arthur [Celtic]
'The noble bear man' or
'Strong as a rock'. The
semi-legendary King of
Britain, who founded the
Round Table.
*(Aurthur, Artair, Artur,
Artus, Art, Artie)*

Artur See **Arthur**

Arundel [Anglo-Saxon]
'Dweller with eagles'.
One who lives with and
shares the keen
sightedness of the eagle.

Arvad [Hebrew]
'The wanderer'.
(Arpad)

Arval [Latin]
'Much lamented'.
(Arvel)

Arvin [Teutonic]
'Friend of the people'.
The first true socialist.

Asa [Hebrew]
'The healer'.

Asaph [Hebrew]
'Gatherer'.

Ascelin [German]
'Of the moon'.
(Aceline)

Ascot [Anglo-Saxon]
'Owner of the east
cottage'.
(Ascott)

Ashburn [Anglo-Saxon]
'The brook by the ash
tree'.

Ashby [Anglo-Saxon]
'Ash tree farm'.

Asher [Hebrew]
'The laughing one'. A
happy lad.

Ashford [Anglo-Saxon]
'One who lives in the ford
by the ash tree'.

Ashley [Anglo-Saxon]
'Dweller in the ash tree
meadow'.
(Lee)

Ashlin [Anglo-Saxon]
'Dweller by the ash tree
pool'.

Ashton [Anglo-Saxon]
'Dweller at the ash tree
farm'.

Ashur [Semitic]
'The martial one'. One of
warlike tendencies.

Astrophel [Greek]
'Star lover'.

Aswin [Anglo-Saxon]
'Spear comrade'.
(Aswine)

Athanasius [Greek]
'Immortal'.

Atherton [Anglo-Saxon]
'Dweller at the spring
farm'.

Athol [Scottish]
Place name.

Atley [Anglo-Saxon]
'One who lives in the
meadow'.

Atwater [Anglo-Saxon]
'One who lives by the
water'.

Atwell [Anglo-Saxon]
'From the spring'. One
who built his home by a
natural well.

Atwood [Anglo-Saxon]
'From the forest'.
(Atwoode, Attwood)

Atworth [Anglo-Saxon]
'From the farm'.

Auberon [Teutonic]
'Noble'.
(Oberon)

Aubert See **Albert**

Aubin [French]
'The blond one'.

Aubin See **Alban**

Aubrey [Teutonic]
'Elf ruler'. The golden
haired king of the spirit
world.

Audley [Old English]
'Prospering'.

Audric [Teutonic]
'Noble ruler'.

Audwin [Teutonic]
'Noble friend'.
*(Aldwin, Aldwyn,
Adalwine)*

Augie See **August**

August [Latin]
'Exalted one'.
*(Augustus, Augustin,
Augustine, Austen, Austin,
Aguistin, Auguste, Gus,
Gussy, Augie)*

Augustin See **August**

Augustus See **August**

Aurelius [Latin]
'Golden friend'.

Auryn [Welsh]
'Gold'.

Austen See **August**

Avan [Hebrew]
'Proud'.
(Evan)

Avenall [French]
'Dweller in the oat field'.
(Avenel, Avenell)

Averill [Anglo-Saxon]
'Boar like' or 'Born in
April'.

*(Averil, Averel, Averell,
Everild)*

Avery [Anglo-Saxon]
'Ruler of the elves'.

Aviv [Hebrew]
'Spring'.

Axel [Teutonic]
'Father of peace'.

Axton [Anglo-Saxon]
'Stone of the sword
fighter'. The whetstone of
the warrior's sword.

Aylmer [Anglo-Saxon]
'Noble and famous'.

Aylward [Anglo-Saxon]
'Awe inspiring guardian'.

Aylworth [Anglo-Saxon]
'Farm belonging to the
awe inspiring one'.

Aymon [Old French]
'Home'.

Ayward [Old English]
'Noble guardian'.

Azarias [Hebrew]
'Whom the Lord helps'.

Azriel [Hebrew]
'Angel of the Lord'.

Girls

Bab [Arabic]
‘From the gateway’. Also
used as dim. of Barbara,
q.v.

Babette See **Barbara**

Balbina [Latin]
‘She who hesitates’.
(Balbine, Balbinia)

Balbine See **Balbina**

Balbinia See **Balbina**

Bambi [Latin]
‘The child’. Suitable
name for one of tiny
stature.
(Orel)

Baptista [Latin]
'Baptized'. A name
symbolic of man's
freedom from sin through
Baptism.
(Baptiste, Batista, Battista)

Barbara [Latin]
'Beautiful stranger'. The
lovely, but unknown
visitor.
*(Bab, Babb, Bas, Barbie,
Barbette, Babette, Barbra)*

Barbetta See **Barbara**

Barbie See **Barbara**

Basilia [Greek]
'Queenly, regal'. Fem. of
Basil.

Bathilda [Teutonic]
'Battle commander'.
Traditionally one who
fought for honour and
truth.
(Bathilde, Batilda, Batilde)

Bathilde See **Bathilda**

Bathsheba [Hebrew]
'Seventh daughter'.
Bathsheba was the wife of
King David in Biblical
times.

Batista [Greek]
'Baptized'.

Bea See **Beata**

Beata [Latin]
'Blessed, divine one'.
Blessed and beloved of
God.
(Bea)

Beatrice [Latin]
'She who brings joy'.
*(Beatrix, Beitris, Bea, Bee,
Trix, Trixie, Trixy)*

Beatrix See **Beatrice**

Beckie See **Rebecca**

Beda [Anglo-Saxon]
'Warrior maiden'.

Bedelia [Celtic]
'Mighty'.
(Delia)

Belicia [Spanish]
'Dedicated to God'.

Belinda [Italian]
'Wise and immortal
beauty'.
*(Bella, Belle, Linda, Lindie,
Lindy)*

Bellance [Italian]
'Blonde beauty'.
(Blanca)

Belle [French]
'Beautiful woman'. Can
also be used as a dim. of
Belinda and Isabelle.
(Bell, Bella, Belva, Belvia)

Belle See **Annabelle**

Belva See **Belle**

Belvia See **Belle**

Bena [Hebrew]
'The wise one'. A woman
whose charm is enhanced
by wisdom.

Benedetta See **Benedicta**

Benedicta [Latin]
'Blessed one'. Fem. of
Benedict.
*(Benedetta, Benedikta,
Benita, Benoîte, Bennie,
Binnie, Dixie)*

Benigna [Latin]
'Gentle, kind and
gracious'. A great lady.

Benilda [Latin]
'Well-intentioned'.

Benita [Spanish]
'Blessed'.
(Benitia)

Bennie See **Benedicta**

Benoite See **Benedicta**

Berdine [Teutonic]
'Glorious one'.

Berengaria [Teutonic]
'Spearer of bears'. A
warrior huntress of
renown.

Berenice See **Bernice**

Bernadette [French]
'Brave as a bear'.
*(Bernadina, Bernadene,
Bernadine, Bernita,
Bernardina, Bernie, Berney)*

Bernadina See
Bernadette

Berneen [Celtic]
'Little one, brave as a
bear'.

Bernia [Latin]
'Angel in armour'.
(Bernie)

Bernice [Greek]
'Herald of victory'.
*(Berenice, Burnice, Berny,
Bunny, Veronica)*

Bernie See **Bernadette**

Bernita See **Bernadette**

Berri See **Beryl**

Berry See **Beverley**

Berta See **Bertha**

Bertha [Teutonic]
'Bright and shining'. The
Teutonic goddess of
fertility.
*(Berthe, Berta, Bertie, Berty,
Bertina)*

Berthe See **Bertha**

Berthilda [Anglo-Saxon]
'Shining warrior maid'.
*(Berthilde, Bertilda,
Bertilde)*

Berthilde See **Berthilda**

Bertina See **Bertha**

Bertrada See **Bertrade**

Bertrade [Anglo-Saxon]
'Shining adviser'.
(Bertrada)

Beryl [Greek]
'Precious jewel'. This
stone is said to bring good
fortune; therefore, the
name is also said to give
good luck to its user.
*(Beryle, Beril, Berri, Berrie,
Berry)*

Bess See **Elizabeth**

Bessy See **Elizabeth**

Beth See **Bethel**

Beth See **Elizabeth**

Bethany [Aramaic]
'House of poverty'.

Bethel [Hebrew]
'House of God'.
(Beth)

Bethesda See **Bethseda**

Bethia [Hebrew]
'Daughter of God'.

Bethinn See **Bevin**

Bethseda [Hebrew]
'House of Mercy'.
(Bethesda)

Betsy See **Elizabeth**

Betta See **Elizabeth**

Bette See **Elizabeth**

Betty See **Elizabeth**

Beulah [Hebrew]
'The married one'. The
traditional wife.
(Beula)

Beverley [Anglo-Saxon]
'Ambitious one'.
*(Beverly, Beverlie, Bev,
Berry)*

Bevin [Gaelic]
'Melodious lady'. One
whose voice is so
beautiful that even the
birds will cease singing to
listen to her.
(Bebhinn)

Bibi [Arabic]
'Lady'.

Biddie See **Bridget**

Bijou [Old French]
'Jewel'.

Billie [Teutonic]
'Wise, resolute ruler'.
Sometimes used as a
diminutive of
Wilhelmina.
(Billy, Willa)

Bina [African]
'To dance'.

Bina See **Sabina**

Binga [Teutonic]
'From the hollow'.

Binnie See **Benedicta** or
Sabina

Birdie [Mod. English]
'Sweet little bird'.

Blaine [Gaelic]
'Thin'.

Blair [Gaelic]
'Dweller on the plain'.

Blake [Old English]
'Fair haired'.

Blanca See **Bellance**

Blanche [French]
'Fair and white'. A very
popular name in
medieval times when it
was supposed to endow
its user with all feminine
virtues.
*(Blanch, Blanca, Blanka,
Blinne, Blinnie, Bluinse,
Branca)*

Blasia [Latin]
'She who stammers'.

Blessin [Old English]
'Consecrated'.
(Blessing)

Blinne See **Blanche**

Blinnie See **Blanche**

Bliss [Old English]
'Gladness, joy'.
(Blita, Blitha)

Blita See **Bliss**

Blitha See **Bliss**

Blodwyn [Welsh]
'White flower'.
(Blodwen)

Blondelle [French]
'Little fair one'.

Blossom [Old English]
'Fragrant as a flower'.

Bluinse See **Blanche**

Bluma See **Anthea**

Blyth [Anglo-Saxon]
'Joyful and happy'.
(Blith, Blithe, Blythe)

Bobette See **Roberta**

Bobina See **Roberta**

Bona See **Bonita**

Bonita [Latin]
'Sweet and good'.
(Bona, Bonne, Bonnie, Nita)

Bonne See **Bonita**

Bonnie See **Bonita**

Branca See **Blanche**

Brandy [Dutch]
'Brandy'.

Branwen [Welsh]
'Beautiful raven'.

Breita See **Bridget**

Brenda [Teutonic]
'Fiery' or (Irish) 'Raven'.
(Bren)

Brenna [Irish]
'Raven haired beauty'.

Briallen [Welsh]
'Primrose'.

Briana [Celtic]
'Strength, virtue, honor'.
(Brianna, Brienne)

Briana See **Bryna**

Bridget [Irish/Celtic]
'Strong and mighty'.
Popular name in Ireland,
where St. Bridget is
Patron Saint.
*(Brigid, Brigette, Brigida,
Brigitte, Breita, Brieta,
Brietta, Brie, Biddie, Biddy,
Bridie, Bridey, Brydie)*

Bridie See **Bridget**

Brienne See **Briana**

Brier [French]
'Heather'.

Brieta See **Bridget**

Brigid See **Bridget**

Brigida See **Bridget**

Briony See **Bryony**

Britannia See **Brittany**

Brittany [Latin]
'Britain'.
(Britannia)

Bronhilde See **Brunhilda**

Bronwen [Welsh/Celtic]
'White bosomed'.
(Bronwyn)

Bronya [Russian]
'Armour'.

Brook [Old English]
'Living near the brook'.
(Brooke)

Brucie [French]
'From the thicket'. Fem.
of Bruce.

Bruelle See **Brunella**

Brunella [Italian]
One with brown hair.
The true brunette.
(Brunelle, Bruella, Bruelle)

Brunelle See **Brunella**

Brunetta [French]
'Dark haired maiden'.

Brunhild See **Brunhilda**

Brunhilda [Teutonic]
'Warrior heroine'.
(Brunhild, Brunhilde)

Bryna [Irish]
'Strength with virtue'.
Fem. of Brian.
(Brina, Briana)

Bryony [Old English]
A twining vine.
(Briony)

Buena [Spanish]
'The good one'.
(Buona)

Bunny [English]
'Little rabbit'.

Bailey [French]
'Steward'. The trusted
guardian of other men's
properties.
(Baillie, Baily, Bayley)

Bainbridge [Anglo-Saxon]
'Bridge over the white
water'.

Baird [Celtic]
'The minstrel'. The
ancient bard.
(Bard)

Balbo [Latin]
'The mutterer'.

Baldemar [Teutonic]
'Bold, famous prince'.

Balder [Norse]
'Prince'. The god of
Peace.
(Baldur, Baldhere)

Baldric [Teutonic]
'Princely ruler'.
(Baudric)

Baldwin [Teutonic]
'Bold, noble protector'.
(Baudouin, Balduin)

Balfour [Gaelic]
'From the pasture'.

Ballard [Teutonic]
'Strong and bold'.

Balthasar [Greek]
'May the Lord protect
the King'.
(Belshazzar)

Bancroft [Anglo-Saxon]
'From the bean field'.

Banning [Gaelic]
'The little golden haired
one'.

Banquo [Gaelic]
'White'.

Barclay [Anglo-Saxon]
'Dweller by the birch tree
meadow'.
(Berkeley, Berkley)

Bard See **Baird**

Barden [Old English]
'One who lives near the
boar's den'.

Bardo See **Bartholomew**

Bardolf [Anglo-Saxon]
'Axe wolf'.
*(Bardolph, Bardolphe,
Bardulf, Bardulph)*

Bardrick [Anglo-Saxon]
'Axe ruler'. One who
lived by the battle axe.
(Baldric, Baldrick)

Barlow [Anglo-Saxon]
'One who lives on the
barren hills'.

Barnabus See **Barnaby**

Barnaby [Hebrew]
'Son of consolation'.
(Barnabas, Barney, Barny)

Barnard See **Bernard**

Barnet See **Bernard**

Barnett [Anglo-Saxon]
'Noble leader'.
(Barnet)

Barney See **Barnaby**

Barnum [Anglo-Saxon]
'Nobleman's house'.
Dwelling place of the
princely.

Baron [Anglo-Saxon]
'Noble warrior'. The

lowest rank of the
peerage.
(Barron)

Barr [Anglo-Saxon]
'A gateway'.

Barret [Teutonic]
'As mighty as the bear'.
(Barrett)

Barris [Celtic]
'Barry's son'.

Barry [Gaelic]
'Spearlike'. One whose
intellect is sword-sharp.
(Barrie)

Bart See **Bartholomew**

Bartel See **Bartholomew**

Barth See **Bartholomew**

Barthelmey See
Bartholomew

Barthol See **Bartholomew**

Bartholomew [Hebrew]
'Son of the furrows;
ploughman'. One of the
twelve apostles.
*(Bartel, Barthelmey,
Bartolome, Bartley, Bardo,
Barth, Barthol, Bart, Bat,
Parlan)*

Bartley [Anglo-Saxon]
'Bartholomew's
meadow'.

Bartley See **Bartholomew**

Bartolome See
Bartholomew

Barton [Anglo-Saxon]
'Barley farmer'.

Baruch [Hebrew]
'Blessed'.
(Barrie, Barry)

Basil [Greek]
'Kingly'. St. Basil the
founder of the Greek
Orthodox Church.
*(Basile, Basilio, Basilius,
Vassily)*

Basilio See **Basil**

Basilius See **Basil**

Baudowin See **Baldwin**

Baudric See **Baldric**

Baxter [Teutonic]
'The baker of bread'.
(Bax)

Bay See **Bayard**

Bayard [Anglo-Saxon]
'Red haired and strong'.
The personification of
knightly courtesy.
(Bay)

Beach See **Beacher**

Beacher [Anglo-Saxon]
'One who lives by the oak
tree'.
(Beecher, Beach, Beech)

Beagan [Gaelic]
'Little one'.
(Beagen)

Beal [French]
'The handsome'. In the
form 'Beau' used to
identify the smart, well
dressed, personable men
of the 17th and early 18th
centuries.
(Beale, Beall, Beau)

Beaman [Anglo-Saxon]
'The bee keeper'.

Beathan See **Benjamin**

Beattie [Gaelic]
'Public provider'. One
who supplies food and
drink for the inhabitants
of a town.
(Beatie, Beaty, Beatty)

Beau See **Beal**

Beaufort [French]
'Beautiful stronghold'.
The name adopted by the
descendants of the union
of John of Gaunt and
Katharine Swynford.

Beaumont [French]
'Beautiful mountain'.

Beauregard [Old French]
'Beautiful in expression'.

Beck [Anglo-Saxon]
'A brook'.
(Bec)

Bede [Old English]
'A prayer'.

Beecher See **Beacher**

Belden [Anglo-Saxon]
'Dweller in the beautiful
glen'.
(Beldon)

Bellamy [French]
'Handsome friend'.

Belshazzar See **Balthasar**

Ben See **Benjamin**

Bendix See **Benedict**

Benedict [Latin]
'Blessed'. One blessed by
God.
*(Bendix, Benito, Benoit,
Benot, Bengt, Benedic,
Benedick, Benedix, Bennet,
Bennett, Ben, Benny, Dixon)*

Bengt See **Benedict**

Beniah [Hebrew]
'Son of the Lord'.

Benito See **Benedict**

Benjamin [Hebrew]
'Son of my right hand'.
The beloved youngest
son.
*(Beathan, Ben, Bennie,
Benjy, Benny)*

Bennet See **Benedict**

Bennett See **Benedict**

Benoit See **Benedict**

Benoni [Hebrew]
'Son of my sorrow'. The
former name of the
Biblical Benjamin.

Benot See **Benedict**

Benson [Hebrew]
'Son of Benjamin'.

Bently [Anglo-Saxon]
'From the farm where the
grass bends'.
(Bentley)

Benton [Anglo-Saxon]
'From the town on the
moors'.

Berenger [Teutonic]
'Bear, spear'.

Beresford [Anglo-Saxon]
'From the barley ford'.

Berg [Teutonic]
'The mountain'.

Berg See **Burgess**

Berger [French]
'The shepherd'.

Berger See **Burgess**

Berk See **Burke**

Berkeley See **Barclay**

Bern See **Bernard**

Bernard [Teutonic]
'As brave as a bear'. A
courageous warrior.
*(Bernhard, Barnard, Barnet,
Barnett, Bern, Burnard,
Bearnard, Barney, Barny,
Bernie, Berny)*

Bernie See **Bernard**

Bert See **Albert**, **Bertram**,
Egbert, **Herbert**,
Berthold

Berthold [Teutonic]
'Brilliant ruler'.
*(Bertold, Berthoud, Bert,
Bertie)*

Berton [Anglo-Saxon]
'Brilliant one's estate'.
(Burton, Burt, Bertie)

Bertram [Anglo-Saxon]
'Bright raven'.
(Bartram, Bertrand)

Bertrand See **Bertram**

Berty See **Albert**

Bevan [Welsh]
'Son of a noble man'.
(Beaven, Beavan, Beven)

Beverley [Anglo-Saxon]
'From the beaver
meadow'.
(Beverly)

Bevis [French]
'Fair view'.
(Beavais)

Bickford [Anglo-Saxon]
'Hewer's ford'.
(Bick)

Bing [Teutonic]
'Kettle shaped hollow'.

Birch [Anglo-Saxon]
'At the birch tree'.
(Birk)

Birk See **Birch**

Birkett [Anglo-Saxon]
'Dweller by the birch
headland'.
(Birket)

Birley [Anglo-Saxon]
'Cattle shed in the field'.

Birney [Anglo-Saxon]
'Dweller on the brook
island'.

Birtle [Anglo-Saxon]
'From the bird hill'.

Bishop [Anglo-Saxon]
'The Bishop'.

Bjorn [Scandinavian]
'Bear'.

Black [Anglo-Saxon]
'Of dark complexion'.

Blade [Anglo-Saxon]
'Prosperity, glory'.

Blagden [Anglo-Saxon]
'From the dark valley'.

Blaine [Gaelic]
'Thin, hungry-looking'.
(Blain, Blayn, Blayne)

Blair [Gaelic]
'A place' or 'From the
plain'.

Blaise [Latin]
'Stammerer' or
'Firebrand'.
(Blase, Blayze, Blaze)

Blake [Anglo-Saxon]
'Of fair complexion'.

Blakeley [Anglo-Saxon]
'From the black
meadow'.

Blakey [Anglo-Saxon]
'Little fair one'.

Bland [Latin]
'Mild and gentle'.

Blandford See **Blanford**

Blane See **Blaine**

Blanford [Anglo-Saxon]
'River crossing belonging
to one with grey hair'.
(Blandford)

Blaze See **Blaise**

Bliss [Anglo-Saxon]
'Joyful one'. One who
always sees the cheerful
side.

Blythe [Anglo-Saxon]
'The merry person'.
(Blyth)

Boaz [Hebrew]
'In the Lord is strength'.
(Boas, Boase)

Bob See **Robert**

Bobbie See **Robert**

Boden [French]
'The herald'. The bringer
of news.

Bogart [Teutonic]
'Strong bow'.

Bonamy [French]
'Good friend'.

Bonar [French]
'Good, gentle and kind'.

Boniface [Latin]
'One who does good'.

Boone [Norse]
'The good one'.

Boot See **Booth**

Booth [Teutonic]
'From a market' or
'Dweller in a hut' or
'Herald'.
(Both, Boothe, Boot, Boote)

Borden [Anglo-Saxon]
'From the valley of the
boar'.

Borg [Norse]
'Dweller in the castle'.

Boris [Slavic]
'A fighter'. A born
warrior.

Boswell [French]
'Forest town'.

Bosworth [Anglo-Saxon]
'At the cattle enclosure'.

Both See **Booth**

Botolf [Anglo-Saxon]
'Herald wolf'.
(Botolph, Botolphe)

Bourke See **Burke**

Bourne [Anglo-Saxon]
'From the brook'.
(Bourn, Burn, Burne, Byrne)

Bowen [Celtic]
'Descendant of Owen'. A
proud Welsh name borne
by descendants of the
almost legendary Owen.

Bowie [Gaelic]
'Yellow haired'.

Boyce [French]
'From the woods'. A
forester.

Boyd [Gaelic]
'Light haired'. The blond
Adonis.

Boyden [Celtic]
'Herald'.

Boyne [Gaelic]
'White cow'. A very rare
person.

Brad See **Bradley**

Bradburn [Anglo-Saxon]
'Broad brook'.

Braden [Anglo-Saxon]
'From the wide valley'.

Bradford [Anglo-Saxon]
'From the broad
crossing'.

Bradley [Anglo-Saxon]
'From the broad
meadow'.
(Bradly, Brad, Lee)

Bradshaw [Old English]
'Large virginal forest'.

Brady [Gaelic]
'Spirited one' or 'From
the broad island'.

Brainard [Anglo-Saxon]
'Bold as a raven'. One
who knows not fear.
(Brainerd)

Bram See **Abraham** or
Bran

Bramwell [Anglo-Saxon]
'From the bramble bush
spring'.

Bran [Celtic]
'Raven'. The spirit of
eternal youth.
(Bram)

Brand [Anglo-Saxon]
'Firebrand'. The
grandson of the god,
Woden.

Brander [Norse]
'Sword of fire'.

Brandon [Anglo-Saxon]
'From the beacon on the hill'.

Brant [Anglo-Saxon]
'Fiery one' or 'Proud one'.

Brawley [Anglo-Saxon]
'From the meadow on the hill slope'.

Brendan [Gaelic]
'Little raven' or 'From the fiery hill'.
(Brendon)

Brendon See **Brendan**

Brent [Anglo-Saxon]
'Steep hill'.

Brett [Celtic]
'Native of Brittany' or 'From the island of Britain'. One of the original Celts.
(Bret)

Brewster [Anglo-Saxon]
'The brewer'.

Brian [Celtic]
'Powerful strength with virtue and honour'. Brian Boru the greatest Irish king.
(Briant, Brien, Bryan, Bryant, Brion, Bryon)

Briant See **Brian**

Brice [Celtic]
'Quick, ambitious and alert'.
(Bryce)

Bridger [Anglo-Saxon]
'Dweller by the bridge'.

Brigham [Anglo-Saxon]
'One who lives where the bridge is enclosed'.

Brinsley [Anglo-Saxon]
'Brin's meadow'.

Brock [Anglo-Saxon]
'The badger'.
(Broc, Brockie, Brok)

Brockie See **Brock**

Brockley [Anglo-Saxon]
'From the badger meadow'.

Broderic See **Roderick**

Broderick [Anglo-Saxon]
'From the broad ridge' or 'Son of Roderick'.
(Broderic)

Brodie [Gaelic]
'A ditch'.
(Brody)

Bromley [Anglo-Saxon]
'Dweller of the broom
meadow'.

Bronson [Anglo-Saxon]
'The brown haired one's
son'.

Brook [Anglo-Saxon]
'One who lives by the
brook'.
(Brooke, Brooks)

Brooks See **Brook**

Brough See **Brougher**

Brougher [Anglo-Saxon]
'The fortified residence'.
(Brough)

Broughton [Anglo-Saxon]
'From a fortified town'.

Bruce [French]
'From the thicket'.
Robert the Bruce,
Scotland's hero-king.

Bruno [Teutonic]
'Brown haired man'.

Bryan/Bryant See **Brian**

Bryce See **Brice**

Brychan [Welsh]
'Freckled'.

Bryn [Welsh]
'Hill'.

Buck [Anglo-Saxon]
'The buck deer'. A fleet
footed youth.

Buckley [Anglo-Saxon]
'One who dwells by the
buck deer meadow'.

Budd [Anglo-Saxon]
'Herald'. The welcome
messenger.

Bundy [Anglo-Saxon]
'Free man'. An
enfranchised serf.

Burbank [Anglo-Saxon]
'Dweller on the castle hill
slope'.

Burch See **Birch**

Burchard [Anglo-Saxon]
'Strong as a castle'.
*(Burckhard, Burkhart,
Burgard)*

Burdett [French]
'Little shield'.

Burdon [Anglo-Saxon]
'One who lives by the
castle on the hill'.

Burford [Anglo-Saxon]
'Dweller at the river
crossing by the castle'.

Burgard See **Burchard**

Burgess [Anglo-Saxon]
'Dweller in a fortified
town'.
*(Bergess, Berger, Berg,
Burg)*

Burke [French]
'From the stronghold'.
*(Berk, Berke, Bourke, Burk,
Birke, Birk)*

Burkett [French]
'From the little fortress'.

Burkhart See **Burchard**

Burl [Anglo-Saxon]
'The cup bearer'. The
wine server.

Burley [Anglo-Saxon]
'Dweller in the castle by
the meadow'.
(Burleigh)

Burnaby [Norse]
'Warrior's estate'.

Burnard See **Bernard**

Burne See **Bourne**

Burnell [French]
'Little one with brown
hair'.

Burnett [Anglo-Saxon]
'Little one with brown
complexion'.

Burney [Anglo-Saxon]
'Dweller on the island in
the brook'.

Burr [Norse]
'Youth'.

Burrell [French]
'One of light brown
complexion'.

Burris [Old English]
'Of the town'.

Burt See **Burton**

Burton [Anglo-Saxon]
'Of bright and glorious
fame' or 'Dweller at the
fortified town'.
(Berton, Bert, Burt)

Busby [Norse]
'Dweller in the thicket'.

Byford [Anglo-Saxon]
'Dweller by the ford'.

Byram [Anglo-Saxon]
'Dweller at the cattle
pen'.
(Byrom)

Byrd [Anglo-Saxon]
'Like a bird'.

Byrle See **Burl**

Byrne See **Bourne**

Byron [French]
'From the cottage' or
'The bear'.

Girls

Cadena See **Cadence**

Cadence [Latin]
'Rhythmic'. One who is
graceful and charming.
(Cadena, Cadenza)

Cadenza See **Cadence**

Caera [Gaelic]
'Spear; ruddy'.

Cailin See **Colleen**

Caireen See **Catherine**

Cairistiona See **Christine**

Cairstine See **Christine**

Caitlin See **Catherine**

Caitrin See **Catherine**

Calandra [Greek]
'Lark'. One who is as
light and gay as a bird.
*(Calandre, Calandria, Cal,
Callie, Cally)*

Calandria See **Calandra**

Calantha [Greek]
'Beautiful blossom'. A
woman of childlike
beauty and innocence.
*(Calanthe, Kalantha,
Kalanthe, Cal, Cally,
Callie)*

Caledonia [Latin]
'Scottish lassie'. One who
comes from the part of
Scotland known in earlier
times as Caledonia.
(Caledonie)

Caledonie See **Caledonia**

Calida [Spanish]
'Ardently loving'. A
woman capable of great
affection.

Calista [Greek]
'Most beautiful of
women'. A name for a girl
thought to be beautiful
beyond the ordinary.
(Calisto, Kallista, Kallisto)

Calisto See **Calistra**

Calla [Greek]
'Beautiful'.

Callie See **Calandra**

Calliope [Greek]
The muse of poetry.

Callula [Latin]
'Little beautiful one'.

Caltha [Latin]
'Yellow flower'.

Calvina [Latin]
'Bald'. Fem. of Calvin.
Name sometimes used in
strongly Calvinistic
families.

Calypso [Greek]
'Concealer'. The
legendary sea nymph
who held Odysseus
captive.
(Kalypso)

Camelia See **Camilla**

Cameo [Italian]
'Sculptured jewel'.

Camilla [Latin]
'Noble and righteous'.
The name given to the
young and beautiful
handmaiden in pagan
ceremonies.

(Camille, Camile, Camella, Camelia, Camellia, Cam)

Camille See **Camilla**

Canace [Latin]
'The daughter of the wind'.
(Kanaka, Kanake)

Candace [Latin]
'Pure, glittering, brilliant white'. One whose purity and virtue is beyond suspicion.
(Candice, Candida, Candie, Candy)

Candice See **Candace**

Candida See **Candace**

Candie See **Candace**

Candra [Latin]
'Luminescent'.

Candra See **Chandra**

Capriccia See **Caprice**

Caprice [Italian]
'Fanciful'.
(Capriccia)

Cara [Celtic/Italian]
'Friend' (Celtic) or 'Dearest one' (Italian). A term of endearment.
(Cariad, Carina, Carine, Kara, Karine, Karina)

Caragh [Irish]
'Love'.

Caressa See **Carissa**

Caresse See **Carissa**

Cari [Turkish]
'Flows like water'.

Cariad See **Cara**

Carina [Latin]
'Keel'.

Carina See **Cara**

Carine See **Cara**

Carissa [Latin]
'Most dear one'.
(Caressa, Caresse, Carisse)

Carisse See **Carissa**

Carita [Latin]
'Beloved little one'.

Carla See **Charlotte**

Carlie See **Charlotte**

Carline See **Caroline**

Carliss See **Corliss**

Carlissa See **Corliss**

Carlotta See **Charlotte**

Carma [Sanskrit]
'Destiny'. From the
Buddhist 'Karma' —
Fate.

Carmacita See **Carmen**

Carmel [Hebrew]
'God's fruitful vineyard'.
(Carmela, Carmelita,
Carmella, Carma, Carmie,
Carmelina, Carmeline,
Melina)

Carmela See **Carmel**

Carmelina See **Carmel**

Carmeline See **Carmel**

Carmelita See **Carmel**

Carmella See **Carmel**

Carmen [Latin]
'Songstress'. One who
has a beautiful voice.
(Carma, Carmia, Carmina,
Carmine, Carmita,
Charmaine, Carmacita,
Carmencita)

Carmencita See **Carmen**

Carmia See **Carmen**

Carmie See **Carmel**

Carmina See **Carmen**

Carmine See **Carmen**

Carmita See **Carmen**

Carnation [French]
'Fresh colour'. One with
perfect features and
colouring.

Caro See **Caroline**

Carol See **Caroline**

Carola See **Caroline**

Carolina See **Caroline**

Caroline [Teutonic]
'Little woman, born to
command'. The power
behind the throne; the
hand which rocks the
cradle and rules the
world. One who is all that
is feminine, but who rules
and controls.
(Carola, Carol, Carole,
Carolina, Carline, Charleen,
Charlene, Charline, Sharleen,
Sharlene, Sharline, Caro,

Lina, Line)
This name is the fem. of
Charles and can also be
used as Charlotte.

Caronwen [Welsh]
'Little fair love'.

Caryl [Welsh]
'Beloved'.
(Carryl, Carys)

Caryn See **Catherine**

Carys See **Caryl**

Casilda [Spanish]
'The solitary one'.
(Casilde)

Casilde See **Casilda**

Cassandra [Greek]
Prophetess ignored by
men.
(Cassandre, Cass, Cassie)

Cassie See **Cassandra**

Casta [Latin]
'Of pure upbringing'.
(Caste)

Caste See **Casta**

Caterina See **Catherine**

Catharina See **Catherine**

Catherine [Greek]
'Pure maiden'. The saint
who was martyred on a
spiked (Catherine) wheel.
*(Caireen, Carine, Catharine,
Catharina, Cathleen,
Catalina, Caterina, Caitlin,
Caitrin, Caryn, Catriona,
Cathy, Cathie, Katharine,
Katherine, Katherina,
Katharina, Katerine,
Kateryn, Kathryn, Katrine,
Katrina, Kate, Katy, Kathy,
Katie, Kit, Kitty)*

Cathy See **Catherine**

Ceara [Irish]
'Spear'. A warrior who
wielded her spear to the
detriment of her enemies.

Cecelia See **Cecilia**

Cecile See **Cecilia**

Cecilia [Latin]
The Patron saint of
Music.
*(Cecelia, Cecile, Cecily,
Celia, Cecil, Cicely, Sisile,
Sisle, Sileas, Sisley, Sissie,
Cele, Ciel, Cissie)*

Cecily See **Cecilia**

Ceinlys [Welsh]
'Sweet gems'.

Ceinwen [Welsh]
'Beautiful gems'.

Ceiridwen [Welsh]
The Goddess of Bardism
(Ceri, Kerridwen)

Celandine [Greek]
'Swallow' or 'yellow
water flower'.
(Celandon)

Celandon See **Celandine**

Cele See **Cecilia** or
Celeste

Celene See **Selena**

Celesta See **Celeste**

Celeste [Latin]
'Heavenly'. A woman of
divine beauty.
*(Celesta, Celestina,
Celestine, Cele)*

Celestina See **Celeste**

Celestine See **Celeste**

Celia See **Cecilia**

Celie See **Selena**

Celina See **Selena**

Celinda See **Selena**

Celosia [Greek]
'Burning flame'.
(Kelosia)

Cerelia [Latin]
'Spring like'. Woman of
spring-blossom beauty.
(Cerealia, Cerellia, Cerelie)

Cerelie See **Cerelia**

Ceri See **Ceiridwen**

Cerian [Welsh]
'Loved one'.

Ceridwen [Welsh]
'Fair poetry'.

Cerys [Welsh]
'Love'.

Chandra [Sanskrit]
'The moon who outshines
the stars'.
(Candra, Chandre, Candre)

Chantal See **Chantelle**

Chantelle [French]
'Little singer'.
(Chantal, Chantel)

Charis [Greek]
'Grace'.

Charissa See **Charity**

Charita See **Charity**

Charity [Latin]
'Benevolent and loving'.
One who gives with
generosity and affection.
*(Charissa, Charita, Charry,
Cherry)*

Charleen See **Caroline**

Charlie See **Charlotte**

Charlotta See **Charlotte**

Charlotte [Teutonic]
See Caroline.
*(Charlotta, Carlotta,
Charlie, Carlie, Carla and
all the variations of Caroline)*

Charmaine [Latin]
'Little song'.
*(Carmen, Charmain,
Charmian)*

Charmaine See **Carmen**

Charry See **Charity**

Charyl See **Charlotte**

Chastity [Latin]
'Purity'.

Cherida See **Cherie** or
Querida

Cherie [French]
'Dear, beloved one'. A
term of endearment.
*(Cheri, Cherida, Cherry,
Cheryl, Sheryl, Sherry,
Sherrie)*

Cherise [Old French]
'Cherrylike'.

Cherry See **Charity**

Cheryl See **Charlotte** or
Cherie

Chesna [Slavic]
'Peaceful'.

Chiquita [Spanish]
'Little one'. A term of
endearment for a small
girl.

Chloe [Greek]
'Fresh young blossom'.
The Greek goddess of
unripened grain.
(Cloe, Kloe)

Chloras See **Chloris**

Chlori See **Chloris**

Chlorinda See **Clorinda**

Chloris [Greek]
'Goddess of the flowers'.
*(Chloras, Chlores, Chlori,
Loris)*

Chloris See **Clarice**

Christabel [Latin]
'Beautiful bright faced
Christian'.
*(Christabelle, Christabella,
Kristabel, Kristabella,
Kristabelle)*

Christabella See
Christabel

Christanta [Colombian]
'A chrysanthemum'.

Christina See **Christine**

Christine [French]
'Christian one'.
*(Cairstine, Cairistiona,
Christina, Christiana,
Christiane, Cristina,
Cristine, Christian, Chrystal,
Crystal, Chris, Chrissie,
Chrissy, Crissie, Crissy)*

Christiana See **Christine**

Chryseis [Latin]
'Golden daughter'.

Ciel See **Cecilia**

Cilla [French]
'The Cilla flower'.

Cinderella [French]
'Girl of the ashes'. From
the fairy tale.
(Cindie, Cindy, Ella)

Cindie See **Cinderella**

Cindy See **Cynthia**

Cipressa See **Cypris**

Claire See **Clara**

Clara [Latin]
'Bright, shining girl'. One
of clear, outstanding
beauty.
*(Clare, Claire, Klara,
Clareta, Clarette, Clarine)*

Clarabella [Latin/French]
'Bright, shining beauty'.
(Clarabelle, Clara, Bella)

Claramae [English]
'Brilliant beauty'.
*(Clarinda, Clorinda,
Chlarinda, Chlorinda)*

Clare See **Clara**

Claresta [English]
'The most shining one'. A
woman to outshine all
others.
(Clarista)

Clareta See **Clara**

Clarette See **Clara**

Clarice [French]
'Little, shining one'.
French form of Clara.
*(Clarissa, Clarisse, Clariss,
Chloris, Chlaris)*

Clarimond [Teutonic]
'Brilliant protector'.
*(Clarimonda, Clarimonde,
Chlarimonda, Chlarimonde)*

Clarimonda See
Clarimond

Clarinda See **Claramae**

Clarine See **Clara**

Clarissa See **Clarice**

Clarista See **Claresta**

Claude See **Claudia**

Claudette See **Claudia**

Claudia [Latin]
'The lame one'. Fem. of
Claud.
*(Claude, Claudette,
Claudina, Claudine,
Claudie, Gladys)*

Claudie See **Claudia**

Claudina See **Claudia**

Claudine See **Claudia**

Cleantha [Greek]
'Glory-flower'.
(Cleanthe)

Cleanthe See **Cleantha**

Clematis [Greek]
'Sweet vine'.

Clemence [Latin]
'Merciful and kind'. One
who tempers justice with
mercy.
*(Clemency, Clementia,
Clementina, Clementine)*

Clemency See **Clemence**

Clementia See **Clemence**

Clementina See
Clemence

Clementine See
Clemence

Cleo See **Cleopatra**

Cleopatra [Greek]
'Her father's glory'. A girl
who will add lustre to her
father's name.
(Cleo)

Cleva [Old English]
'Cliff dweller'. Fem. of
Clive.

Cliantha [Greek]
'Flower of glory'.
*(Cleantha, Cleanthe,
Clianthe)*

Clio [Greek]
'She who proclaims'. The
Greek Muse of History.

Clorinda [Latin]
'Famed for her beauty'.
*(Chlorinda, Chlorinde,
Clorinde, Clarinda,
Clarinde)*

Clorinda See **Claramae**

Clotilda [Teutonic]
'Famous battle maiden'.
A warrior who fought
alongside her father and
brothers. *(Clotilde,
Clothilda, Clothilde)*

Clover [English]
'Meadow blossom'. From
the flower.
(Clovie)

Clovie See **Clover**

Clydia [Greek]
'Glorious'.

Clymene [Greek]
'Fame and renown'.

Clytie [Greek]
'Splendid daughter'. The
mythical nymph who was
turned into a heliotrope,
so that she could worship
the sun.

Cody [Old English]
'A cushion'.

Colette [Latin]
'Victorious'. A form of
Nicolette.
(Collette, Collete)

Colleen [Gaelic]
'Girl'. The name given to
a young girl in Ireland.
*(Coleen, Colene, Colline,
Coline, Cailin)*

Columba [Latin]
'The dove'. One of a
peaceful disposition.
*(Coline, Columbine,
Columbia, Colombe, Colly)*

Comfort [French]
'One who gives comfort'.
One of the virtue names
popular with English and
American Puritan
families.

Con See **Constance**

Conceptia See
Conception

Conception [Latin]
'Beginning'.
*(Conceptia, Concepcion,
Conchita, Concha)*

Concetta [Italian]
'An ingenious thought'.

Concha See **Conception**

Conchita See **Conception**

Concordia [Latin]
'Harmony and Peace'.
*(Concordina, Concordie,
Concordy)*

Concordie See **Concordia**

Concordina See
Concordia

Conrada See **Conradine**

Conradina See **Conradine**

Conradine [Teutonic]
'Bold and wise'. Fem. of
Conrad.
*(Conradina, Conrada,
Connie)*

Consolata [Latin]
'One who consoles'.
(Consolation)

Consolation See
Consolata

Constance [Latin]
'Constant'. One who is
firm and unchanging.
*(Constantia, Constantina,
Constanta, Constantine,
Constancy, Constanza,
Connie, Con)*

Constancy See **Constance**

Constanta See **Constance**

Constantia See **Constance**

Constantina See
Constance

Constantine See
Constance

Constanze See **Constance**

Consuela [Spanish]
'Consolation'. The
Friend when in need.
(Consuelo, Connie)

Consuelo See **Consuela**

Cora [Greek]
'The maiden'. From
Kore, the daughter of
Demeter.
*(Corella, Corett, Corette,
Corina, Corrina, Corinna,
Corinne, Corin, Correna,
Coretta, Corrie, Corie)*

Corabella [Combination
Cora/Bella]
'Beautiful maiden'.
(Corabelle)

Corabelle See **Corabella**

Coral [Latin]
'Sincere' or 'From the
sea'.
(Corale, Coraline, Coralie)

Coralie See **Coral**

Coraline See **Coral**

Cordelia [Welsh]
'Jewel of the sea'. The
daughter of Lear, the Sea
King.
(Cordelie, Cordie, Delia)

Cordelie See **Cordelia**

Cordie See **Cordelia**

Corella See **Cora**

Corett See **Cora**

Coretta See **Cora**

Corey [Gaelic]
'From the hollow'.

Corina See **Cora**

Corinne See **Cora**

Corissa [Latin/Greek]
'Most modest maiden'.
(Corisse)

Corisse See **Corissa**

Corliss [English]
'Cheerful and kind-
hearted'.
(Carliss, Carlissa, Corlissa)

Corlissa See **Corliss**

Cornela See **Cornelia**

Cornelia [Latin]
'Womanly virtue'.
(*Cornela, Cornelle, Cornelie,
Cornie, Nela, Nelie, Nelli*)

Cornelie See **Cornelia**

Cornelle See **Cornelia**

Cornie See **Cornelia**

Corona [Spanish]
'Crowned maiden'.
(*Coronie*)

Coronie See **Corona**

Correna See **Cora**

Cosetta See **Cosette**

Cosette [French]
'Victorious army'.
(*Cosetta*)

Cosima See **Cosina**

Cosina [Greek]
'World harmony'.
(*Cosima*)

Courtney [Old English]
'From the court'.

Crescent [French]
'The creative one'.
(*Crescentia, Crescenta*)

Crescenta See **Crescent**

Crescentia See **Crescent**

Cresseide See **Cressida**

Cressida [Greek]
'The golden one'.
(*Cresseide*)

Crisiant [Welsh]
'Crystal'.

Crispina [Latin]
'Curly haired'. Fem. of
Crispin. (*Crispine*)

Crystal [Latin]
'Clear'. Also form of
Christine.
(*Cristal, Chrystal, Krystal*)

Cynara [Greek]
'Artichoke'. A beautiful
maiden, protected by
thorns.

Cynth See **Cynthia**

Cynthia [Greek]
'Moon Goddess'.
Another name for Diana,
Goddess of the Moon,
born on Cynthos.
(*Cindy, Cyn, Cynth,
Cynthie*)

Cynthie See **Cynthia**

Cypris [Greek]
'Born in Cyprus'.
(Cypres, Cipressa, Cypressa)

Cyrena [Greek]
'From Cyrene'. A water
nymph, beloved of
Apollo.
(Cyrenia, Kyrena, Kyrenia)

Cyrenia See **Cyrena**

Cyrilla [Latin]
'Lordly one'. Fem. of
Cyril. *(Cirilla, Cirila)*

Cytherea [Greek]
'From Cythera'. Another
name for Aphrodite.
*(Cytheria, Cytherere,
Cytherine)*

Cytherere See **Cytherea**

Cytherine See **Cytherea**

Cadby [Norse]
'Warrior's settlement'.

Cadda See **Chad**

Caddock [Celtic]
'Keenness in battle'. An
eager warrior.

Cadell [Celtic]
'Battle spirit'.

Cadeyrn [Welsh]
'Battle king'.

Cadfan [Welsh]
'Battle peak'.

Cadman [Celtic]
'Battle man'.

Cadmus [Greek]
'Man from the east'. The
legendary scholar who
devised the Greek
alphabet.

Cadwallader [Celtic]
'Battle leader'.

Caesar [Latin]
'Emperor'. Source of all
names meaning Emperor
— Tsar, Kaiser, Shah,
etc.
(Cesare, Cesar)

Cain [Hebrew]
'The possessed'. The
original murderer.

Calder [Anglo-Saxon]
'The brook'.

Caldwell [Anglo-Saxon]
'The cold spring (or
well)'.

Cale See **Caleb**

Caleb [Hebrew]
'The bold one'. The
impetuous hero.
(Cal, Cale)

Caley [Gaelic]
'Thin, slender'.

Calhoun [Gaelic]
'From the forest strip'.

Callum See **Columba**

Calvert [Anglo-Saxon]
'Calf minder'.

Calvert See **Calvin**

Calvin [Latin]
'Bald'.
(Calvert, Calvino, Cal)

Calvino See **Calvin**

Camden [Gaelic]
'From the valley which
winds'.

Cameron [Celtic]
'Crooked nose'. The
founder of the Scottish
Clan.
(Cam, Camm)

Camm See **Cameron**

Campbell [Celtic]
'Crooked mouth'.
Founder of Clan
Campbell.

Cannon See **Channing**

Canute [Norse]
'The knot'. Name of the
king who tried to hold
back the waves.
(Knut, Knute)

Caradoc [Celtic]
'Beloved'.

Carey [Celtic]
'One who lives in a
castle'.
(Cary)

Carl See **Charles**

Carleton [Anglo-Saxon]
'Farmers' meeting place'.
(Carlton, Carl)

Carlin [Gaelic]
'Little champion'.
(Carling)

Carling See **Carlin**

Carlisle [Anglo-Saxon]
'Tower of the castle'.
(Carlile, Carlyle, Carlysle)

Carlo See **Charles**

Carlos See **Charles**

Carmichael [Celtic]
'From St. Michael's
castle'.

Carney [Gaelic]
'Victorious'. The warrior
who never lost a battle.
(Carny, Kearney)

Carol [Gaelic]
'The champion'. The
unbeatable fighter.
(Carroll)

Carol See **Charles**

Carollan [Gaelic]
'Little champion'.

Carr [Norse]
'One who dwells beside a marsh'.
(Karr, Kerr)

Carrick [Gaelic]
'The rocky cape'.

Carroll See **Carol**

Carson [Anglo-Saxon]
'Son of the marsh-dweller'.

Carswell [Anglo-Saxon]
'The water cress grower'.

Carter [Anglo-Saxon]
'The cart driver'. One who transports cattle and goods.

Cartland [Celtic]
'The land between the rivers'.

Carvell [French]
'Estate in the marshes'.
(Carvel)

Carver [Old English]
'Woodcarver'.

Carvey [Gaelic]
'The athlete'.
(Carvy)

Cary See **Carey** or **Charles**

Casey [Gaelic]
'Brave and watchful'.
The warrior who never slept.

Cash See **Cassius**

Casimir [Slavic]
'The proclaimer of peace'.
(Cass, Cassie, Cassy, Kazimir, Kasimir)

Caspar [Persian]
'Master of the treasure'.
One trusted to guard the most precious possessions.
(Casper, Gaspar, Gasper)

Cassidy [Gaelic]
'Ingenuity' or 'curly-haired'.

Cassius [Latin]
'Vain and conceited'.
Never far from a mirror.

Castor [Greek]
'The beaver'. An industrious person.

Cathmor [Gaelic]
'Great warrior'.

Cato [Latin]
'The wise one'. One with
great worldly knowledge.

Cavan [Gaelic]
'The handsome'. The
Irish Adonis!
(Kavan)

Cavell [French]
'Little lively one'. Always
up and doing.

Cawley [Norse]
'Ancestral relic'.

Cecil [Latin]
'The unseeing one'.
(Sissil)

Cedric [Celtic]
'Chieftain'.

Cephas [Aramaic]
'Rock'.

Cerwyn [Welsh]
'Fair love'.

Chad [Anglo-Saxon]
'Warlike; bellicose'.
(Cadda, Chadda)

Chadda See **Chad**

Chadwick [Anglo-Saxon]
'Town of the warrior'.

Chaim [Hebrew]
'Life'.

Chalmer [Celtic]
'The chamberlain's son'
or 'King of the
household'.
(Chalmers)

Chalmers See **Chalmer**

Chan See **Channing**

Chance [Anglo-Saxon]
'Good fortune'.
(Chaunce, Chauncey)

Chancellor [Anglo-Saxon]
'King's counsellor'. A
man trusted with the
highest state secrets.
*(Chaunceler, Chaunceller,
Chanceller)*

Chandler [French]
'The candle maker'.

Chaney [French]
'Oak wood'.

Channing [French]
'The canon'.
(Chan, Cannon)

Chapman [Anglo-Saxon]
'The merchant'. The
travelling salesmen of
medieval times.

Charles [Teutonic]
'The strong man'. The
personification of all that
is masculine.
(Carl, Carlos, Carol, Carrol,
Charley, Charlie, Chas,
Carlo, Cary, Carey, Chuck,
Karl, Karol, Tearlach)

Charley See **Charles**

Charlton [Anglo-Saxon]
'Charles's farm'.
(Charleton)

Chas See **Charles**

Chase [French]
'The hunter'. One who
enjoys the chase.

Chatham [Anglo-Saxon]
'Land of the soldier'.

Chauncey [French]
'Chancellor; record
keeper'. Also var. of
Chance and Chancellor.
(Chancey, Chaunce)

Chauncey See **Chance**

Cheiro [Greek]
'Hand'.

Cheney [French]
'Oak forest dweller'. A
woodman.
(Cheyney)

Ches See **Chester**

Chester [Latin]
'The fortified camp'.
(Cheston, Ches, Chet)

Cheston See **Chester**

Chet See **Chester**

Chetwin [Anglo-Saxon]
'Cottage dweller by the
winding path'.
(Chetwyn)

Chevalier [French]
'Knight'.

Cheyney See **Cheney**

Chilton [Anglo-Saxon]
'From the farm by the
spring'.
(Chelton)

Chris See **Christopher**

Christian [Latin]
'Believer in Christ; a
Christian'.
*(Chris, Christy, Christie,
Kristian, Kristin, Kit)*

Christophe See
Christopher

Christopher [Greek]
'The Christ carrier'. The
man who carried the
infant Christ across the
river.
*(Chris, Christophe, Kit,
Kester, Kris, Kriss,
Gillecirosd)*

Christy See **Christian**

Chrysander [Greek]
'Golden man'.

Chuck See **Charles**

Churchill [Anglo-Saxon]
'Dweller by the church on
the hill'.

Cian [Gaelic]
'The ancient one'. One
who lives long.

Cicero [Latin]
'The chick-pea'.

Clare [Latin]
'Famous one' (Latin) or
'Bright, illustrious'
(Anglo-Saxon).
(Clair)

Clarence [Latin/Anglo-
Saxon]
'Famous, illustrious one'.
(Clavance)

Clark [French]
'Wise and learned
scholar'.
(Clarke)

Claud [Latin]
'The lame'.
(Claude)

Claus See **Nicholas**

Clavance See **Clarence**

Clay [Anglo-Saxon]
'From the clay pit'.

Clay See **Clayborne**

Clayborne [Anglo-Saxon]
'From the brook by the
clay pit'.
*(Clay, Claiborn,
Claybourne)*

Clayton [Anglo-Saxon]
'From the clay town' or
'Mortal man'.

Cleary [Gaelic]
'The scholar'.

Cledwyn [Welsh]
'Blessed sword'.

Clem See **Clement**

Clemence See **Clement**

Clemens See **Clement**

Clement [Latin]
'Kind and merciful'.
(Clemence, Clemens, Clem,
Clemmy, Clim)

Clemmy See **Clement**

Cleve See **Clive**

Cleveland [Anglo-Saxon]
'From the cliff land'.

Cliff See **Clifford**

Clifford [Anglo-Saxon]
'From the ford by the
cliff'.
(Clif, Cliff)

Clifton [Anglo-Saxon]
'From the farm by the
cliff'.

Clim See **Clement**

Clint See **Clinton**

Clinton [Anglo-Saxon]
'From the farm on the
headland'.
(Clint)

Clive [Anglo-Saxon]
'Cliff'.
(Cleve, Cleeve, Clyve)

Clovis [Teutonic]
An early form of Lewis
(Louis) — 'Famous
warrior'.

Cluny [Gaelic]
'From the meadow'.

Clydai [Welsh]
'Fame'.

Clyde [Celtic]
'Warm' (Welsh Celtic),
'Heard from the distance'
(Scots Celtic)

Cobb See **Jacob**

Cody [Old English]
'A cushion'.

Coel [Welsh]
'Trust'.
(Cole)

Colan See **Colin**

Colbert [Anglo-Saxon]
'Brilliant seafarer' or
'Cool and calm'.
(Colvert, Culbert)

Colby [Norse]
'From the dark country'.

Cole See **Coleman** or
Nicholas

Coleman [Anglo-Saxon/
Celtic]
'Follower of Nicholas'
(Anglo-Saxon) or
'Keeper of the Doves'
(Celtic).
(Colman, Col, Cole)

Colin [Gaelic]
'Strong and virile' or
'The young child' or
'Victorious army'.
(Collin, Colan, Cailean,
and all der. of *Nicholas)*

Colis See **Collier**

Colley [Old English]
'Swarthy'.

Collier [Anglo-Saxon]
'Charcoal merchant'.
(Colier, Colis, Collyer,
Colyer)

Colm See **Columba**

Colman See **Coleman**

Colter [Anglo-Saxon]
'The colt herder'. A lover
of horses.

Colton [Anglo-Saxon]
'From the dark town'.

Columba [Latin]
'Dove'.
(Callum, Colum, Colm)

Colver See **Culver**

Colvert See **Colbert**

Con See **Conrad**

Conal See **Conan**

Conan [Celtic]
'High and mighty' or
'Wisely intelligent'.
(Conal, Conant, Connall,
Connel, Con, Conn, Kynan,
Quinn)

Conant See **Conan**

Conlan [Gaelic]
'The hero'.
(Conlin, Conlon)

Conlin See **Conlan**

Conlon See **Conlan**

Conn See **Conan**

Connel See **Conan**

Connie See **Conrad**

Connor [Old English]
'Wise aid'.

Conrad [Teutonic]
'Brave counsellor'. One
who told what was right;
not what the receiver
wanted to hear.
*(Con, Connie, Cort, Curt,
Konrad, Kort, Kurt)*

Conroy [Gaelic]
'The wise one'.

Constant See **Constantine**

Constantin See
Constantine

Constantine [Latin]
'Firm and unwavering'.
Always constant.
*(Constantin, Konstantin,
Konstantine, Constant,
Conn)*

Conway [Gaelic]
'Hound of the plain'.

Coop See **Cooper**

Cooper [Anglo-Saxon]
'Barrel maker'.
(Coop)

Corbett [French]
'The raven'. From the
raven device worn by the
ancient Vikings.
*(Corbet, Corbin, Corbie,
Corby)*

Corbie See **Corbett**

Corbin See **Corbett**

Corcoran [Gaelic]
'Reddish complexion'.
(Corquoran)

Cordell [French]
'Rope maker'.

Corey [Gaelic]
'Dweller in a ravine'.
(Cory)

Cormac See **Cormick**

Cormick [Gaelic]
'The charioteer'.
(Cormac, Cormack)

Cornelius [Latin]
'Battle horn'.
*(Cornell, Cornel, Cornall,
Cornal, Neal, Neil)*

Cornell See **Cornelius**

Cort See **Conrad**

Corty See **Courtenay**

Corwin [French]
'Friend of the heart'.
(Corwen)

Corydon [Greek]
'The helmeted man'.

Cosimo See **Cosmo**

Cosme See **Cosmo**

Cosmo [Greek]
'The perfect order of the universe'.
(Cosme, Cosimo)

Court See **Courtland**

Courtenay [French]
'A place'.
(Courtney, Court, Cort, Cortie, Corty)

Courtland [Anglo-Saxon]
'One who dwelt on the court land'.
(Court)

Covell [Anglo-Saxon]
'Dweller in the cave on the slope'.
(Covill)

Covill See **Covell**

Cowan [Gaelic]
'Hollow in the hillside'.

Coyle [Gaelic]
'Battle follower'.
(Coile)

Craddock [Celtic]
'Abundance of love'.
(Caradoc, Caradock)

Craig [Celtic]
'From the stony hill'.

Crandell [Anglo-Saxon]
'Dweller in the valley of the crane'.
(Crandall)

Cranley [Anglo-Saxon]
'From the crane meadow'.

Cranog [Welsh]
'Heron'.

Cranston [Anglo-Saxon]
'From the farmstead where the cranes gather'.

Crawford [Anglo-Saxon]
'From the crow ford'.
(Crowford)

Creighton [Anglo-Saxon]
'From the farm by the creek'.
(*Crayton*)

Crepin See **Crispin**

Crisp See **Crispin**

Crispin [Latin]
'Curly haired'. St. Crispin, the patron saint of shoemakers.
(*Crispen, Crisp, Crepin*)

Cromwell [Anglo-Saxon]
'One who lives by a winding spring'. The small rivulet that twists and winds through the countryside.

Crosby [Anglo-Saxon/ Norse]
'Dweller at the crossroads' (Anglo-Saxon) or 'Dweller by the shrine of the cross' (Norse).
(*Crosbey, Crosbie*)

Crosley [Anglo-Saxon]
'From the meadow with the cross'.

Crowford See **Crawford**

Culbert See **Colbert**

Cullen [Gaelic]
'Handsome one'.
(*Cullan, Cullin*)

Culley [Gaelic]
'From the woodland'.
(*Cully*)

Culver [Anglo-Saxon]
'Gentle as the dove, peaceful'. The symbol of peace.
(*Colver*)

Curran [Gaelic]
'The resolute hero'. One who would die defending the right.
(*Curren, Currey, Currie, Curry*)

Curren See **Curran**

Curt See **Conrad**

Curtis [French]
'The courteous one'. A gentleman with perfect manners.
(*Curtis, Curt, Kurt*)

Cuthbert [Anglo-Saxon]
'Famous and brilliant'. One famed for his high intellect.

Cyndeyrn [Welsh]
'Chief lord'.

Cynfael [Welsh]
'Chief metal'.

Cynfor [Welsh]
'Great chief'.

Cyngen [Welsh]
'Chief son'.

Cynric [Anglo-Saxon]
'From the royal line of
kings'.

Cynyr [Welsh]
'Chief hero'.

Cyprian [Greek]
'Man from Cyprus'. The
birthplace of Venus.
(Ciprian, Cyprien)

Cyrano [Greek]
'From Cyrene'.
(Cyrenaica)

Cyrenaica See **Cyrano**

Cyril [Greek]
'The lord'.
(Cyrill, Cyrille)

Cyrus [Persian]
'The sun god'. The
founder of the Persian
Empire.

Girls

Dacia [Greek]
'From Dacia'.

Daffodil [Greek]
'Golden spring flower'.

Dagmar [Norse]
'Glory of the Danes'.

Dahlia
'Of the valley'. From the
flower of the same name.

Daisy [Anglo-Saxon]
'The day's eye'. Also a
nickname for Margaret
(Marguerite), the name
of the daisy in French.

Dale [Teutonic]
'From the valley'. An
earlier form of Dahlia.

Dallas [Gaelic]
'Wise'.

Damara [Greek]
  'Gentle girl'.
  (Damaris, Mara, Maris)

Damaris See **Damara**

Damita [Spanish]
  'Little noble lady'.

Dana [Scandinavian]
  'From Denmark'.

Danae [Greek]
  Mother of Perseus.

Danella See **Danielle**

Danelle See **Danielle**

Danica [Norse]
  'The morning star'.

Daniela See **Danielle**

Danielea See **Danielle**

Danielle [Hebrew]
  'God is my judge'. Fem.
  of Daniel.
  (Danielea, Danella, Danelle, Daniela)

Danuta [Polish]
  'Young deer'.

Daphne [Greek]
  'Bay tree'. Symbol of
  victory. The nymph who
  was turned into a laurel
  bush to escape the
  attentions of Apollo.

Dara [Hebrew]
  'Charity, compassion and
  wisdom'.

Darcia See **Darcy**

Darcie [French]
  'From the fortress'. Fem.
  of D'Arcy.
  (D'Arcie)

Darcy [Celtic]
  'Girl of dark hair'.
  (Darcia, Dercy)

Darees See **Darice**

Darel [Anglo-Saxon]
  'Little dear one'. Another
  form of Darlene.
  (Darelle, Darrelle, Darry, Daryl)

Daria [Greek]
  'Wealthy queen'. Fem. of
  Darius.

Darice [Persian]
  'Queenly'.
  (Dareece, Darees)

Darlene [Anglo-Saxon]
'Little darling'.
(Darleen, Darline, Daryl)

Daron [Gaelic]
'Great'.

Darry See **Darel**

Daryl See **Darlene**

Davina [Hebrew]
'Beloved'. Fem. of David.

Dawn [Anglo-Saxon]
'The break of day'. One
who lightens the
darkness.

Deane See **Dena**

Deanna See **Diana**

Debby See **Deborah**

Deborah [Hebrew]
'The bee'. An industrious
woman who looks only
for what is sweet in life.
*(Debora, Debra, Debbie,
Debby)*

Decima [Latin]
'Tenth daughter'.
'Dark beauty'. Also a
dim. of Diana.

Dee See **Audrey** or **Diana**

Deel See **Dorothy**

Deirdre [Gaelic]
'Sorrow'. A legendary
Irish beauty — 'Deirdre
of the Sorrows'.
(Deidre)

Dela See **Adelaide**

Delcine See **Dulcie**

Delfina See **Delfine**

Delfine [Greek]
'The larkspur or
delphinium flower'.
*(Delfina, Delphina, Delveen,
Delphine)*

Delia [Greek]
'Visible'. Another name
for the Moon Goddess.
Also one who came from
Delos.

Delia See **Bedelia**

Delicia [Latin]
'Delightful maiden'.
'Spirit of delight'.

Delight [French]
'Pleasure'. One who
brings happiness to her
family.

Delilah [Hebrew]
'The gentle temptress'.
Betrayer of the Biblical
Samson.
(Delila, Dalila, Lila)

Della See **Adelaide**

Delma [Spanish]
'Of the Sea'.
(Delmar, Delmare)

Delmar See **Delma**

Delmare See **Delma**

Delora [Latin]
'From the seashore'.
(Dellora)

Delora See **Dolores**

Delores See **Dolores**

Deloris See **Dolores**

Delorita See **Dolores**

Delphine [Greek]
'Calmness and serenity'.
(Delfine)

Delta [Greek]
'Fourth daughter'. The
fourth letter of the Greek
alphabet.

Delwen [Welsh]
'Neat, fair'.

Delyth [Welsh]
'Neat, pretty'.

Demeter See **Demetria**

Demetria [Greek]
'Fertility'. The Goddess
of Fertility.
(Demeter)

Dena [Anglo-Saxon]
'From the valley'.
(Deana, Deane)

Denise [French]
'Wine goddess'. Fem. of
Dionysus, God of wine.
(Denice, Denys)

Dercia See **Darcy**

Dercy See **Darcy**

Derryth [Welsh]
'Of the oak'.

Desdemona [Greek]
'One born under an
unlucky star'. After the
heroine of Shakespeare's
Othello.
(Desmona)

Desiree [French]
'Desired one'.

Desma [Greek]
'A pledge'.

Desmona See **Desdemona**

Desta See **Modesty**

Destinee [Old French]
'Destiny'.

Deva [Sanskrit]
'Divine'. The Moon
Goddess.

Devin [Gaelic]
'Poet'.

Devona [English]
'From Devon'. Someone
born in that county, the
name of which means
'People of the deep valley'.

Dextra [Latin]
'Skilful, adept'.

Diamanta [French]
'Diamond like'. One who
is as precious as the rarest
jewel.

Diana [Latin]
'Divine Moon Goddess'.
Roman Goddess of the
Moon and the Chase.
*(Deanna, Diane, Dianna,
Dyana, Dyanna, Dyane, Di,
Dian, Dee)*

Diane See **Diana**

Diantha [Greek]
'Divine flower of Zeus'.
(Dianthe, Dianthia)

Dianthe See **Diantha**

Dianthia See **Diantha**

Dido [Greek]
'Teacher'.

Dilys [Welsh]
'Perfect'.

Dinah [Hebrew]
'Judgement'. One whose
understanding is
complete.

Dione [Greek]
'The daughter of heaven
and earth'.

Disa [Norse or Greek]
'Lively spirit' (Norse) or
'Double' (Greek).

Dixie [French]
'The tenth'.
(Dixey, Dixy, Dixil)

Dixie See **Benedicta**

Dixil See **Dixie**

Doanna [Combination Dorothy/Anna]

Docie See **Endocia**

Docila [Latin]
'Gentle teacher'.

Dodi See **Doris**

Dodie [Hebrew]
'Beloved'.

Dolley See **Dorothy**

Dolly See **Dolores** or **Dorothy**

Dolores [Spanish]
'Lady of Sorrow'.
Deriving from 'Our Lady of Sorrows', which depicts the seven sad occasions in the Virgin's life.
(Delores, Delora, Deloris, Delorita, Dolly, Lola, Lolita)

Domina [Latin]
'The lady'. One of noble birth.

Dominica [Latin]
'Belonging to the Lord'.
Fem. of Dominic.
(Dominique, Domenica, Dominga)

Dominique See **Dominica**

Dominga See **Dominica**

Donalda [Gaelic]
'Ruler of the world'. Fem. of Donald.

Donata [Latin]
'The gift'.

Donna [Italian]
'Noble lady'.
(Dona)

Dora See **Dorothy** or **Eudora**

Dorcas [Greek]
'Graceful'. A girl with the grace of a gazelle.

Dore [French]
'Golden maiden'.

Dore See **Dorothy**

Doreen [Gaelic]
'Golden girl', alternatively 'The sullen one'.
(Dorene, Dorine, Dori, Dorie, Dory, Dora)

Doretta See **Dorothy**

Dori See **Doreen**

Dorinda [Greek/Spanish]
'Beautiful golden gift'.

Doris [Greek]
'From the sea'. The
daughter of Oceanus.
*(Dora, Dorice, Dorise,
Dorris, Dodi)*

Dorothea See **Dorothy**

Dorothoe See **Dorothy**

Dorothy
'Gift of God'. A form of
Theodora.
*(Dorothoe, Dora, Doretta,
Dorothea, Dorothi, Dorthea,
Dorthy, Deel, Dolley, Dollie,
Dolly, Dore, Dot, Dotty,
Theodora)*

Dot See **Dorothy**

Dotty See **Dorothy**

Douna [Slavic]
'Valley'.

Dove [English]
'Bird of peace'.

Doxie See **Endocia**

Druella [Teutonic]
'Elfin vision'.
(Druilla)

Drusilla [Latin]
'The strong one'. One
with patience and
fortitude.

Duana [Gaelic]
'Little dark maiden'.
(Duna, Dwana)

Duena [Spanish]
'Chaperon'. A name
given to women of good
birth who were
responsible for the
manners and morals of
the young girls in their
charge.
(Duenna)

Dulce See **Dulcie**

Dulcea See **Dulcie**

Dulciana See **Dulcie**

Dulcibella See **Dulcie**

Dulcibelle See **Dulcie**

Dulcie [Latin]
'Sweet and charming'.
One who believes that
love is the sweetest thing.
*(Dulciana, Dulcibelle,
Dulcibella, Delcine, Dulce,
Dulcea, Dulcine, Dulcinea)*

Dulcine See **Dulcie**

Dulcinea See **Dulcie**

Durene [Latin]
'The enduring one'.

Duscha [Russian]
'Soul'.

Dwana See **Duana**

Dyane See **Diana**

Dympha See **Dymphia**

Dymphia [Latin]
'Nurse'.
(Dimphia, Dympha)

Dympna [Irish]
'Eligible'.
(Dymphna)

Dysis [Greek]
'Sunset'.

Dacey [Gaelic]
'The southerner'.
(Dacy)

Dag [Norse]
'Day of brightness'.

Dagan [Semitic]
'The earth' or 'The small
fish'.
(Dagon)

Dagwood [Anglo-Saxon]
'Forest of the shining
one'.

Dal See **Dallas**

Dalbert [Anglo-Saxon]
'From the shining valley'.
(Delbert)

Dale [Teutonic]
'Dweller in the valley'.

Dallas [Celtic]
'Skilled' or 'From the
water field'.
(Dal)

Dalston [Old English]
'From Daegal's place'.

Dalton [Anglo-Saxon]
'From the farm in the
valley'.

Daly [Gaelic]
'The counsellor'.

Dalziel [Celtic]
'From the little field'.
(Dalziell)

Damek [Slavic]
'Man of the earth'.

Damien See **Damon**

Damon [Greek]
'Tame and
domesticated'. The true
friend.
(Damien)

Dana [Anglo-Saxon]
'Man from Denmark'.
(Dane)

Danby [Norse]
'From the settlement of
the Danish'.

Dane See **Dana**

Daniel [Hebrew]
'The Lord is my judge'.
*(Daniell, Danielle, Dane,
Darnell, Dan, Danny)*

Danny See **Daniel**

Dante See **Durant**

Darby [Gaelic]
'Freeman'.
(Derby)

Darcy [French]
'From the fortress'.
*(Darcie, D'Arcy, Darsey,
Darsy)*

Darien [Spanish]
A place name.

Darius [Greek]
'The wealthy man'.

Darnell [French]
'From the hidden nook'.

Darnell See **Daniel**

Darrell [French]
'Beloved one'.
(Daryl, Darryl)

Darren [Gaelic]
'Little great one'.

Darton [Anglo-Saxon]
'From the deer forest'.

Darwin [Old English]
'Beloved friend'.

Dave See **David**

David [Hebrew]
'The beloved one'. St.
David, the patron saint of
Wales.
(Dave, Davie, Davy, Davis)

Davin [Scandinavian]
'Brightness of the Finns'.

Davis [Anglo-Saxon]
David's son.

Davis See **David**

Davy See **David**

Dean [Anglo-Saxon]
'From the valley'.
(Deane, Dene)

Dearborn [Anglo-Saxon]
'Beloved child' or 'From
the deer brook'.

Deck See **Dexter**

Dedrick [Teutonic]
'Ruler of the people'.

Deems [Anglo-Saxon]
'The judge's son'.

Delaney [Gaelic]
'Descendant of the
challenger'.

Delano [French]
'From the nut tree
woods'.

Delbert See **Albert**

Delling [Norse]
'Very shining one'.

Delmar [Latin]
'From the sea'.
(Delmer, Delmore)

Delmore See **Delmar**

Delwyn [Anglo-Saxon]
'Bright friend from the
valley'.
(Delwin)

Demas [Greek]
'The popular person'.

Demetrius [Greek]
'Belonging to Demeter'.
(Dimitri, Dmitri, Demmy)

Demmy See **Demetrius**

Demos [Greek]
'The spokesman of the
people'.

Demosthenes [Greek]
'Strength of the people'.

Dempsey [Gaelic]
'The proud one'.

Dempster [Anglo-Saxon]
'The judge'.

Den See **Dennis**

Denby [Norse]
'From the Danish
settlement'.

Denley [Anglo-Saxon]
'Dweller in the meadow
in the valley'.

Denman [Anglo-Saxon]
'Resident in the valley'.

Dennie See **Dennis**

Dennis [Greek]
'Wine lover'. From
Dionysus, the God of
Wine.
*(Denis, Denys, Dennison,
Denzil, Dion, Den, Dennie,
Denny, Deny)*

Dennison [Anglo-Saxon]
'Son of Dennis'.
(Denison)

Dennison See **Dennis**

Denton [Anglo-Saxon]
'From the farm in the
valley'.

Denver [Anglo-Saxon]
'From the edge of the
valley'.

Denzil [Cornish]
'High stronghold'.

Denzil See **Dennis**

Deodatus [Latin]
'God-given'.

Derby See **Darby**

Derek [Teutonic]
'Ruler of the people'.
*(Derrick, Derk, Dirk,
Derry)*

Derk See **Derek**

Dermot [Gaelic]
'Free man'.

Derry [Gaelic]
'The red one'.

Derry See **Derek**

Derward [Anglo-Saxon]
'Guardian of the deer'.

Derwin [Anglo-Saxon]
'Dearest friend'.

Desmond [Gaelic]
'Man of the world;
sophisticated'.

Deverell [Celtic]
'From the river bank'.

Devin [Celtic]
'A poet'.

Devlin [Gaelic]
'Fierce bravery'.

Dewey [Celtic]
'The beloved one'. The
Celtic form of David.

De Witt [Flemish]
'Fair haired one'.

Dex See **Dexter**

Dexter [Latin]
'The right handed man;
dextrous'.
(Deck, Dex)

Diamond [Anglo-Saxon]
'The shining protector'.

Diccon See **Richard**

Dick See **Richard**

Dickie See **Richard**

Dickon See **Richard**

Diego See **Jacob**

Dieter [German]
'From strong people'.

Digby [Norse]
'From the settlement by
the dyke'.

Diggory [French]
'Strayed, lost'.

Dillon [Gaelic]
'Faithful'. A true and
loyal man.

Dimitri See **Demetrius**

Dinsmore [Gaelic]
'From the fortified hill'.

Diomede [Greek]
'Divine ruler'.

Dion See **Dennis**

Dirk See **Derek**

Dixon [Anglo-Saxon]
'Son of Richard' (Dick's
son).
(Dickson)

Dixon See **Benedict**

Doane [Celtic]
'From the sand dune'.

Dolan [Gaelic]
'Black haired'.

Dolf See **Adolph**

Dolph See **Adolph**

Dom See **Dominic**

Domingo See **Dominic**

Dominic [Latin]
'Belonging to the Lord;
born on the Lord's day'.
*(Dominic, Domingo,
Dominy, Dom, Nic, Nick,
Nickie, Nicky)*

Dominy See **Dominic**

Don See **Donald**

Donahue [Gaelic]
'Warrior clad in brown'.
(Don, Donn)

Donal See **Donald**

Donald [Celtic]
'Ruler of the world'. The
founder of Clan Donald
(MacDonald).
*(Donal, Donnall, Donnell,
Don, Donn, Donnie, Donny)*

Donato [Latin]
'A gift'.

Donnell See **Donald**

Donnelly [Gaelic]
'Brave dark man'.

Donny See **Donald**

Donovan [Irish]
'Dark brown'.

Doran [Celtic]
'The stranger'.

Dorcas [Hebrew]
'From the forest'.

Dore See **Theodore**

Dorian [Greek]
'Man from Doria'.

Dory [French]
'The golden haired'.

Doug See **Douglas**

Dougal See **Douglas**

Douggie See **Douglas**

Douglas [Celtic]
'From the dark stream'.
One of the largest
Scottish clans.
*(Duglass, Dougal, Dugal,
Dugald, Doug, Douggie,
Douggy, Duggie, Duggy)*

Dow [Gaelic]
'Black haired'.

Doyle [Gaelic]
'The dark haired
stranger'.

Drake [Anglo-Saxon]
'The dragon'.

Drew [Celtic]
'The wise one'. Also dim.
of Andrew.

Driscoll [Celtic]
'The interpreter'.
(Driscol)

Drostan See **Tristan**

Druce [Celtic]
'Son of Drew'.

Drury [French]
'The dear one'.

Dryden [Anglo-Saxon]
'From the dry valley'.

Duane See **Dwayne**

Duddie See **Dudley**

Dudley [Anglo-Saxon]
'From the people's
meadow'.
*(Dudly, Dud, Duddie,
Duddy)*

Duff [Gaelic]
'Dark complexion'.

Dugal See **Douglas**

Dugald See **Douglas**

Dugan [Gaelic]
'Dark skinned'. The
suntanned man.
(Dougan, Doogan)

Duke [French]
'The leader'.

Duke See **Marmaduke**

Duncan [Celtic]
'Brown warrior'.
(Dunc)

Dunham [Celtic]
'Dark man'.

Dunley [Anglo-Saxon]
'From the meadow on the
hill'.

Dunmore [Celtic]
'From the fortress on the
hill'.

Dunn [Anglo-Saxon]
'Dark skinned'.

Dunstan [Anglo-Saxon]
'From the brown stone
hill'.

Durand See **Durant**

Durant [Latin]
'Enduring'. One whose
friendship is lasting.
(Durand, Dante)

Durward [Anglo-Saxon]
'The gate keeper'. The
guardian of the
drawbridge.

Durwin [Anglo-Saxon]
'Dear friend'.
(Durwyn)

Dustin [Old German]
'Valiant fighter'.

Dwayne [Gaelic/Celtic]
'The small dark man'
(Gaelic) or 'The singer'
(Celtic).
(Duane)

Dwight [Teutonic]
'The light haired one'.

Dyfan [Welsh]
'Tribe ruler'.

Dylan [Welsh]
'Man from the sea'.

Dynawd [Welsh]
'Given'.

Girls

Eadwine See **Edwina**

Earlene [Anglo-Saxon]
'Noble woman'. Fem. of
Earl.
*(Earlie, Earley, Earline,
Erlene, Erline)*

Earlie See **Earlene**

Earline See **Earlene**

Eartha [Old English]
'Of the earth'.
*(Ertha, Erda, Herta,
Hertha)*

Easter [Old English]
'Born at Easter'. The pre-
Christian Goddess of
Spring.
(Eastre, Eostre)

Eastre See **Easter**

Ebba [Anglo-Saxon]
Form of Eve, *q.v.*

Ebony [Greek]
'A hard, dark wood'.

Echo [Greek]
'Repeating sound'. From
the Greek nymph who
pined away for love.

Eda [Anglo-Saxon/
Greek]
'Poetry' (Anglo-Saxon).
'Loving mother of many'
or 'Prosperous' (Greek).
(Eada, Edda)

Eda See **Edith**

Edana [Gaelic]
'Little fiery one'. A
warmly loving child,
whose ardent nature is
said to have been
bestowed by God himself.
(Aiden, Aidan, Eidann)

Ede See **Edith**

Edelina See **Adelaide**

Edeline See **Adelaide**

Eden [Hebrew]
'Enchanting'. The
epitome of all female
charm.

Edina [Scottish]
Another form of Edwina,
q.v.

Edina See **Edwina**

Edith [Teutonic]
'Rich gift'.
*(Eadith, Eda, Edythe,
Eadie, Eaidie, Eady, Ede,
Edie, Edithe, Ediva, Editha)*

Editha See **Edith**

Ediva See **Edith**

Edlyn [Anglo-Saxon]
'Noble maiden'.

Edmonda [Anglo-Saxon]
'Rich protector'. Fem. of
Edmund.
(Edmunda)

Edna [Hebrew]
'Rejuvenation'. One who
knows the secret of
eternal youth.
(Edny, Ed, Eddie)

Edny See **Edna**

Edra See **Edrea**

Edrea [Anglo-Saxon]
'Powerful and
prosperous'. Fem. of
Edric.
(Andrea, Eadrea, Edra)

Edwardina [Anglo-Saxon]
'Rich guardian'. Fem. of
Edward.

Edwina [Anglo-Saxon]
'Rich friend'.
*(Eadwina, Eadwine,
Edwine, Edina, Win, Wina,
Winnie)*

Effie [Greek]
'Famous beauty'.
(Effy)

Effie See **Euphemia**

Egberta [Anglo-Saxon]
'Bright, shining sword'.
Fem. of Egbert.
*(Egbertha, Egberthe,
Egberte, Egbertina,
Egbertine)*

Egberte See **Egberta**

Egberthe See **Egberta**

Egbertina See **Egberta**

Egbertine See **Egberta**

Eglantina See **Eglantine**

Eglantine [French]
'The wild rose'.
*(Eglantina, Eglintyne,
Eglyntine)*

Eiblin [Gaelic]
'Pleasant'.
(Eveleen)

Eileen [Celtic] See **Helen**

Eilwen [Welsh]
'Fair brow'.

Eir [Norse]
'Peace and mercy'. The
goddess of healing.

Eirena See **Irene**

Eirian [Welsh]
'Silver'.

Eiric See **Henrietta**

Eirlys [Welsh]
'Snowdrop'

Eirwen [Welsh]
'Snow-white'.

Eister See **Esther**

Ekaterina See **Catherine**

Elaine [French] See
Helen

Elana [Hebrew]
'Oak tree'.

Elata [Latin]
'Lofty, noble'. A woman
of high birth and beauty.

Eldora [Spanish]
'Gilded one'. From El
Dorado, the land of gold.

Eldrida [Teutonic]
'Old and wise adviser'.
Fem. of Eldred.
(Aeldrida)

Eleanor [French]
A medieval form of
Helen.
*(Eleanore, Eleanora, Elinor,
Elinore, Elinora, Eleonor,
Eleonora, Eleonore, Elnore,
Leonora, Leonore, Lenora,
Lenore, Leanor)*

Eleanor See **Helen**

Eleanora See **Eleanor**

Electra [Greek]
'Brilliant one'.

Elfreda [Teutonic]
'Wise counsellor'. See
also Alfreda.
(Elfrida, Elfrieda, Aelfreda)

Elga [Slav]
'Consecrated'.
(Olga)

Elga See **Alfreda**

Elga See **Olga**

Elinora See **Helen**

Elisa See **Elizabeth**

Elise See **Elizabeth**

Elissa See **Elizabeth**

Elita See **Melita**

Elizabeth [Hebrew]
'Consecrated to God'.
Isabel is another version
of this name.
*(Elisabeth, Elisa, Elise,
Elissa, Eliza, Elyse, Elysa,
Elsie, Elsa, Else, Elsbeth,
Elspeth, Bess, Bessie, Bessy,
Beth, Betsy, Betty, Betta,
Bette, Betina, Liza, Lizzy,
Lizabeta, Lisbeth, Lizbeth,
Libby)*. And all the
various forms of Isabel/
Isabella.

Elke See **Alice**

Ella [Teutonic]
'Beautiful fairy maiden'.
Beauty bestowed by
fairies as a birth gift. Also
form of Helen.

Ellen See **Helen**

Ellice [Greek]
'Jehovah is God'. Fem. of
Elias.
(Ellis)

Elma [Greek]
'Pleasant and amiable'.

Elmina [Old German]
'Awe-inspiring fame'.

Elmira See **Almira**

Elna See **Helen**

Elnore See **Eleanor**

Elodie [Greek]
'Fragile flower'.

Eloisa See **Louise**

Eloise See **Louise**
'Noble one'. Also form of
Elizabeth.

Elrica [Teutonic]
'Ruler of all'.
(Ulrica)

Elsa [Anglo-Saxon]

Elsa See **Elizabeth**

Elsbeth See **Elizabeth**

Else See **Elizabeth**

Elsie See **Elizabeth**

Elspeth See **Elizabeth**

Elswyth [Old English]
'Noble strength'.

Eluned [Welsh]
'Idol'.

Elva [Anglo-Saxon]
'Friend of the elves'.
(Elvia, Elvie, Elfie, Elvina)

Elva See **Alfreda**

Elvera See **Elvira**

Elvia See **Elva**

Elvie See **Elva**

Elvira [Latin]
'White woman'.
(Albinia, Elvera, Elvire)

Elwy [Welsh]
'Benefit'.

Elysia [Latin]
'Blissful sweetness'. From
Elysium.

Ema See **Emma**

Embla [Scandinavian]
The first woman (in
Norse mythology).

Emelina See **Amelia** or
Emma

Emeline See **Emma**

Emerald [French]
'The bright green jewel'.
*(Emerant, Emeraude, Esme,
Esmeralda, Esmeralde)*

Emerande See **Emerald**

Emerant See **Emerald**

Emily See **Amelia**

Emina [Latin]
'Highly placed maiden'.
Daughter of a noble
house.

Emma [Teutonic]
'One who heals the
universe'. A woman of
command.
*(Emmeline, Emelina,
Emeline, Emelyne,
Emmaline, Ema)*

Emmanuela [Hebrew]
'God with us'.

Emmeline See **Emma**

Emogene See **Imogen**

Ena [Gaelic]
'Little ardent one'. Also
dim. of Eugenia.

Ena See **Eugenia**

Endocia [Greek]
'Of spotless reputation'.
*(Docie, Doxie, Doxy,
Eudosia, Eudoxia)*

Engacia See **Grace**

Engelberga See **Engelberta**

Engelbert See **Engleberta**

Engelberta [Teutonic]
'Bright angel'. One of the
bright defenders of
legend.
*(Engelberga, Engelbertha,
Engelberthe, Engelbert)*

Enid [Celtic]
'Purity of the soul'.

Enrica [Italian]
Italian form of Henrietta,
q.v.

Eolande See **Yolande**

Ernaline See **Erna**

Eranthe [Greek]
'Flower of spring'.

Erda See **Eartha**

Erica [Norse]
'Powerful ruler'. Symbol
of royalty. Fem. of Eric.
(Erika)

Erin [Gaelic]
'From Ireland'. One born
in the Emerald Isle.

Erlina [Old English]
'Little elf'

Erma [Teutonic]
'Army maid'.
*(Erminia, Ermina, Erminie,
Hermia, Hermine,
Hermione)*

Erme See **Irma**

Ermina See **Erma**

Erminia See **Erma**

Erminie See **Armina** or
Erma

Erna [Anglo-Saxon]
'Eagle'. Also variation of

Ernestine.
(Ernaline)

Ernestine [Anglo-Saxon]
'Purposeful one'.
(Erna)

Ertha See **Eartha**

Erwina [Anglo-Saxon]
'Friend from the sea'.

Esme See **Emerald**

Esmeralda See **Emerald**

Esmeralde See **Emerald**

Essa See **Esther**

Essylt [Welsh]
'Beautiful to behold'.

Esta [Italian]
'From the East'.

Estaphania [Greek]
'Crown'.

Estella See **Estelle**

Estelle [French]
'Bright star'.
*(Estella, Estrella, Estrelita,
Stella, Stelle)*

Esther [Hebrew]
'The star'.
(Essa, Etty, Eister, Hester, Hesther, Hetty, Hessy)

Estrelita See **Estelle**

Estrella See **Estelle**

Eswen [Welsh]
'Strength'.

Esyllt See **Isolde**

Ethel [Teutonic]
'Noble maiden'. The daughter of a princely house.
(Ethelda, Ethelinda, Etheline, Ethylyn, Ethyl)

Ethelda See **Ethel**

Ethelinda [Teutonic]
'Noble Serpent'. The symbol of immortality.

Ethelinda See **Ethel**

Etheline See **Ethel**

Ethylyn See **Ethel**

Etta See **Henrietta**

Etty See **Esther**

Euclea [Greek]
'Glory'.

Eudora [Greek]
'Generous gift'.
(Eudore, Dora)

Eudosia See **Endocia**

Eugenia [Greek]
'Well born'. A woman of a noble family.
(Eugenie, Genie, Gene, Gina, Gena, Ena)

Eugenie See **Eugenia**

Eula See **Eulalia**

Eulalia [Greek]
'Fair spoken one'.
(Eulalie, Eula, Lallie)

Eunice [Greek]
'Happy and victorious'.

Euphemia [Greek]
'Of good reputation'.
(Euphemie, Effie, Effy, Phemie)

Euphemie See **Euphemia**

Euphrasia [Greek]
'Delight'.

Eurwen [Welsh]
'Gold-fair'.

Eurydice [Greek]
   'Broad'.

Eustacia [Latin]
   'Tranquil maiden'.
   'Fruitful'.
   (Eustacie, Stacey, Stacy,
   Stacie)

Eustacie See **Eustacia**

Evadne [Greek]
   'Fortunate'.

Evangelina See
   Evangeline

Evangeline [Greek]
   'Bearer of glad tidings'.
   (Evangelina, Eva, Vangie,
   Vancy)

Evanthe [Greek]
   'Lovely flower'.

Eve [Hebrew]
   'Life giver'.
   (Eva, Eveleen, Evelina,
   Eveline, Evelyn, Evita,
   Evonne, Evie)

Eveleen See **Eiblin** or **Eve**

Evelina See **Eve**

Evelyn See **Eve**

Evie See **Eve**

Evita See **Eve**

Evonne See **Eve**

Eachan [Gaelic]
'Little horse'.
(Eacheann)

Eachan See **Hector**

Eamonn See **Edmond**

Eanruig See **Henry**

Earl [Anglo-Saxon]
'Nobleman; chief'.
*(Erle, Earle, Erl, Errol,
Early)*

Early See **Earl**

Eaton [Anglo-Saxon]
'From the estate by the
river'.

Eben [Hebrew]
'Stone'.

Ebenezer [Hebrew]
'Stone of help'.

Eberhard See **Everard**

Eberhart See **Everard**

Edan [Celtic]
'Flame'.

Edbert [Anglo-Saxon]
'Prosperous; brilliant'.

Edd See **Edwin**

Edel [Teutonic]
'The noble one'.

Edelmar [Anglo-Saxon]
'Noble and famous'.

Eden [Hebrew]
'Place of delight and
pleasure'. The original
paradise.

Edgar [Anglo-Saxon]
'Lucky spear warrior'.
*(Ed, Eddie, Eddy, Edgard,
Ned)*

Edgard See **Edgar**

Edison See **Edson**

Edlin See **Edwin**

Edmonn See **Edmund**

Edmund [Anglo-Saxon]
'Rich guardian'.
*(Edmond, Edmon, Edmonn,
Ed, Eddie, Eddy, Ned)*

Edolf [Anglo-Saxon]
'Prosperous wolf'.

Edric [Anglo-Saxon]
'Fortunate ruler'.

Edryd [Welsh]
'Restoration'.

Edsel [Anglo-Saxon]
'A prosperous man's
house' or 'Profound
thinker'.

Edson [Anglo-Saxon]
'Edward's son'.
(Edison)

Edwald [Anglo-Saxon]
'Prosperous ruler'.

Edward [Anglo-Saxon]
'Prosperous guardian'.
*(Eduard, Ed, Eddie, Eddy,
Ned, Neddie, Neddy, Teddy)*

Edwin [Anglo-Saxon]
'Prosperous friend'.
(Edlin, Edd, Eddie, Eddy)

Edwy [Old English]
'Richly beloved'.

Egan [Gaelic]
'Formidable, fiery'.

Egbert [Anglo-Saxon]
'Bright, shining sword'.
The name of the first king
of all England'.

Ehren [Teutonic]
'Honourable one'.

Einar [Norse]
'Warrior leader'.

Eiros [Welsh]
'Bright'.

Elaeth [Welsh]
'Intelligent'.

Elbert See **Albert**

Elden [Anglo-Saxon]
'Elf Valley'.

Elder [Anglo-Saxon]
'One who lives by an
elder tree'.

Eldon [Anglo-Saxon/
Teutonic]
'From the holy hill'
(Anglo-Saxon) or
'Respected elder'
(Teutonic).

Eldrid See **Eldridge**

Eldridge [Anglo-Saxon]
'Wise adviser'.
*(Eldrid, Eldwyn, Eldwin,
Eldred)*

Eldwin [Old English]
'Old friend'.

Eldwyn See **Eldridge**

Eleazar [Hebrew]
'Helped by God'.
(Elizer, Lazarus, Lazar)

Eleutherios [Greek]
'A free man'.

Elfed [Welsh]
'Autumn'.

Elgar [Old English]
'Noble spearman'.

Eli [Hebrew]
'The highest'.
(Ely)

Elian [Hebrew]
'Bright'.

Elias [Hebrew]
'The Lord is God'.
*(Elihu, Elijah, Eliot,
Elliott, Ellis)*

Elidr [Welsh]
'Brass'.

Elihu See **Elias**

Elijah See **Elias**

Eliot See **Elias**

Elisha [Hebrew]
'God is my salvation'.

Elizer See **Eleazar**

Elkanah [Hebrew]
'God has created'.

Ellard [Anglo-Saxon]
'Noble, brave'.

Ellery [Teutonic]
'From the elder tree'.
(Elery, Ellerey)

Elliot See **Elias**

Ellis See **Elias**

Ellison [Anglo-Saxon]
'Son of Elias'.

Ellsworth [Anglo-Saxon]
'A farmer; lover of the
land'.

Elmer [Anglo-Saxon]
'Noble; famous'.
(Aylmer)

Elmo [Italian/Greek]
'Protector' (Italian) or
'Friendly' (Greek).

Elmore [Anglo-Saxon]
'Dweller by the elm tree
on the moor'.

Elroy [French]
'The king'. The name is
supposed to be an
anagram of Le Roi or it
may be from the Spanish
El Rey, either meaning
The King.

Elsdon [Anglo-Saxon]
'Hill belonging to the
noble one'.

Elson See **Ellison**

Elston [Anglo-Saxon]
'Estate of the noble one'.

Elsworth [Anglo-Saxon]
'Estate of the noble one'.

Elton [Anglo-Saxon]
'From the old farm'.

Elvis [Norse]
'All wise'. The prince of
wisdom.

Elvy [Anglo-Saxon]
'Elfin warrior'. Though
small in stature he had
the heart of a lion.

Elwell [Anglo-Saxon]
'From the old well'.

Elwin [Anglo-Saxon]
'Friend of the elves'.

Elwood [Anglo-Saxon]
'From an ancient forest'.

Ely See **Eli**

Emerson See **Emery**

Emery [Teutonic]
'Industrious ruler' or
'Joint ruler'.
*(Emmery, Emory, Emerson,
Emmerich, Amerigo, Emery,
Merrick)*

Emil [Teutonic]
'Industrious'.
(Emile, Emilio, Emlyn)

Emilio See **Emil**

Emlyn [Welsh]
'A border dweller'.

Emlyn See **Emil**

Emmanuel [Hebrew]
'God is with us'.
(Emanuel, Immanuel,
Manuel, Mannie, Manny)

Emmerich See **Emery**

Emmet [Anglo-Saxon]
'The industrious ant'.
(Emmett, Emmit, Emmot,
Emmott, Emmy)

Emmit See **Emmet**

Emmot See **Emmet**

Emmy See **Emmet**

Emory See **Emery**

Emry [Welsh]
'Honour'.

Emrys See **Ambrose**

Eneas See **Aeneas**

Engelbert [Old German]
'Bright as an angel'.

Ennis [Gaelic]
'The only choice'.

Enoch [Hebrew]
'Consecrated; dedicated;
devoted'.

Enos [Hebrew]
'The mortal'.

Ephraim [Hebrew]
'Abounding in
fruitfulness'.
(Efrem, Eph)

Erasme See **Erasmus**

Erasmus [Greek]
'Worthy of being loved'.
(Erasme, Ras, Rasmus)

Erastus [Greek]
'The beloved'.
(Ras)

Eric [Norse]
'All powerful ruler'.
'Kingly'.
(Erich, Erick, Erik, Rick,
Ricky)

Erin [Gaelic]
'Peace'.

Erland [Anglo-Saxon]
'Land of the nobleman'.

Erle See **Earle**

Erling [Anglo-Saxon]
'Son of the nobleman'.

Ermin See **Herman**

Ernest [Anglo-Saxon]
'Sincere and earnest'.
(Ernst, Ernie, Erny)

Ernie See **Ernest**

Ernst See **Ernest**

Errol See **Earl**

Erskine [Celtic]
'From the cliff's height'.

Erwin [Old English]
'Army friend'.

Esmond [Anglo-Saxon]
'Gracious protector'.

Este [Italian]
'Man from the East'.
(Estes)

Estes See **Este**

Ethan [Hebrew]
'Steadfast and firm'.

Ethelbert [Teutonic]
'Noble, bright'.

Ethelred [Teutonic]
'Noble counsel'.

Euclid [Greek]
'True glory'.

Eugene [Greek]
'Nobly born'.
(Gene)

Eurwyn [Welsh]
'Gold-fair'.

Eusebius [Greek]
'Honourable'.

Eustace [Greek]
'Stable, tranquil' or
'Fruitful'.

Evan [Gaelic]
'Well born young
warrior'. Also Welsh
form of John.
(Ewan, Ewen, Owen)

Evaristus [Greek]
'Most excellent'.

Evelyn [English]
A surname.

Everard [Anglo-Saxon]
'Strong as a boar'.
*(Evered, Everett, Eberhard,
Eberhart, Ev, Eb)*

Evered See **Everard**

Everett See **Everard**

Everild See **Averill**

Everley [Anglo-Saxon]
'Field of the wild boar'.

Ewald [Anglo-Saxon]
'Law powerful'.

Ewert [Anglo-Saxon]
'Ewe herder'. One who
tended the ewes in lamb'.

Ewing [Anglo-Saxon]
'Friend of the law'.

Ezekiel [Hebrew]
'Strength of God'.
(Zeke)

Ezra [Hebrew]
'The one who helps'.
(Esra, Ez)

Girls

Fabia [Latin]
'Bean grower'.
*(Fabiana, Fabianna,
Fabienne)*

Fabiana See **Fabia**

Fabienne See **Fabia**

Fabrianna See **Fabrianne**

Fabrianne [Latin]
'Girl of resourcefulness'.
*(Fabriane, Fabrianna,
Fabrienne)*

Faine [Old English]
'Joyful'.

Faith [Teutonic]
'Trust in God'. One who
is loyal and true.
(Fae, Fay, Faye)

Fallon [Gaelic]
'Grandchild of the ruler'.

Fan See **Frances**

Fanchon [French]
'Free being'. A derivative
of Francoise.

Fanny See **Frances**

Farica See **Frederica**

Farrah [Middle English]
'Beautiful'.

Fatima [Arabic]
'Unknown'.

Fausta See **Faustine**

Faustina See **Faustine**

Faustine [Latin]
'Lucky omen'.
(Fausta, Faustina)

Favor [French]
'The helpful one'.
(Favora)

Favora See **Favor**

Fawn [French]
'Young deer'. A lithe,
swift footed girl.

Fay [French]
'A fairy' or 'A raven'
(Irish). A fairy-like
person. Also dim. of
Faith.
(Fae, Faye, Fayette)

Faye See **Faith**

Fayette See **Fay**

Fayme [French]
'Of high reputation'.
Beyond reproach.

Feadore See **Theodora**

Fealty [French]
'Faithful one'. One who is
loyal to God, sovereign,
country and friend.

Fedora See **Theodora**

Fedore See **Theodora**

Felda [Teutonic]
'From the field'. For one
born at harvest time.

Felice See **Felicia**

Felicia [Latin]
'Joyous one'. Fem. of
Felix.
*(Felice, Felicity, Felis,
Felicie, Felise, Felicidad)*

Felicidad See **Felicia**

Felicity See **Felicia**

Fenella [Gaelic]
'White shouldered'.
(Finella, Fionnula)

Feodora See **Theodora**

Ferdinanda See **Fernanda**

Fern [Anglo-Saxon]
'Fernlike'.

Fernanda [Teutonic]
'Adventurous'. One who
is daring and courageous.
(Ferdinanda, Fernandina)

Fernandina See **Fernanda**

Fidela [Latin]
'Faithful one'.
(Fidelia, Fidele)

Fidele See **Fidela**

Fidelia See **Fidela**

Fifi See **Josephine**

Filipa See **Philippa**

Filma [Anglo-Saxon]
'Misty veil'. An ethereal
type of beauty.
(Pholma, Philmen)

Fiona [Gaelic]
'Fair one'.
(Fionn, Fionna)

Fionn See **Fiona**

Fionnula See **Fenella**

Fiora See **Florence**

Firoenza See **Florence**

Flanna [Gaelic]
'Red haired'.

Flavia [Latin]
'Yellow haired'.

Fleta [Anglo-Saxon]
'The swift one'.

Fleur [French]
'A flower'. French version
of Florence.
(Fleurette)

Fleurdelice [French]
'Iris or lily'.

Fleurette See **Fleur**

Flo See **Florence**

Flora See **Florence**

Florance See **Florence**

Flore See **Florence**

Florence [Latin]
'A flower'.
*(Flora, Flore, Floria, Flor,
Fiora, Florance, Florinda,
Floris, Florine, Firoenza,
Florencia, Florentia, Flo,
Florrie, Florry, Flossie)*

Florencia See **Florence**

Florentia See **Florence**

Floria See **Florence**

Florida [Latin]
'Flowery'.

Florimel [Greek]
'Flower honey'.

Florinda See **Florence**

Florine See **Florence**

Floris See **Florence**

Florrie See **Florence**

Flossie See **Florence**

Flower [English]
The English version of
Florence.

Fonda [English]
'Affectionate'.

Fortuna See **Fortune**

Fortune [Latin]
'Fate'. The woman of
destiny.
(Fortuna)

Fossetta [French]
'Dimpled'.

Fran See **Frances**

Frances [Latin]
'Free' or 'Girl from
France'.
*(Francine, Francyne,
Francoise, Francesca,
Francisca, Fan, Fanny,
Fran, Frannie, Franny,
Francy, Frankie)*

Francesca See **Frances**

Francine See **Frances**

Francoise See **Frances**

Francy See **Frances**

Frankie See **Frances**

Frannie See **Frances**

Freda [Teutonic]
'Peace'. One who is calm
and unflurried.
*(Frieda, Freida, Frida,
Friedie, Freddie)*

Freda See **Alfreda**

Frederica [Teutonic]
'Peaceful ruler'.
(Frederika, Frederique,
Friederik, Fredericka,
Frerike, Frerika, Farica,
Freddie, Freddy)

Frederique See **Frederica**

Freida See **Halfrida**

Frerika See **Frederica**

Freya [Norse]
'Noble goddess'. The
Norse Goddess of Love —
the Norse equivalent of
the Greek Aphrodite.

Friedie See **Freda**

Fritzi See **Frederica**

Frodis See **Fronde**

Fronde [Latin]
'Leaf of the fern'.
(Frodis, Frond)

Fulvia [Latin]
'Golden girl'. The
daughter born at high
summer.

Fabe See **Fabian**

Fabian [Latin]
'The bean grower' or
'Prosperous farmer'.
(Fabien, Fabe)

Fabre See **Fabron**

Fabron [French]
'The little blacksmith'.
(Fabre, Faber)

Fagan [Gaelic]
'Little, fiery one'.
(Fagin)

Fairfax [Anglo-Saxon]
'Fair haired one'.

Fairley [Anglo-Saxon]
'From the far meadow'.
*(Farley, Fairly, Fairlie,
Farl)*

Falkner [Anglo-Saxon]
'Falcon trainer'. One who
trained the birds used in
the hunt.
*(Faulkner, Faulkener,
Fowler)*

Fane [Anglo-Saxon]
'Glad, joyful'.

Faramond [Teutonic]
'Journey protection'.

Farand [Teutonic]
'Pleasant and attractive'.
(Farant, Farrand, Ferrand)

Farant See **Farand**

Farl See **Fairley**

Farley [Old English]
'From the bull meadow'.

Farman See **Firman**

Farnell [Anglo-Saxon]
'From the fern slope'.
(Farnall, Fernald, Fernall)

Farnley [Anglo-Saxon]
'From the fern meadow'.
(Fernley)

Farold [Anglo-Saxon]
'Mighty traveller'.

Farquhar [Celtic]
'Man; friendly'.

Farr [Anglo-Saxon]
'The traveller'.

Farrell [Celtic]
'The valorous one'.
(Farrel, Ferrell)

Farris See **Ferris**

Faust [Latin]
'Lucky, auspicious'.

Favian [Latin]
'A man of understanding'.

Fay [Gaelic]
'The raven'. Symbol of
great wisdom.
(Fayette)

Fayette See **Fay**

Felice See **Felix**

Felix [Latin]
'Fortunate'.
(Felice)

Felton [Anglo-Saxon]
'From the town estate'.

Fenton [Anglo-Saxon]
'Dweller of the
marshland'. One who
lived by the fens.

Feodor See **Theodore**

Ferant See **Ferrand**

Ferd See **Ferdinand**

Ferdie See **Ferdinand**

Ferdinand [Teutonic]
'Bold, daring adventurer'.
*(Fernando, Fernand,
Hernando, Ferd, Ferdie,
Ferdy)*

Fergie See **Fergus**

Fergus [Gaelic]
'The best choice'.
(Fergie, Feargus)

Fermin [Spanish]
'Firm'.

Fernald See **Farnell**

Fernand See **Ferdinand**

Fernando See **Ferdinand**

Ferrand [French]
'One with iron grey hair'.
(Ferant, Ferrant, Ferand)

Ferris [Gaelic]
'The rock'.
(Farris)

Fidel [Latin]
'Advocate of the poor'.
(Fidele, Fidelio)

Fidelio See **Fidel**

Fielding [Anglo-Saxon]
'One who lives near the field'.

Filbert [Anglo-Saxon]
'Very brilliant one'.
(Philbert)

Filmer [Anglo-Saxon]
'Very famous one'.
(Filmore, Fillmore)

Filmore See **Filmer**

Fin See **Finlay**

Findlay See **Finlay**

Finlay [Gaelic]
'Fair soldier'.
(Finley, Findlay, Findley, Fin, Lee)

Finn [Gaelic]
'Fair haired'.

Firman [Anglo-Saxon]
'Long distance traveller'.
(Farman)

Firmin [French]
'The firm, strong one'.

Fiske [Anglo-Saxon]
'Fish'.

Fitch [Anglo-Saxon]
'The marten'.

Fitz [Anglo-French]
'Son'. Originally in the form of Fils (French for son) the present form was introduced into Britain by the Normans.

Fitzgerald [Anglo-Saxon]
'Son of Gerald'.

Fitzhugh [Anglo-French]
'Son of Hugh'.

Fitzroy [French]
'King's son'.

Flann [Gaelic]
'Lad with red hair'.

Flavian See **Flavius**

Flavius [Latin]
'Yellow haired one'.
(Flavian)

Fleming [Anglo-Saxon]
'The Dutchman'.

Fletcher [French]
'The arrow maker'.

Flinn [Gaelic]
'Son of the redhaired one'.
(Flynn)

Flint [Anglo-Saxon]
'A stream'.

Florian [Latin]
'Flowering; blooming'.
(Flory)

Flory See **Florian**

Floyd See **Lloyd**

Flynn See **Flinn**

Forbes [Gaelic]
'Man of prosperity;
owner of many fields'.
The great landowner.

Ford [Anglo-Saxon]
'The river crossing'.

Forester See **Forrest**

Forrest [Teutonic]
'Guardian of the forest'.
*(Forest, Forester, Forrester,
Forster, Foster, Forrie, Foss)*

Forrie See **Forrest**

Forster See **Forrest**

Fortune [French]
'The lucky one'. Child of
many blessings.

Foss See **Forrest**

Foster See **Forrest**

Fowler See **Falkner**

Fowler See **Falkner**

Fran See **Francis**

Franchot See **Francis**

Francis [Latin]
'Free man'.
*(Frank, Franchot, Franz,
Frankie, Fran)*

Francklin See **Franklin**

Frank See **Francis or
Franklin**

Frankie See **Francis**

Franklin [Anglo-Saxon]
'Free-holder of property'.
He owned his own land to
use as he wished.
*(Frank, Franklyn,
Francklin, Francklyn,
Frankie)*

Franz See **Francis**

Fraser [French]
'Strawberry' or 'Curly
haired one'.
(Frazer, Frasier, Frazier)

Frayne [Anglo-Saxon]
'Stranger'.
(Fraine, Frean, Freen, Freyne)

Frean See **Frayne**

Fred See **Frederick**

Freddy See **Frederick**

Frederick [Teutonic]
'Peaceful ruler'. One who
used diplomacy not war'.
(Frederic, Fredric, Fredrick, Friedrich, Fritz, Frederik, Fred, Freddie, Freddy)

Freeman [Anglo-Saxon]
'Born a free man'.

Freen See **Frayne**

Fremont [Teutonic]
'Free and noble
protector'.

Frewin [Anglo-Saxon]
'Free, noble friend'.
(Frewen)

Frey [Anglo-Saxon]
'The lord of peace and
prosperity'. From the Old
Norse God.

Frick [Anglo-Saxon]
'Bold man'.

Fridolf [Anglo-Saxon]
'Peaceful wolf'.

Fritz See **Frederick**

Fulbert See **Fulbright**

Fulbright [Old German]
'Very bright'.
(Fulbert)

Fuller [Anglo-Saxon]
'Cloth thickener'.

Fulton [Anglo-Saxon]
'From the field' or
'Dweller by the fowl-pen'.

Fyfe [Scottish]
'Man from Fife'.
(Fife, Fyffe)

Girls

Gabriella See **Gabrielle**

Gabrielle [Hebrew]
'Woman of God'. The
bringer of good news.
*(Gabriel, Gabriella,
Gabriele, Gabriela, Gaby,
Gabbie)*

Gaby See **Gabrielle**

Gaea [Greek]
'The earth'. The Goddess
of the Earth.
(Gaia)

Gael See **Abigail**

Gail See **Abigail**

Galatea [Greek]
'Milky white'.

Gale See **Abigail**

Galiena [Teutonic]
'Lofty maiden'. A tall girl
of lofty mien.
(Galiana)

Galilah [Hebrew]
Place name in Galilee.

Galina See **Helen**

Garda See **Gerda**

Gardenia [Latin]
'White, fragrant flower'.

Garland [French]
'Crown of blossoms'.

Garnet [English]
'Deep red haired beauty'.
(Garnette)

Gartred See **Gertrude**

Gavrila [Hebrew]
'Heroine'.

Gay [French]
'Lively'.
(Gai, Gaye)

Gayle See **Abigail**

Gaynor See **Genevieve**

Gazella [Latin]
'The antelope'. One who
is graceful and modest.

Gelasia [Greek]
'Laughing water'. One
who is like a fresh and
gurgling stream.
(Gelasie)

Gelasie See **Gelasia**

Gemini [Greek]
'Twin'.

Gemma [Latin]
'Precious stone'.
(Gemmel)

Gemmel See **Gemma**

Gena See **Eugenia**

Gene See **Eugenia**

Genesa See **Genesia**

Genesia [Latin]
'Newcomer'.
(Genesa, Genisia, Jenesia)

Geneva [French]
'Juniper tree'. Also var. of
Genevieve.
(Genvra, Genevre)

Genevieve [French]
'Pure white wave'.
*(Genevra, Genevre, Gaynor,
Ginevra, Jennifer, Guinevere,
Guenevere, Vanora, Ginette)*

Genevra See **Genevieve**

Genevre See **Geneva**

Genie See **Eugenia**

Genvra See **Geneva**

Georgana See **Georgina**

Georgene See **Georgina**

Georgette See **Georgina**

Georgia See **Georgina**

Georgiana See **Georgina**

Georgina [Greek]
'Girl from the farm'.
Fem. of George.
*(Georgiana, Georgana,
Georgia, Georgene,
Georgette, Georgine, Girogia,
Georgy, Georgie)*

Georgy See **Georgina**

Geralda See **Geraldine**

Geraldina See **Geraldine**

Geraldine [Teutonic]
'Noble spear carrier'.
*(Geraldina, Gerhardine,
Geralda, Gerry, Giralda,
Jeraldine, Jeroldine, Jerri,
Jerry)*

Geranium [Greek]
'Bright red flower'.

Gerda [Norse]
'Protected one'. One who
has been strictly brought
up.

Gerda See **Gertrude**

Gerhardine See
Geraldine

Germaine [French]
'From Germany'.
(Germain)

Gerry See **Geraldine**

Gert See **Gertrude**

Gertie See **Gertrude**

Gertruda See **Gertrude**

Gertrude [Teutonic]
'Spear maiden'. One of
the Valkyrie.
*(Gertruda, Gertrud,
Gertrudis, Gert, Gertie,*

Gerty, Gerda, Trudie, Trudy, Gartred)

Gertrudis See **Gertrude**

Ghislaine [French]

Giacinta See **Hyacinth**

Gianina [Hebrew]
'The Lord's grace'.

Gigi See **Gilberta**

Gilah [Hebrew]
'Joy'.

Gilberta [Teutonic]
'Bright pledge'. Fem. of
Gilbert.
*(Gilberte, Gilbertha,
Gilberthe, Gilbertina,
Gilbertine, Gigi, Gillie,
Gilly)*

Gilberte See **Gilberta**

Gilbertina See **Gilberta**

Gilbertine See **Gilberta**

Gilda [Celtic]
'God's servant'.

Gill See **Gillian**

Gillian [Latin]
'Young nestling'. Also
der. of Juliana.
*(Jillian, Jill, Jillie, Gill,
Gillie)*

Gillie See **Gilberta** or
Gillian

Gina See **Eugenia** or
Regina

Ginette See **Genevieve**

Ginger See **Virginia**

Giorsal See **Grace**

Girogia See **Georgina**

Gisella See **Gisselle**

Giselle [Teutonic]
'A promise'. One who
stands as a pledge for her
family.
(Gisella, Gisela, Gisele)

Gitana [Spanish]
'The gipsy'.

Githa See **Gytha**

Gittle [Hebrew]
'Innocent flatterer'.
(Gittle, Gytle)

Glad See **Gladys**

Gladdie See **Gladys**

Gladine See **Gladys**

Gladys [Celtic]
'Frail delicate flower'.
Celtic version of Claudia
(the lame).
*(Gladine, Gladis, Gladdie,
Glad, Gwyladys, Gwladys,
Gleda)*

Gleda [Anglo-Saxon]
Old English version of
Gladys.

Gleda See **Gladys**

Glenda See **Glenna**

Glenn See **Glenna**

Glenna [Celtic]
'From the valley'. One of
the oldest names on
record.
(Glenda, Glynis, Glenn)

Glenys [Welsh]
'Holy'.

Gloire See **Gloria**

Gloria [Latin]
'Glorious one'. An
illustrious person. This
name was often used of
Queen Elizabeth I by her
sycophantic courtiers.
*(Gloire, Glori, Glory,
Gloriana, Glorianna,
Gloriane, Glorianne)*

Gloriana See **Gloria**

Glorianna See **Gloria**

Glorianne See **Gloria**

Glory See **Gloria**

Glynis See **Glenna**

Goda See **Guda**

Godgifu See **Godiva**

Godiva [Anglo-Saxon]
'Gift of God'.
(Godgifu)

Golda See **Goldie**

Goldie [Anglo-Saxon]
'Pure gold'.
(Golda)

Grace [Latin]
'The graceful one'.
*Gracia, Grazia, Gracie,
Grayce, Giorsal, Engracia)*

Gracia See **Grace**

Gracie See **Grace**

Grainne [Irish]
'Love'.
(Grania)

Grania See **Grainne**

Grazina [Italian]
'Grace, charm'.

Greer [Greek]
'The watchful mother'.
The eternal matriarch.
(Gregoria)

Gregoria See **Greer**

Greta See **Margaret**

Gretchen See **Margaret**

Grete See **Margaret**

Griselda [Teutonic]
'Grey heroine'.
*(Griselde, Grishelda,
Grishelde, Grishilda,
Grishilde, Grizelda, Selda,
Zelda)*

Griselde See **Griselda**

Grishilda See **Griselda**

Grishilde See **Griselda**

Guadalupe [Arabic]
'River of black stones'.

Guda [Anglo-Saxon]
'The good one'.
(Goda)

Gudrun [German]
'War; rune'.

Guida [Latin]
'The guide'.

Guilla See **Wilhelmina**

Guinevere [Celtic]
'White phantom'.
*(Guinivere, Guenevere,
Gwenhwyvar, Jennifer)*

Guinevere See
Genevieve

Gunhilda [Norse]
'Warrior maid'.
(Gunhilde)

Gunhilde See **Gunhilda**

Gussy See **Gustava**

Gustava [Scandinavian]
'Staff of the Goths'.
(Gustave, Gussie, Gussy)

Gustave See **Gustava**

Gwen See **Gwendoline**

Gwenda See **Gwendoline**

Gwendoline [Celtic]
  'White browed maid'.
  (Gwendolen, Gwendolene,
  Gwendolyn, Gwendolyne,
  Gwenda, Gwennie, Gwen,
  Gwyn, Wendy)

Gwendydd [Welsh]
  'Morning star'.

Gweneira [Welsh]
  'White snow'.

Gwenllian [Welsh]
  'Fair, Flaxen'.

Gwennie See **Gwendoline**

Gwenonwyn [Welsh]
  'Lily of the valley'.

Gwyladys See **Gladys**

Gwyn See **Gwendoline**

Gwyneth [Welsh]
  'Blessed'.

Gwynne [Old Welsh]
  'White or fair one'.

Gypsy [Anglo-Saxon]
  'The wanderer'. See also
  Gitana.
  (Gipsy)

Gytha [Anglo-Saxon]
  'The war like'.
  (Githa)

Gabbie See **Gabriel**

Gabe See **Gabriel**

Gable [French]
'The small Gabriel'.

Gabriel [Hebrew]
'Messenger of God'. The
archangel who
announced the birth of
Christ.
*(Gabe, Gabbie, Gabie,
Gabby)*

Gage [French]
'A pledge'. The glove that
was given as an earnest of
good faith.

Gair [Gaelic]
'Short one'.

Gaius [Latin]
'Rejoiced'.

Galahad [Hebrew]
'Gilead'.

Gale [Celtic]
'The lively one'.
(Gail, Gayle)

Galen [Gaelic]
'Little bright one' or
(Greek) 'The helper'.

Gallagher [Gaelic]
'Eager helper from
overseas'.

Gallard See **Gaylord**

Galloway [Celtic]
'Man from the stranger
gaels'.
(Galway, Gallway)

Galton [Anglo-Saxon]
'Lease holder of an
estate'.

Galvan See **Galvin**

Galvin [Gaelic]
'Bright, shining white' or
'The sparrow'.
(Galvan, Galven)

Galway See **Galloway**

Gamaliel [Hebrew]
'The recompense of the
Lord'.

Gannon [Gaelic]
'Little blond one'.

Ganymede [Greek]
'Rejoicing in mankind'.

Gardiner [Teutonic]
'A gardener; a flower
lover'.
(Gardner, Gardener)

Gardner See **Gardiner**

Gareth [Welsh]
'Gentle'.

Garey See **Gary**

Garfield [Anglo-Saxon]
'War or battle field'.

Garland [Anglo-Saxon]
'From the land of the
spears'.

Garman [Anglo-Saxon]
'The spearman'.

Garmon See **Garmond**

Garmond [Anglo-Saxon]
'Spear protector'.
(Garmon, Garmund)

Garner [Teutonic]
'Army guard; noble
defender'.

Garnet [Latin]
'A red seed; pomegranate
seed'.

Garnett [Anglo-Saxon]
'Compulsive spear man'.
He struck first and
challenged afterwards.

Garnock [Celtic]
'One who dwells by the
river alder'.

Garrett [Anglo-Saxon]
'Mighty spear warrior'.
*(Garett, Garret, Garritt,
Gerard, Garrard, Jarrett)*

Garrick [Anglo-Saxon]
'Spear ruler'.

Garroway [Anglo-Saxon]
'Spear warrior'.
(Garraway)

Garth [Norse]
'From the garden'.

Garton [Anglo-Saxon]
'The dweller by the
triangular shaped farm'.

Garvey [Gaelic]
'Rough peace'. Peace
obtained after victory!
(Garvie)

Garvin [Teutonic]
'Spear friend'.
(Garwin)

Garwin See **Garvin**

Garwood [Anglo-Saxon]
'From the fir trees'.

Gary [Anglo-Saxon]
'Spearman'.
(Gari, Garey, Garry)

Gaspar [Persian]
'Master of the treasure'.
One of the Magi.
*(Caspar, Casper, Gasper,
Kaspar, Kasper, Jasper)*

Gaspar See **Casper**

Gaston [French]
'Man from Gascony'.

Gavin See **Gawain**

Gawain [Celtic]
'The battle hawk'.
*(Gawaine, Gavin, Gavan,
Gaven, Gawen)*

Gayle See **Gale**

Gaylor See **Gaylord**

Gaylord [French]
'The happy noble man'.
(Gayler, Galor, Gallard)

Gaynor [Gaelic]
'Son of the blond haired
one'.

Gearalt See **Gerald**

Geary [Anglo-Saxon]
'The changeable'.
(Gearey, Gery)

Gemmel [Scandinavian]
'Old'.

Gene See **Eugene**

Geof See **Geoffrey**

Geoffrey [Teutonic]
'God's Divine peace'.
*(Godfrey, Jeffery, Jeffrey,
Jeffry, Jeffers, Jeff, Geof,
Geoff)*

Geordie See **George**

George [Greek]
'The farmer'. The Patron
Saint of England.
*(Georges, Georgie, Geordie,
Gordie, Gordy, Georgy,
Georg, Jorge, Jorin, Joris,
Jurgen, Yorick)*

Georges See **George**

Georgie See **George**

Ger See **Gerald**

Geraint [Welsh]
'Old'.

Gerald [Teutonic]
'Mighty spear ruler'.
*(Geraud, Giraud, Gearalt,
Garold, Gereld, Gerrald,
Jereld, Jerold, Jerald,
Jerrold, Gerry, Gery, Jerry,
Ger, Jer)*

Gerard [Anglo-Saxon]
'Spear strong; spear
brave'.
*(Gerrard, Gerhard,
Gerhardt, Gearard, Gerry)*

Gerard See **Garrett**

Geraud See **Gerald**

Gerhardt See **Gerard**

Gerry See **Gerard**

Gervase [Teutonic]
'Spear vassal'.
*(Gervais, Jarvis, Jervis,
Jarvey, Jarv, Ger)*

Gerwyn [Welsh]
'Fair love'.

Gethin [Welsh]
'Dark skinned'.

Ghislaine [French]
'A pledge'.

Gian See **John**

Gib See **Gilbert**

Gibson [Anglo-Saxon]
'Son of Gilbert'.

Gideon [Hebrew]
'Brave indomitable spirit'
or 'The destroyer'.

Gifford [Teutonic]
'The gift'.
(Giffard, Gifferd)

Gilbert [Anglo-Saxon]
'Bright pledge; a
hostage'.
*(Gil, Gill, Gillie, Gib,
Gibb, Bert, Gilibeirt,
Gilleabart)*

Gilby [Norse]
'The pledge; a hostage'.
(Gilbey)

Gilchrist [Gaelic]
'The servant of Christ'.
(Gilecriosd)

Gilecriosd See **Gilchrist**

Giles [Latin/French]
'Shield bearer' (Latin)
or 'Youthful shaveling'
(French).
(Gilles, Gil)

Gill See **Gilbert**

Gilleabart See **Gilbert**

Gilleasbuig See
Archibald

Gillecirosd See
Christopher

Gillet [French]
'Little Gilbert'.

Gillie See **Gilbert**

Gilmer [Anglo-Saxon]
'Famous hostage'. An
eminent knight taken
captive in battle.

Gilmore [Gaelic]
'St. Mary's servant'.
(Gillmore, Gilmour)

Gilroy [Latin/Gaelic]
'The king's servant'
(Latin) or 'The red-
haired one's servant'
(Gaelic).

Girvin [Gaelic]
'Little rough one'.
(Girvan, Girven)

Gladwin [Anglo-Saxon]
'Kind friend'.

Glanville [French]
'Dweller on the oak tree
estate'.
(Glanvil)

Glen [Celtic]
'From the valley'.
(Glenn, Glyn, Glynn)

Glendon [Celtic]
'From the fortress in the
Glen'.

Glyn See **Glenn**

Glynn See **Glen**

Godart See **Goddard**

Goddard [Teutonic]
'Divinely firm'. Firm in
belief and trust in God.
(Godard, Godart, Goddart)

Godfrey See **Geoffrey**

Golding [Anglo-Saxon]
'Son of the golden one'.

Goldwin [Anglo-Saxon]
'Golden friend'.

Gomez [Spanish]
'Man'.

Goodwin [Anglo-Saxon]
'Good friend; God's
friend'.
*(Godwin, Godwine,
Godewyn)*

Gordie See **Gordon**

Gordon [Anglo-Saxon]
'From the cornered hill'.
*(Gordan, Gorden, Gordie,
Gordy)*

Gorman [Gaelic]
'Small, blue eyed lad'.

Gouveneur [French]
'The Governor; the
ruler'.

Gower [Celtic]
'The pure one'.

Grady [Gaelic]
'Illustrious and noble'.

Graham [Teutonic]
'From the grey lands'.
One from the country
beyond the mists.
(Graeme)

Granger [Anglo-Saxon]
'The farmer'.

Grant [French]
'The great one'.

Grantham [Old English]
'From the big meadow'.

Grantland [Anglo-Saxon]
'From the great lands'.

Granville [French]
'Dweller in the big town'.
*(Grandville, Granvil,
Grandvil, Greville)*

Grayson [Anglo-Saxon]
'The bailiff's son'.

Greeley [Anglo-Saxon]
'From the grey meadow'.

Greg See **Gregory**

Gregor See **Gregory**

Gregory [Greek]
'The watchful one'.
Someone ever vigilant.
*(Greg, Gregor, Gregg,
Greiogair, Greagoir)*

Greiogair See **Gregory**

Gresham [Anglo-Saxon]
'From the grazing
meadow'.

Greville See **Granville**

Griff See **Rufus**

Griffin See **Griffith**

Griffith [Celtic]
'Fierce, red haired
warrior'.
(Griffin, Gruffydd, Rufus)

Griffith See **Rufus**

Grimbald [Teutonic]
'Fierce power'.

Griswold [Teutonic]
'From the grey forest'.

Grover [Anglo-Saxon]
'One who comes from the
grove'.

Guido See **Guy**

Gunnar See **Gunther**

Gunter See **Gunther**

Gunther [Teutonic]
'Bold warrior'.
*(Gunnar, Gunner, Gunter,
Gunar, Guntar, Gunthar)*

Gurion [Hebrew]
'Dwelling place of God'.

Gus See **August** or
Gustave

Gustave [Scandinavian]
'Staff of the Goths'.
*(Gustav, Gustaf, Gustavus,
Gus)*

Gustavus See **Gustave**

Guthrie [Celtic]
'War serpent; war hero'
or 'From the windy
country'.
(Guthry)

Guy [French/Teutonic/
Latin]
'The guide' (French);
'The warrior' (Teutonic);
'Life' (Latin).
*(Guido, Guyon, Wiatt,
Wyatt)*

Guyon See **Guy**

Gwylim See **William**

Gwynfor [Welsh]
'Fair place'.

Gwynllyw [Welsh]
'Blessed leader'.

Gwynn [Celtic]
'The blond one'.
(Gwynn, Guin)

Girls

Hadria See **Adrienne**

Hadwisa See **Avice**

Hafwen [Welsh]
  'Summer-beautiful'.

Hagar [Hebrew]
  'Forsaken'.

Haidee [Greek]
  'Modest, honoured'. A
  maid renowned for her
  natural modesty.

Halcyone [Greek]
  'The king fisher'. The
  mythological Greek who
  was turned into a bird
  when she drowned
  herself.
  (Halcyon)

Haldana [Norse]
'Half Danish'.

Haley [Scandinavian]
'Hero'.

Halfrida [Teutonic]
'Peaceful heroine'. A
diplomat not a warrior.
*(Halfreida, Halfrieda,
Hallie, Frida, Freida,
Frieda)*

Halimeda [Greek]
'Sea thoughts'. One who
is drawn to the sea.
(Hallie, Meda)

Halla [African]
'Unexpected gift'.

Hallie See **Halfrida**

Halona [North American
Indian]
'Fortunate'.

Hannah See **Anne**

Happy [English]
'Happy'.

Haracia See **Horatia**

Haralda [Norse]
'Army ruler'. Fem. of
Harold.
*(Haraldina, Harolda,
Haroldina)*

Haraldina See **Haralda**

Harika [Turkish]
'Most beautiful'.

Harley [Old English]
'From the long field'.

Harmonia See **Harmony**

Harmony [Latin]
'Concord and harmony'.
(Harmonia, Harmonie)

Harriet See **Henrietta**

Hattie See **Henrietta**

Hayley [English]
From the surname.

Hazel [English]
'The hazel tree'.
(Aveline)

Heather [Anglo-Saxon]
'Flower of the moors'.

Hebe [Greek]
Goddess of Youth

Hedda [Teutonic]
'War'. A born fighter.
(Heddi, Heddy, Hedy)

Heddi See **Hedda**

Heidi See **Hilda**

Helen [Greek]
'Light'. According to
tradition, the most
beautiful woman, Helen
of Troy. There are so
many variations of this
name, that it is not
possible to list them all. A
representative selection:
*(Helena, Helene, Eleanor,
Eleanore, Elinor, Elenor,
Elinore, Elinora, Elenore,
Elenora, Elaine, Elane,
Ella, Ellen, Ellyn, Ellene,
Elena, Galina, Ileane, Ilena,
Ilona, Illona, Illone, Aileen,
Aisleen, Eileen, Isleen,
Leonora, Leonore, Lenora,
Leora, Lora, Lana, Leona,
Nora, Norah, Nell, Lena,
Lina)*

Helena See **Helen**

Helga [Teutonic]
'Pious, religious and
holy'. Var. of Olga.

Helianthe [Greek]
'Bright flower;
sunflower'.

Helice [Greek]
'Spiral'.
(Helixa)

Helixa See **Helice**

Helma [Teutonic]
'A helmet'.
(Hilma)

Helma See **Wilhelmina**

Heloise See **Louise**

Hendrika See **Henrietta**

Henrietta [Teutonic]
'Ruler of home and
estate'. Fem. of Henry.
*(Harriet, Harriette, Harriot,
Harriotte, Henriette,
Henrika, Hattie, Hatty,
Hettie, Hetty, Etta, Netta,
Netie, Yetta, Eiric, Minette,
Hendrika)*

Henriette See **Henrietta**

Henrika See **Henrietta**

Hera [Latin]
'Queen of the heaven'.
The wife of the ruler of
the Heaven, Zeus.

Herleva See **Arlene**

Hermia See **Hermione**

Hermina See **Hermione**

Herminia See **Hermione**

Hermione [Greek]
'Of the earth'. The
daughter of Helen of
Troy'.
*(Hermia, Hermina,
Hermine, Herminia)*

Hermosa [Spanish]
'Beautiful'.

Herta See **Eartha**

Hertha See **Eartha**

Hesper [Greek]
'The evening star'.
(Hespera, Hesperia)

Hespera See **Hesper**

Hesperia See **Hesper**

Hessy See **Esther**

Hester See **Esther**

Hestia [Greek]
'A star'.

Hettie See **Henrietta**

Hetty See **Esther**

Heulwen [Welsh]
'Sunshine'.

Heutte [Old English]
'Brilliant'.
(Hughette, Hugette, Huetta)

Hiberna [Latin]
'Girl from Ireland'.
(Hibernia)

Hibernia See **Hiberna**

Hibiscus [Latin]
'The marshmallow plant'.

Hilaria See **Hilary**

Hilary [Latin]
'Cheerful one'. One who
is always happy.
(Hilaria, Hilaire)

Hild See **Hilda**

Hilda [Teutonic]
'Battle maid'. A
handmaiden of the
warriors of Valhalla.
*(Heidi, Hilde, Hildie, Hild,
Hildy, Heidy, Hidie)*

Hildegarde [Teutonic]
'Battle stronghold'.

Hildemar [Teutonic]
'Battle celebrated'.

Hildie See **Hilda**

Hildreth [Teutonic]
'Battle adviser'.
(Hildretha)

Hildretha See **Hildreth**

Hilma See **Helma**

Hina [Hebrew]
'Female deer'.

Hippolyta [Greek]
'Horse destruction'.

Holda [Norse]
'Muffled'
(Holde, Holle, Hulda)

Holde See **Holda**

Holle See **Holda**

Holly [Anglo-Saxon]
'Bringer of good luck'.
The child born during the
Christmas season.
(Hollie)

Honey [English]
'Sweet one'. A term of
endearment, especially in
the U.S.

Honey See **Honora**

Honor See **Honora**

Honora [Latin]
'Honour'.
*(Honor, Honour, Honoria,
Honey, Noreen, Norine,
Nora, Norah, Norrey, Norrie,
Norry)*

Honoria See **Honora**

Hope [Anglo-Saxon]
'Cheerful optimism'.
Another 'virtue' name.

Horatia [Latin]
'Keeper of the hours'.
Fem. of Horace.
(Haracia, Horacia)

Hortense [Latin]
'Of the garden'. One with
green fingers.
(Hortensia)

Hortensia See **Hortense**

Huberta [Teutonic]
'Brilliant mind'. One
with intelligence above
the ordinary.
(Hubertha, Huberthe)

Hubertha See **Huberta**

Huberthe See **Huberta**

Huetta See **Heutte**

Huetta See **Huette**

Huette [Anglo-Saxon]
'Brilliant thinker'. Fem.
of Hugh'.
(Hugette, Huetta)

Hugette See **Huette**

Hulda See **Holda**

Hyacinth [Greek]
'Hyacinth flower'.
*(Hyacintha, Hyacinthia,
Jacintha, Jacinthia, Cynthie,
Cynthis, Jackie, Giacinta)*

Hyacintha See **Hyacinth**

Hyacinthia See **Hyacinth**

Hypatia [Greek]
'Highest'.

Haakon [Scandinavian]
'Noble kin'.

Habakkuk [Hebrew]
'Embrace'.

Hackett [Teutonic]
'The small woodsman'.
The apprentice forester.
(Hacket)

Hacon [Old Norse]
'Useful'.

Hadden [Anglo-Saxon]
'From the heath valley'.
(Haddan, Haddon)

Hadley [Anglo-Saxon]
'From the heath
meadow'.

Hadwin [Anglo-Saxon]
'Battle companion'.

Hafiz [Arabic]
'He who remembers'.

Hagen [Gaelic]
'The young one'.
(Hagan, Haggan, Haggen)

Haggai [Hebrew]
'Festive'.

Hagley [Anglo-Saxon]
'From the hedged
meadow'.

Haig [Anglo-Saxon]
'One who lives in an
enclosure'. Popular name
for boys during early part
of 20th century, in
compliment to the Field
Marshal Lord Haig.

Haines [Old German]
'From a vined cottage'.

Hakeem [Arabic]
'Wise'.
(Hakim)

Hako See **Hakon**

Hakon [Norse]
'From an exalted race'.
(Haakon, Hako)

Hal See **Harold, Henry**

Halbert [Anglo-Saxon]
'Brilliant hero'.

Haldane See **Halden**

Halden [Norse]
'Half Danish'.
*(Haldan, Halfdan,
Haldane)*

Hale [Anglo-Saxon]
'From the hall'.

Haley [Gaelic]
'The ingenious one'. One
with a scientific
intelligence.

Halfdan See **Halden**

Halford [Anglo-Saxon]
'From the ford by the
manor house'.

Hall [Anglo-Saxon]
'Dweller at the manor
house'.

Hallam [Anglo-Saxon]
'One who lives on the hill
slopes'.

Halley [Anglo-Saxon]
'From the Manor House
meadow' or 'Holy'.

Halliwell [Anglo-Saxon]
'The dweller by the holy
well'.

Hallward [Anglo-Saxon]
'Guardian of the Manor
House'.
(Halward)

Halsey [Anglo-Saxon]
'From Hal's island'.
(Halsy)

Halstead [Anglo-Saxon]
'From the manor house'.
(Halsted)

Halton [Anglo-Saxon]
'From the estate on the
hill slope'.

Ham [Hebrew]
'South'.

Hamal [Arabic]
'The lamb'. A very gentle
person.

Hamar [Norse]
'Symbol of ingenuity'. A
great gift for invention.
(Hammar)

Hamid [Arabic]
'Thanking God'.

Hamilton [Anglo-Saxon/
French]
'Sheep enclosure' (Anglo-
Saxon) or 'From the
mountain village'
(French).

Hamish See **James**

Hamlet [Teutonic]
'Little village'.

Hamlin [Teutonic]
'Small home lover'.
*(Hamelin, Hamlyn,
Hamelyn)*

Hamlin See **Henry**

Hamon [Greek]
'Faithful'.

Handley See **Hanley**

Hanford [Anglo-Saxon]
'From the high ford'.

Hank See **Henry**

Hanley [Anglo-Saxon]
'From the high meadow'.
(Handley, Henleigh, Henley)

Hannibal
The hero Carthage

Hanraoi See **Henry**

Hans See **John**

Hansel [Scandinavian]
'Gift from the Lord'.

Harailt See **Harold**

Harbert See **Herbert**

Harbin See **Herbert**

Harcourt [French]
'From a fortified court'.

Harden [Anglo-Saxon]
'From the valley of the
hare'.

Harden See **Harley**

Harding [Anglo-Saxon]
'Son of the hero'.

Hardwin [Anglo-Saxon]
'Brave friend'.
*(Harwin, Hardwyn,
Harwyn)*

Hardy [Teutonic]
'Bold and daring'.
(Hardey, Hardie, Hardi)

Harford [Anglo-Saxon]
'From the hare ford'.
*(Herford, Hereford,
Hareford)*

Hargrave See **Hargrove**

Hargreave See **Hargrove**

Hargreaves See **Hargrove**

Hargrove [Anglo-Saxon]
'From the hare grove'.
*(Hargrave, Hargreave,
Hargreaves)*

Hark See **Henry**

Harl See **Harley**

Harland See **Harlon**

Harley [Anglo-Saxon]
'From the hare meadow'.
*(Arley, Harden, Harleigh,
Hartley, Hartleigh, Arlie,
Harl, Hart)*

Harley See **Arlie**

Harlon [Teutonic]
'From the battle land'.
(Harland)

Harlow [Anglo-Saxon]
'The fortified hill'. An
army camp on the
hillside.

Harman/Harmon See
Herman

Harold [Anglo-Saxon]
'Army commander'. A
mighty general.

*(Harald, Herold, Hereld,
Herrick, Harailt, Hal,
Harry)*

Harper [Anglo-Saxon]
'The harp player'. The
wandering minstrel.

Harris [Anglo-Saxon]
'Harold's son'.
(Harrison)

Harrison See **Harris**

Harry See **Harold, Henry**

Hart [Anglo-Saxon]
'The hart deer'.

Hart See **Harley**

Hartford [Anglo-Saxon]
'The river crossing of the
deer'.
(Hertford)

Hartley [Anglo-Saxon]
'Meadow of the hart
deer'.

Hartley See **Harley**

Hartman [Teutonic]
'Strong and austere'. The
original stoic. Also
'Keeper of the stags'
(Anglo-Saxon).
(Hartmann)

Hartwell [Anglo-Saxon]
'Well where the deer
drink'.
*(Harwell, Hartwill,
Harwill, Hart)*

Hartwill See **Hartwell**

Hartwood [Anglo-Saxon]
'Forest of the hart deer'.
(Harwood)

Harve See **Harvey**

Harvey [Teutonic/French]
'Army warrior'
(Teutonic) or 'Bitter'
(French).
*(Hervey, Harve, Harv,
Herve, Herv)*

Harwell See **Hartwell**

Harwill See **Hartwell**

Harwin See **Hardwin**

Harwood See **Hartwood**

Hashim [Arabic]
'Destroyer of evil'.

Haslett [Anglo-Saxon]
'Hazel tree grove on the
headland'.
(Haslitt, Hazlett, Hazlitt)

Haslitt See **Haslett**

Hassan [Arabic]
'Handsome'.

Hastings [Anglo-Saxon]
'Son of violence'.

Havelock [Norse]
'Sea battle'.
(Havlock)

Haven [Anglo-Saxon]
'A place of safety'.

Hawley [Anglo-Saxon]
'From the hedged
meadow'.

Hayden [Teutonic]
'From the hedged valley'.
(Haydon)

Hayes [Old English]
'From the hedged forest'.

Hayward [Anglo-Saxon]
'Keeper of the hedged
field'.
(Heyward)

Haywood [Anglo-Saxon]
'From the hedged forest'.
(Heywood)

Hearne See **Ahern**

Heath [Anglo-Saxon]
'Heathland'.

Heathcliff [Anglo-Saxon]
'From the heather cliff'.
(Heathcliffe)

Hebert See **Herbert**

Heck See **Hector**

Hector [Greek]
'Steadfast, unswerving;
holds fast'.
*(Eachan, Eachann, Eachunn,
Heck)*

Heddwyn [Welsh]
'Blessed peace'.

Hedley [Old English]
'Blessed peace'.

Heinrich See **Henry**

Henderson [Old English]
'Son of Henry'.

Hendrick See **Henry**

Henley See **Hanley**

Henry [Teutonic]
'Ruler of the estate'. Lord
of the Manor.
*(Hamlin, Heinrich,
Heinrick, Hendrick, Henri,
Henrik, Eanruig, Hanraoi,
Harry, Hal, Hank)* ·

Herald See **Harold**

Herb See **Herbert**

Herbert [Teutonic]
'Brilliant warrior'.
*(Harbert, Hebert,
Hoireabard, Herb, Herbie,
Bert)*

Herbie See **Herbert**

Hercules [Latin]
'Glory of Hera'.

Hereford See **Harford**

Herm See **Herman**

Herman [Teutonic]
'Army warrior'.
*(Harman, Harmon,
Hermann, Ermin, Armand,
Herm, Hermie, Armin,
Armond, Armyn, Hermon)*

Hermie See **Herman**

Hermon See **Herman**

Hernando See **Ferdinand**

Herold See **Harold**

Herrick [Teutonic]
'Army ruler'.

Herrick See **Harold**

Herschel [Hebrew]
  'Deer'.

Herv See **Harvey**

Hervey See **Harvey**

Herwin [Teutonic]
  'Lover of war; battle
  companion'.

Hewe See **Hugh**

Hewett [Anglo-Saxon]
  'Little Hugh'.

Heywood See **Haywood**

Hezekiah [Hebrew]
  'God is strength'. Belief
  in God arms this man
  against all adversity.

Hiatt See **Hyatt**

Hilary [Latin]
  'Cheerful and merry'.
  (Hillary, Hillery, Hilaire)

Hildebrand [Teutonic]
  'Sword of war'.

Hillel [Hebrew]
  'Greatly praised'.

Hilliard [Teutonic]
  'War guardian; brave in
  battle'.
  (Hillier, Hillyer)

Hillier See **Hilliard**

Hilton [Anglo-Saxon]
  'From the hill farm'.
  (Hylton)

Hiram [Hebrew]
  'Most noble and exalted
  one'.
  (Hyram, Hi, Hy)

Hobart See **Hubert**

Hobbard See **Hubert**

Hogan [Celtic]
  'Youth'.

Hoibeard See **Hubert**

Hoireabard See **Herbert**

Holbrook [Anglo-Saxon]
  'From the brook in the
  valley'.

Holcomb [Anglo-Saxon]
  'Deep valley'.
  *(Holcombe, Holecomb,
  Holecombe)*

Holden [Anglo-Saxon/
Teutonic]
'From the valley' or
'Kind'.

Holgate [Anglo-Saxon]
'Gatekeeper'.

Holger [Scandinavian]
'Faithful warrior'.

Hollis [Anglo-Saxon]
'Dweller in the holly
grove'.

Holman [Dutch]
'Man from the hollow'.

Holmes [Anglo-Saxon]
'From the island in the
river'.

Holt [Anglo-Saxon]
'From the forest'.

Homer [Greek]
'A pledge'.

Horace [Latin]
'Time keeper; hours of
the sun'.
(Horatio, Horatius, Race)

Horatio See **Horace**

Horatius See **Horace**

Horst [German]
'From the thicket'.

Horton [Anglo-Saxon]
'From the grey farm'.

Hosea [Hebrew]
'Salvation'.

Houghton [Anglo-Saxon]
'From the estate on the
cliff'.

Houston [Anglo-Saxon]
'From the town in the
mountains'.

Howard [Anglo-Saxon]
'Chief guardian'.
(Howie)

Howe [Teutonic]
'The eminent one'. A
personage of high birth.

Howell [Celtic]
'Little, alert one'.
(Hywel, Hywell)

Howie See **Howard**

Howland [Anglo-Saxon]
'Dweller on the hill'.

Hoyt See **Hubert**

Hube See **Hubert**

Hubert [Teutonic]
'Brilliant, shining mind'.
(Hobart, Hubbard, Hoyt,
Hugh, Hube, Bert,
Hoibeard, Hugo, Hughes,
Huey, Hughy, Hughie, Aodh,
Aoidh)

Hudson [Anglo-Saxon]
'Son of the hoodsman'.

Huey See **Hubert**

Hugh See **Hubert**

Hughes See **Hubert**

Hugo See **Hubert**

Hulbard See **Hulbert**

Hulbert [Teutonic]
'Graceful'.
(Hulbard, Hulburd,
Hulburt)

Humbert [Teutonic]
'Brilliant Hun' or 'Bright
home'.
(Umberto, Humbie, Bert,
Bertie, Berty)

Humbie See **Humbert**

Humph See **Humphrey**

Humphrey [Teutonic]
'Protector of the peace'.
(Humfrey, Humfry, Hump,
Humph)

Hunt See **Hunter**

Hunter [Anglo-Saxon]
'A hunter'.
(Hunt)

Huntingdon [Anglo-
Saxon]
'Hill of the hunter'.

Huntington [Anglo-
Saxon]
'Hunting estate'.

Huntly [Anglo-Saxon]
'From the hunter's
meadow'.
(Huntley)

Hurlbert [Teutonic]
'Brilliant army leader'.

Hurley [Gaelic]
'Sea tide'.

Hurst [Anglo-Saxon]
'One who lives in the
forest'.
(Hearst)

Hussein [Arabic]
'Little and handsome'.

Hutton [Anglo-Saxon]
'From the farm on the ridge'.

Huxford [Anglo-Saxon]
'Hugh's Ford'.

Huxley [Anglo-Saxon]
'Hugh's meadow'.

Hy See **Hiram**

Hyatt [Anglo-Saxon]
'From the high gate'.
(Hiatt)

Hyde [Anglo-Saxon]
'From the hide of land'.
An old unit of measurement of land'.

Hyman [Hebrew]
'Life'. The divine spark.
(Hymen, Hymie, Hy)

Hymie See **Hyman**

Hywel See **Howell**

Hywell See **Howell**

Girls

Ian See **Ianthe**

Iantha See **Ianthe**

Ianthe [Greek]
'Violet coloured flower'.
*(Iantha, Ianthina, Ian,
Janthina, Janthine)*

Ianthina See **Ianthe**

Ida [Teutonic]
'Happy'. Name comes
from Mount Ida in Crete,
where Jupiter is supposed
to have been hidden.
*(Idalia, Idaline, Idalina,
Idelea, Idelia, Idalia, Idella,
Idalle, Idelle)*

Idalia See **Ida**

Idalina See **Ida**

Idaline See **Ida**

Idalle See **Ida**

Idelea See **Ida**

Idelia [Teutonic]
'Noble'.

Idella See **Ida**

Idelle See **Ida**

Idonia See **Iduna**

Idonie See **Iduna**

Iduna [Norse]
'Lover'. The keeper of the
golden apples of youth.
(Idonia, Idonie)

Ierne [Latin]
'From Ireland'.

Ignatia [Latin]
'Fiery ardour'. Fem. of
Ignatius.
(Ignacia)

Ignatia See **Iniga**

Ila [French]
'From the island'.
(Ilde)

Ilde See **Ila**

Ileana [Greek]
'Of Ilion (Troy)'.

Ilena See **Helen**

Ilka [Slavic]
'Flattering'.

Illona See **Aileen**

Ilona See **Helen**

Ilse See **Elizabeth**

Imelda [Latin]
'Wishful'.
(Imalda, Melda)

Imogene [Latin]
'Image of her mother'.
(Imogen)

Imperial [Latin]
'Imperial one'.

Ina See **Agnes**

Ines See **Agnes**

Inez See **Agnes**

Inga See **Ingrid**

Ingaberg See **Ingrid**

Ingeborg See **Ingrid**

Ingrid [Norse]
'Hero's daughter'. Child
of a warrior.
*(Inga, Inger, Ingunna,
Ingaberg, Ingeborg,
Ingebiorg, Ingibiorg)*

Ingunna See **Ingrid**

Iniga [Latin]
'Fiery ardour'.
(Ignatia)

Iola [Greek]
'Colour of the dawn
cloud'.
(Iole)

Iolanthe [Greek]
'Violet flower'.
(Yolanda, Yolande)

Iolanthe See **Violet**

Iole See **Iola**

Iona See **Ione**

Ione [Greek]
'Violet coloured stone'.
(Iona)

Iphigenia [Greek]
'Sacrifice'.

Irene [Greek]
'Peace'. The Goddess of
Peace.
*(Eirene, Eirena, Erena,
Irena, Irina, Irenna, Renata,
Rena, Rene, Reini, Rennie,
Renny)*

Irenna See **Irene**

Ireta [Latin]
'Enraged one'.
(Iretta, Irette, Irete)

Irette See **Ireta**

Iris [Greek]
'The rainbow'. The
messenger of the Gods.

Irma [Latin or Teutonic]
'Noble person' (Latin);
'Strong' (Teutonic).
*(Erma, Erme, Irmina,
Irmine, Irme)*

Irmina See **Irma**

Irmine See **Irma**

Irvetta See **Irvette**

Irvette [English]
'Sea friend'.
(Irvetta)

Isa [Teutonic]
'Lady of the iron will'. A
determined lass.

Isabeau See **Isabel**

Isabel [Hebrew]
Spanish form of
Elizabeth, *q.v.*
*(Isabella, Isabelle, Isobel,
Isbel, Ishbel, Ysabel,
Isabeau, Ysabeau, Ysobel,
Ysabella, Ysabelle, Ysobella,
Ysobelle, Bella, Belle, Bel}*
and the variations of
Elizabeth

Isabella See **Isabel**

Isadora [Greek]
'The gift of Isis'.
*(Isidora, Isidore, Isadore,
Dora, Dori, Dory, Issie,
Issy, Izzy)*

Isadore See **Isadora**

Isbel See **Isabel**

Isidora See **Isadora**

Isis [Egyptian]
'Supreme goddess'. The
Goddess of Fertility.

Isleen See **Aileen**

Ismena [Greek]
'Learned'.

Isoda See **Isolde**

Isola [Latin]
'The isolated one'. A
'loner'.

Isolabella [Combination
Isola/Bella]
'Beautiful lonely one'.
(Isolabelle)

Isolabelle See **Isolabella**

Isolde [Celtic]
'The fair one'.
*(Isoda, Ysolda, Ysolde,
Yseult, Iseult, Esyllt)*

Issie See **Isadora**

Ita [Caelic]
'Desire for truth'.
(Ite)

Ite See **Ita**

Iva [French]
'The yew tree'.
(Ivanna, Ivanne)

Ivanna See **Iva**

Ivanne See **Iva**

Iverna [Latin]
An old name for Ireland.

Ivonne See **Yvonne**

Ivory [Welsh]
'Highborn lady'.

Ivy [English]
'A vine'. The sacred plant
of the ancient religions.

Ian [Celtic]
'God is gracious'. See also John.
(Iain, Iaian)

Ibrahim See **Abraham**

Icarus [Greek]
'Dedicated to the moon'.

Ichabod [Hebrew]
'The glory has departed'.

Idris [Welsh]
'Fiery Lord'.

Idwal [Welsh]
'Wall lord'.

Iestin See **Justin**

Ignace See **Ignatius**

Ignacio See **Ignatius**

Ignate See **Ignatius**

Ignatius [Latin]
'The ardent one'. A fiery patriot.
(Inigo, Ignace, Ignate, Ignacio, Ignatius)

Igor [Scandinavian]
'The hero'.

Ike See **Isaac**

Ikey See **Isaac**

Illtyd [Welsh]
'Ruler of a district'.

Immanuel See **Emmanuel**

Ingemar [Norse]
'Famous son'.
(Ingmar)

Inger [Norse]
'A son's army'.
(Ingar, Ingvar)

Inglebert [Teutonic]
'Brilliant angel'.
(Englebert, Engelbert)

Ingram [Teutonic]
'The raven' or 'The raven's son'.
(Ingraham)

Ingvar See **Inger**

Inigo See **Ignatius**

Inir [Welsh]
'Honour'.

Inness [Celtic]
'From the island in the
river'.
(Innes, Innis, Iniss)

Iorweth [Welsh]
'Lord Worth'.

Iorwyn [Welsh]
'Fair lord'.

Ira [Hebrew]
'The watcher'.

Irfon [Welsh]
'Annointed one'.

Irvin See **Irving**

Irving [Anglo-Saxon/
Celtic]
'Sea friend' (Anglo-
Saxon) or 'White river'
(Welsh/Celtic)
(Irvin, Irvine, Irwin, Erwin)

Irwin See **Irving**

Isaac [Hebrew]
'The laughing one'.
*(Isaak, Izaak, Ike, Ikey,
Ikie)*

Isaiah [Hebrew]
'God is my helper'.

Isham [Anglo-Saxon]
'From the estate of the
iron man'.

Ishmael [Hebrew]
'The wanderer'.

Isidore [Greek]
'The gift of Isis'.
*(Isidor, Isador, Isadore, Issy,
Iz, Izzy, Izzie)*

Isoep See **Joseph**

Israel [Hebrew]
'The Lord's soldier'. The
warrior of god.
(Issie, Izzie)

Ithel [Welsh]
'Lord-generous'.

Ivan See **John**

Ivar [Norse]
'Battle archer'. The
warrior with the long
bow.
*(Iver, Ivor, Ives, Ivon, Ivo,
Ives, Iven)*

Iven See **Ivar**

Ives [Anglo-Saxon]
'Son of the archer' or der.
of Ivar.

Ives See **Ivar**

Ivo See **Ivar**

Ivon See **Ivar**

Ivor [Welsh]
  'Lord'.
  (Ifor)

Ivor See **Ivar**

Iz See **Isidore**

Izzie See **Isidore**

Girls

Jacenta See **Jacinda**

Jacinda [Greek]
'Beautiful and comely'.
Also a var. of Hyacinth.
(Jacenta)

Jacinth See **Hyacinth**

Jacintha See **Hyacinth**

Jacinthia See **Hyacinth**

Jackie See **Hyacinth** or **Jacqueline**

Jacoba [Latin]
'The supplanter'. The understudy who is better than the star.
(Jacobina, Jacobine)

Jacobina See **Jacoba**

Jacobine See **Jacoba**

Jacqueline [Hebrew]
'The supplanter'.
*(Jacqueleine, Jacquelyn,
Jacquetta, Jacketta, Jackelyn,
Jackeline, Jackie, Jacky,
Jamesina, Jacobina)*

Jacquetta See **Jacqueline**

Jade [Spanish]
'Daughter'. A mother's
most precious jewel.

Jaime [French]
'I love'.
(Jaimee, Jamie, Jamey)

Jaimey See **Jaime**

Jamesina See **Jacqueline**

Jamila [Muslim]
'Beautiful'.

Jan See **Jane**

Jana See **Jane**

Jane [Hebrew]
'God's gift of grace'. With
Mary the most

consistently popular girl's
name, defying fashion
and whim. A selection of
variations:
*(Jan, Jana, Janet, Janette,
Janetta, Janice, Janina,
Janna, Jayne, Jean, Jeanne,
Jeannette, Jeanette, Jenette,
Joan, Joana, Joanna, Joanne,
Johanna, Johanne, Juana,
Juanita, Sinead, Shena,
Sheena, Sine, Sean, Seon,
Seonaid)*

Janet See **Jane**

Janetta See **Jane**

Janice See **Jane**

Janina See **Jane**

Janna See **Jane**

Janthina See **Ianthe**

Janthine See **Ianthe**

Jarmila [Slavic]
'Spring'.

Jarvia [Teutonic]
'Keen as a spear'.

Jasmin [Persian]
'Fragrant flower'.
(Jasmina, Jasmine,
Jessamine, Jessamyn,
Jessamy, Jessamie, Yasmin,
Yasmina)

Jasmina See **Jasmin**

Jayne [Sanskrit]
'God's victorious smile'.
Also a var. of Jane.

Jean See **Jane**

Jeanette See **Jane**

Jemie See **Jemina**

Jemina [Hebrew]
'The dove'. Symbol of
peace.
(Jemie, Jemmie, Mina)

Jena [Arabic]
'A small bird'.

Jennifer See **Genevieve** or
Guinevere

Jeremia [Hebrew]
'The Lord's exalted'.
Fem. of Jeremiah.
(Jeri, Jerrie, Jerry)

Jeri See **Geraldine** or
Jeremia

Jerri See **Geraldine**

Jerusha [Hebrew]
'The married one'. The
perfect wife.
(Yerusha)

Jessalyn See **Jessica**

Jessamine See **Jasmin**

Jessamy See **Jasmin**

Jessica [Hebrew]
'The rich one'.
(Jessalyn)

Jewel [Latin]
'Most precious one'. The
ornament of the home.

Jill See **Julia** or **Gillian**

Jillie See **Gillian**

Jinny See **Virginia**

Jinx [Latin]
'Charming spell'. One
who can enchant with her
beauty and grace.
(Jynx)

Joakima [Hebrew]
'The Lord's Judge'.
(Joachima)

Joan See **Jane**

Joana See **Jane**

Joanne See **Jane**

Jobina [Hebrew]
'The afflicted'. Fem. of
Job.
(Jobyna)

Jocasta [Greek]
'Shining moon'.

Joccoaa [Latin]
'The humorous one'. Girl
with a lively wit.

Jocelyn [Latin]
'Fair and just'. Fem. of
Justin.
*(Jocelyne, Joceline, Jocelin,
Joscelyn, Joscelyne, Joscelin,
Josceline, Joslin, Josline,
Joselin, Joseline, Joselyn,
Joselyne, Joselen, Joselene,
Josilin, Josiline, Josilyn,
Josilyne, Josilen, Josilene,
Justine, Justina, Lyn, Lynne)*

Jodie See **Judith**

Jody See **Judith**

Joelle [Hebrew]
'The Lord is willing'.

Joette See **Josephine**

Johanna See **Jane**

Jolene [Middle English]
'He will increase'.

Jolie [French]
'Pretty'.

Jonquil [Latin]
'Flower-name'.

Jordana [Hebrew]
'The descending'.

Joseline See **Jocelyn**

Josepha See **Josephine**

Josephina See **Josephine**

Josephine [Hebrew]
'She shall add'. Fem. of
Joseph.
*(Josepha, Josephina, Joette,
Josette, Josetta, Jo, Josie,
Fifi, Yusepha, Yosepha)*

Josetta See **Josephine**

Josette See **Josephine**

Josie See **Josephine**

Joslin See **Jocelyn**

Jovita [Latin]
'The joyful one'. The fem.
of Jove the bringer of
jollity.

Joy See **Joyce**

Joyce [Latin]
'Gay and joyful'.
*(Joy, Joice, Joyous, Joycelyn,
Joicelin, Joicelyn, Joycelin)*

Joyous See **Joyce**

Juana See **June**

Juanita See **Jane**

Judith [Hebrew]
'Admired, praised'. One
whose praises cannot be
sufficiently sung.
*(Juditha, Judie, Judy, Jodie,
Judy, Siobhan, Siuban)*

Juditha See **Judith**

Judy See **Judith**

Julia [Greek]
'Youthful'. Young in
heart and mind.
*(Julie, Juliana, Juliane,
Julianna, Julianne, Juliet,
Julietta, Julina, Juline, Jill,
Juli, Sile, Sileas)*

Juliana See **Julia**

Juliane See **Julia**

Julie See **Julia**

Juliet See **Julia**

Julietta See **Julia**

Julina See **Julia**

Juline See **Julia**

Juna See **June**

June [Latin]
'Summer's child'. One
born in the early summer.
*(Juna, Junia, Juniata,
Junette, Junine, Juana)*

Junette See **June**

Junia See **June**

Juniata See **June**

Junine See **June**

Juno [Latin]
'Heavenly being'. The
wife of Jupiter, ruler of
the heavens.

Justina See **Jocelyn**

Justine See **Jocelyn**

Jabez [Hebrew]
'Cause of sorrow'.

Jack See **John**

Jackie See **John**

Jackson [Old English]
'Son of Jack'.

Jacob [Hebrew]
'The supplanter'.
(Jacobus, Jacques, Jamie,
Jim, Jimmie, Jimmy, Jas,
Hamish, Diego, Seamus,
Shamus, Jem, Jemmie,
Jemmy, Jock, Jocko)

Jacobus See **Jacob**

Jacques See **Jacob**

Jael [Hebrew]
'To ascend'.

Jagger [Northumbrian]
'A carter'.

Jamal [Arabic]
'Beauty'.

James See **Jacob**

Jamie See **Jacob**

Jamil [Arabic]
'Handsome'.

Jan See **John**

Janos See **John**

Jared [Hebrew]
'The descendant'.

Jarman [Teutonic]
'The German'.
(Jerman, Jermyn)

Jaroslav [Slavic]
'Praise of spring'.

Jarrett See **Garrett**

Jarv See **Gervase**

Jarvey See **Gervase**

Jarvis See **Gervase**

Jas See **Jacob**

Jason [Greek]
'The healer'.

Jasper See **Gaspar**

Javier See **Xavier**

Jay [Anglo-Saxon]
'Jay or crow'. Also used
as dim. for any name
beginning with J.

Jean See **John**

Jed See **Jedediah**

Jedediah [Hebrew]
'Beloved by the Lord'.
(Jed, Jedidiah, Jeddy)

Jeffers See **Geoffrey**

Jefferson [Anglo-Saxon]
'Jeffrey's son'.

Jeffrey See **Geoffrey**

Jehoshaphat [Hebrew]
'The Lord judges'.

Jem See **Jacob**

Jemmie See **Jacob**

Jeremiah See **Jeremy**

Jeremias See **Jeremy**

Jeremy [Hebrew]
'Exalted by the Lord'.
(Jeremiah, Jeremias, Jerry)

Jermyn See **Jarman**

Jerome [Latin]
'Sacred; holy'. A man of
God.
(Jerome, Gerome, Jerry)

Jerrold See **Gerald**

Jerry See **Jeremy**

Jervis See **Gervase**

Jervoise See **Gervase**

Jesse [Hebrew]
'God's gift'. *(Jess)*

Jethro [Hebrew]
'Excellent; without
equal'.

Jevon See **John**

Jim See **Jacob**

Jimmy See **Jacob**

Joachim [Hebrew]
'Judgement of the Lord'.

Job [Hebrew]
'The persecuted; the
afflicted'.

Jock See **Jacob**, **James** or
John

Jocko See **Jacob**

Joe See **Joel**

Joel [Hebrew]
'The Lord is God'.
(Joe, Joey)

Joey See **Joel**

Johan See **John**

John [Hebrew]
'God's gracious gift'. The
most consistently popular
boy's name.
*(Jon, Jean, Jack, Jock, Jevon,
Jan, Janos, Johan, Johann,
Jackie, Johnnie, Johnny,
Sean, Shawn, Shane, Sian,
Evan, Ivan, Ian, Gian,
Hans, Zane, Iain, Iaian,
Eoin, Seain, Seann)*

Johnnie See **John**

Joliet See **Julius**

Jolyon See **Julius**

Jon See **Jonathan**

Jonah [Hebrew]
'Peace'.

Jonas [Hebrew]
'Dove'. A man of peace
and tranquillity'.

Jonathan [Hebrew]
'Gift of the Lord'.
(Jon, Jonathon)

Jordan [Hebrew]
'The descending river'.
(Jordon, Jourdain)

Jorin See **George**

Joris See **George**

Joseph [Hebrew]
'He shall add'.
*(Joe, Joey, Jose, Isoep,
Seosaidh, Josiah)*

Josh See **Joshua**

Joshua [Hebrew]
'God's salvation'. A man
saved by his belief in
God.
(Josh)

Josiah See **Joseph**

Jotham [Hebrew]
'God is perfect'.

Judah See **Judd**

Judd [Hebrew]
'Praised; extolled'.
(Judah, Jude)

Jude See **Judd**

Jule See **Julius**

Jules See **Julius**

Julian See **Julius**

Julie See **Julius**

Julius [Latin]
'Youthful shaveling'.
*(Jules, Julian, Joliet, Jule,
Julie, Jolyon)*

Junius [Latin]
'Born in June'.

Jurgen See **George**

Just See **Justin**

Justin [Latin]
'The just one'. One of
upright principles and
morals.
(Justus, Just, Iestin)

Justis [French]
'Justice'. A strict
upholder of the moral
laws.

Justus See **Justin**

Girls

Kali [Sanskrit]
'Energy'.

Kalila [Arabic]
'Beloved'.
(Kally, Kaylee, Kylila)

Kalinda [Sanskrit]
'Sun'.

Kally See **Kalila**

Kama [Sanskrit]
'Love'. The Hindu god of
love, like Cupid.

Kanaka See **Canace**

Kanake See **Canace**

Kara See **Cara**

Karen See **Katherine**

Karena See **Katherine**

Karin See **Katherine**

Kasmira [Slavic]
'Commands peace'.
(Casmira)

Kate See **Catherine**

Katherina See **Katherine**

Katherine [Greek]
'Pure maiden'. Another
spelling of Catherine.
*(Katharine, Katharina,
Katherina, Katheryn,
Kathryn, Katrin, Katrina,
Katryn, Kathleen, Kathlene,
Kitty, Katie, Kathie, Kay,
Kate, Kara, Karen, Karena,
Karin, Karyn* and all var.
of Catherine)

Kathie See **Katherine**

Kathleen See **Katherine**

Kathryn See **Katherine**

Katie See **Katherine**

Katrin See **Katherine**

Katrina See **Catherine** or
Katherine

Katryn See **Katherine**

Katy See **Catherine**

Kay See **Katherine**

Kaylee See **Kalila**

Keely [Gaelic]
'The beautiful one'.

Kelda [Norse]
'Bubbling spring'.
(Kelly)

Kelly [Irish Gaelic]
'Warrior maid'.

Kelsey [Scandinavian]
'From the ship island'.

Kendra [Old English]
'Knowledgeable'.

Keren [Hebrew]
'Horn of antimoney'.

Kerridwen See **Ceiridwen**

Kerry [Gaelic]
'Dark one'.
(Kerri)

Kesia [African]
'Favourite'.

Ketti See **Katherine**

Ketura [Hebrew]
'Incense'.

Kevin [Gaelic]
'Gentle and lovable'.
(Kelvina)

Kiah [African]
'Season's beginning'.

Kim [Origin not known]
'Noble chief'.

Kimberley [English]
'From the royal meadow'.

Kineta [Greek]
'Active and elusive'.

Kinnnereth [Hebrew]
'From the Sea of Galilee'.

Kira [Persian]
'Sun'.

Kirstie See **Kirstin**

Kirstin [Norse]
'The annointed one'.
(Kirstina, Kirstie, Kirsty)

Kirstina See **Kirstin**

Kit See **Catherine**

Kitty See **Catherine**

Koren [Greek]
'Beautiful maiden'.

Kyla [Gaelic]
'Comely'.
(Kilah, Kylah, Kylie)

Kylie See **Kyla**

Kyna [Gaelic]
'Great wisdom'.

Kyrenia See **Cyrena**

Kalil [Arabic]
'Good friend'.

Kane [Celtic]
'Little, warlike one' or
'Radiant brightness'.

Kareem [Arabic]
'Noble'.

Karl See **Charles**

Karney See **Kearney**

Karr See **Carr**

Kaspar See **Gaspar**

Kavan See **Cavan**

Kay [Celtic]
'Rejoiced in'. Also dim.
for any name beginning
with K.

Kean [Irish]
'Fast'.

Keane [Anglo-Saxon]
'Bold and handsome'. A
sharp witted man.

Kearney See **Carney**

Kedar [Arabic]
'Powerful'.

Keefe [Celtic]
'Handsome, noble and
admirable'.

Keegan [Celtic]
'Little fiery one'.

Keelan [Celtic]
'Little slender one'.

Keeley [Celtic]
'Little, handsome one'.

Keenan [Celtic]
'Little ancient one'.

Keith [Celtic]
'A place' or 'From the
forest' (Welsh).

Kell [Norse]
'From the well'.

Keller [Gaelic]
'Little companion'.

Kelly [Gaelic]
'The warrior'.
(Kelley)

Kelsey [Norse/Teutonic]
'Dweller on the island'
(Norse) or 'From the
water' (Teutonic).

Kelvin [Gaelic]
'From the narrow
stream'.
(Kelvan, Kelven)

Kembell See **Kimball**

Kemp [Anglo-Saxon]
'The warrior champion'.

Ken See **Kendall** or
Kenneth

Kendall [Celtic]
'Chief of the valley'.
(Kendal, Kendell, Ken)

Kendrick [Gaelic/
Anglo-Saxon]
'Son of Henry' (Gaelic)
or 'Royal ruler' (Anglo-
Saxon)

Kenelm [Anglo-Saxon]
'Brave helmet'. A
courageous protector.

Kenley [Anglo-Saxon]
'Owner of a royal
meadow'.

Kenn [Celtic]
'Clear as bright water'.

Kennard [Anglo-Saxon]
'Bold and vigorous'.

Kennedy [Gaelic]
'The helmeted chief'.

Kennet See **Kenneth**

Kenneth [Celtic]
'The handsome' or
'Royal oath'.
*(Keneth, Kennet, Ken,
Kenny, Kent)*

Kenny See **Kenneth**

Kenrick [Anglo-Saxon]
'Bold ruler'.

Kent [Celtic]
'Bright and white'. Also
dim. of Kenneth.

Kent See **Kenneth**

Kenton [Anglo-Saxon]
'From the royal estate'.

Kenward [Anglo-Saxon]
'Bold guardian'.

Kenway [Anglo-Saxon]
'Bold or royal warrior'.

Kenyon [Celtic]
'White haired'.

Kermit [Celtic]
'A free man'.
(Dermot, Derry, Kerry)

Kern [Gaelic]
'Little dark one'.

Kerr See **Carr** or **Kirby**

Kerry [Gaelic]
'Son of the dark one'.

Kerry See **Kermit**

Kerwin [Gaelic]
'Small black haired one'.

Kester [Anglo-Saxon]
'From the army camp'.
Also used as dim. of
Christopher.

Kevan See **Kevin**

Kevin [Gaelic]
'Gentle, kind and
lovable'.
(Kevan, Keven, Kev)

Key [Gaelic]
'Son of the fiery one'.

Kieran [Gaelic]
'Small and dark skinned'.
(Kieron, Kerrin, Kerry)

Killian [Gaelic]
'Little warlike one'.

Kim See **Kimball**

Kimball [Celtic]
'Royally brave' or
'Warrior chief'.
*(Kimble, Kimbell, Kemble,
Kim)*

Kincaid [Celtic]
'Battle chief'.

King [Anglo-Saxon]
'The sovereign'. The
ruler of his people.

Kingsley [Anglo-Saxon]
'From the king's
meadow'.

Kingston [Anglo-Saxon]
'From the king's farm'.

Kingswell [Anglo-Saxon]
'From the king's well'.

Kinnard [Gaelic]
'From the high
mountain'.
(Kinnaird)

Kinnell [Gaelic]
'Dweller on the top of the
cliff'.

Kinsey [Anglo-Saxon]
'Royal victor'.

Kipp [Anglo-Saxon]
'Dweller on the pointed hill'.

Kirby [Teutonic]
'From the church village'.
(Kerby, Kerr)

Kirk [Norse]
'Dweller at the church'.

Kirkley [Anglo-Saxon]
'From the church meadow'.

Kirkwood [Anglo-Saxon]
'From the church wood'.

Kirwin See **Kerwin**

Kit See **Christopher**

Knight [Anglo-Saxon]
'Mounted soldier'.

Knox [Anglo-Saxon]
'From the hills'.

Knut See **Canute**

Knute See **Canute**

Konrad See **Conrad**

Krishna [Hindu]
'Delightful'.

Kristian See **Christian**

Kristin See **Christian**

Kurt See **Conrad/Curtis**

Kwasi [African]
'Born on Sunday'.

Kyle [Gaelic]
'From the strait'.

Kynan See **Conan**

Kyne [Anglo-Saxon]
'The royal one'.

Girls

La Roux [French]
'The red haired one'.
(Larousse, Roux)

Labhaoise See **Louise**

Lacey See **Larissa**

Ladonna [French]
'The lady'.

Lala [Slavic]
'The tulip flower'.

Lalage [Greek]
'Gentle laughter'.

Lalita [Sanskrit]
'Without guile'.

Lalota [Sanskrit]
'Pleasing'.

Lana See **Alana**

Lane [Middle English]
'From the narrow road'.

Lanelle [Old French]
'From the little lane'.

Lani [Hawaiian]
'The sky'.

Lara [Latin]
'Famous'.

Laraine See **Lorraine**

Lareena See **Larine**

Larentia [Latin]
'Foster mother'.
(*Laurentia*)

Larianna See **Larine**

Larina See **Lorraine**

Larine [Latin]
'Girl of the sea'.
(*Lareena, Larena, Larianna*)

Larine See **Lorraine**

Larissa [Greek]
'Cheerful maiden'. One
who is as happy as a lark.
(*Lacey*)

Lark [English]
'Singing bird'.

Lasca [Latin]
'Weary one'.

Lassie [Scots]
'Little girl'.

Latona See **Latonia**

Latonia [Latin]
'Belonging to Latona'.
Was the mother of Diana.
(*Latona, Latoya*)

Latoya See **Latonia**

Laura [Latin]
'Laurel wreath'. The
victor's crown of laurels.
(*Laurel, Lauren, Laureen,
Laurena, Laurene, Lauretta,
Laurette, Lora, Loren,
Lorena, Loretta, Lorette,
Lorita, Lorna, Laure,
Lorenza, Loralie, Lorelie,
Lorinda, Lorine, Lori, Loree,
Lorie, Lorrie, Laurie*)

Laure See **Laura**

Laureen See **Laura**

Laurel See **Laura**

Lauren See **Laura**

Laurena See **Laura**

Laurentia See **Larentia**

Lauretta See **Laura**

Laurette See **Laura**

Laveda [Latin]
'One who is purified'.
(Lavetta, Lavette)

Lavelle [Latin]
'Cleansing'.

Lavender [English]
'Sweet smelling flower'.
(Lavvie)

Laverna See **Laverne**

Laverne [French]
'Spring like' or 'Alder
tree'.
*(Laverna, Verna, Verne,
Vern)*

Lavetta See **Laveda**

Lavette See **Laveda**

Lavina See **Lavinia**

Lavinia [Latin]
'Lady of Rome'.
(Lavina, Vina, Vinia)

Lavvie See **Lavender**

Leah [Hebrew]
'The weary one'.
(Lea, Lee, Leigh)

Leala [French]
'The true one'. One who
is true to home, family
and friends.

Leandra [Latin]
'Like a lioness'.

Leane See **Liana**

Leatrice [Combination
Leah/Beatrice]
'Tired but joyful'.
(Leatrix)

Leatrix See **Leatrice**

Leda [Greek]
'Mother of beauty'. The
mother of Helen of Troy.

Leda See **Alida**, **Letha** or
Letitia

Lee [English]
'From the fields'. Also a
var. of Leah.

Lee See **Leila**

Leela See **Leila**

Leigh [Old English]
'From the meadow'.

Leila [Arabic]
'Black as the night'.
*(Leilia, Lela, Lilia, Leilah,
Lilah, Leela, Lee)*

Leila See **Lilian**

Leilani [Hawaiian]
'Heavenly blossom'. The
tropical flower of the
Islands.
(Lullani, Lillani)

Leilia See **Leila**

Lela See **Leila** or **Lilian**

Lelia See **Lilian**

Lemuela [Hebrew]
'Dedicated to God'. A
daughter dedicated to the
service of God.
(Lemuella)

Lena [Latin]
'Enchanting one'. Also a
dim. of Caroline,
Madeleine, Helena.
(Lina)

Lena See **Helen**

Lene See **Lenis**

Lenis [Latin]
'Smooth and white as the
lily'.
*(Lene, Lenta, Lenita, Leneta,
Lenos)*

Lenita See **Lenis**

Lennie See **Leona**

Lenora See **Helen**

Lenore See **Eleanor**

Lenos See **Lenis**

Lenta See **Lenis**

Leoda [Teutonic]
'Woman of the people'.
(Leola, Leota)

Leola See **Leoda**

Leoma [Anglo-Saxon]
'Bright light'. One who
casts radiance around
her.

Leona [Latin]
'The lioness'.
*(Leola, Leonie, Leone,
Leoni, Lennie, Lenny)*

Leona See **Helen**

Leonarda [French]
'Like a lion'.
(Leonarde, Leonardina, Leonardine)

Leonarde See **Leonarda**

Leonardina See **Leonarda**

Leonardine See **Leonarda**

Leone See **Leona**

Leonie See **Leona**

Leonora See **Eleanor**

Leontina See **Leontine**

Leontine [Latin]
'Like the lion'.
(Leontina, Leontyne)

Leopolda See **Leopoldina**

Leopoldina [Teutonic]
'The people's champion'.
Fem. of Leopold.
(Leopoldine, Leopolda)

Leopoldine See **Leopoldina**

Leora See **Helen**

Leota See **Leoda**

Les See **Lesley**

Lesley [Celtic]
'Keeper of the grey fort'.
(Leslie, Lesli, Lesly, Les)

Leta See **Letha** or **Letitia**

Letha [Greek]
'Sweet oblivion'. Lethe
the river of forgetfulness.
(Lethia, Lethitha, Leithia, Leda, Leta)

Lethia See **Letha**

Lethitha See **Letha**

Letitia [Latin]
'Joyous gladness'.
(Laetitia, Leticia, Letizia, Lettice, Lettie, Leta, Leda, Tish)

Lettice See **Letitia**

Lettie See **Letitia**

Levana [Latin]
'The sun of the dawn'.
The Goddess of
childbirth.
(Levania)

Levania See **Levana**

Levina [English]
'A bright flash'. One who
passes like a comet.

Lewanna [Hebrew]
'As pure as the white
moon'.
(Luanna)

Lexie See **Alexandra**

Lexine See **Alexandra**

Leya [Spanish]
'Loyalty to the law'. A
strict upholder of morals
and principles.

Liana [French]
'The climbing vine'.
*(Leane, Leana, Leanna,
Lianna, Lianne)*

Libby See **Elizabeth**

Libusa [Russian]
'Beloved'.

Lida [Slavic]
'Beloved of the people'.

Lila See **Leila**

Lilac [Persian]
'Dark mauve flower'.

Lilais See **Lilian**

Lilian [Latin]
'A lily'. One who is pure
in thought, word and
deed.

*(Lillian, Liliana, Lilliana,
Liliane, Lilliane, Lilyan,
Lillyan, Lily, Lili, Lilli,
Lilly, Lilias, Lilais, Lillis,
Lela, Lelah, Lelia, Leila,
Lila, Lilah, Lilia, Lilla)*

Lilias See **Lilian**

Lilith [Arabic]
'Woman of the night'.
According to Eastern
belief, Lilith was the first
wife of Adam and the first
woman in the world; Eve
was his second wife.

Lily See **Lilian**

Lina See **Caroline**

Lind See **Linda**

Linda [Spanish]
'Pretty one'. Also dim. of
Belinda, Rosalinda, etc.
*(Lind, Linde, Lindie, Lindy,
Lynda, Lynd)*

Linda See **Belinda**

Lindie See **Belinda** or
Linda

Lindsay [Old English]
'From the linden tree
island'.
(Lindsey)

Line See **Caroline**

Linetta See **Linnet**

Linnea [Norse]
'The lime blossom'.

Linnet [French]
'Sweet bird'.
*(Linnette, Linette, Linetta,
Linnetta, Lynette, Lynnette)*

Liorah [Hebrew]
'I have light'.

Lisa See **Elizabeth**

Lisbeth See **Elizabeth**

Lisha [Arabic]
'The darkness before
midnight'.

Lissie See **Alida**

Lita See **Alida**

Liusade See **Louise**

Livi See **Olga**

Livia See **Olga**

Liza See **Elizabeth**

Lizabeta See **Elizabeth**

Lizzy See **Elizabeth**

Llawela [Welsh]
'Like a ruler'.
(Llawella)

Lodema [English]
'Leader or guide'.

Lodie See **Melody**

Lois See **Louise**

Lola [Spanish]
'Strong woman'.
(Loleta, Lolita, Lollie)

Lola See **Dolores**

Loleta See **Lola**

Lolita See **Dolores**

Lollie See **Lola**

Lomasi [North American
Indian]
'Pretty flower'.

Lona [Anglo-Spanish]
'Solitary watcher'.

Lora See **Helen** or **Laura**

Loralie See **Laura**

Lorelei [Teutonic]
'Siren of the river'. The
Rhine maiden who lured
unwary mariners to their
deaths.
(Lorelie, Lorelia, Lurleen)

Lorelia See **Lorelei**

Lorelle [Latin]
'Little'.

Loren See **Laura**

Lorena See **Laura**

Lorenza See **Laura**

Loretta See **Laura**

Lori See **Laura**

Lorinda See **Laura**

Lorine See **Laura**

Loris See **Chloris**

Lorita See **Laura**

Lorna See **Laura**

Lorraine [Teutonic/
French]
'Renowned in battle'
(Teutonic); 'The Queen'
(French).

*(Loraine, Laraine, Larraine,
Larayne, Larine, Larina)*

Lotus [Greek]
'Flower of the sacred
Nile'.

Louella See **Luella**

Louisa See **Louise**

Louise [Teutonic]
'Famous battle maid'.
One who leads victorious
armies into battle.
*(Louisa, Luise, Lois, Loise,
Louisitte, Labhaoise,
Liusade, Loyce, Eloise,
Eloisa, Heloise, Aloisa,
Aloisia, Aloysia, Alison,
Allison)*

Louisitte See **Louise**

Love [English]
'Tender affection'.

Loyce See **Louise**

Luana [Teutonic]
'Graceful army maiden'.
*(Luane, Louanna, Louanne,
Luwana, Luwanna,
Luwanne)*

Luane See **Luana**

Luba [Russian]
'Love'.

Lucette See **Lucy**

Lucia See **Lucy**

Luciana See **Lucy**

Lucianna [Combination
Lucy/Anne]

Lucida See **Lucy**

Lucile See **Lucy**

Lucinda See **Lucy**

Lucrece See **Lucretia**

Lucretia [Latin]
'A rich reward'.
(Lucrezia, Lucrece, Lucrecia)

Lucy [Latin]
'Light'. One who brings
the lamp of learning to
the ignorant.
*(Luciana, Lucida, Lucinda,
Lucile, Lucille, Lucette,
Lucia, Luisadh, Luighseach)*

Ludella [Anglo-Saxon]
'Pixie maid'.

Ludmilla [Slavic]
'Beloved of the people'.
(Ludmila)

Luella [Anglo-Saxon]
'The appeaser'.
(Louella, Loella, Luelle)

Luelle See **Luella**

Luighseach See **Lucy**

Luisadh See **Lucy**

Luna See **Lunetta**

Lunetta [Latin]
'Little Moon'.
(Luna, Luneta)

Lupe [Spanish]
'She wolf'. A fierce
guardian of the home.

Lura See **Lurline**

Lurleen See **Lorelei**

Lurlette See **Lurline**

Lurlina See **Lurline**

Lurline [Teutonic]
'Siren'. A version of
Lorelie.
*(Lurlina, Lura, Lurleen,
Lurlene, Lurlette)*

Luvena [Latin]
'Little beloved one'.

Lydia [Greek]
'Cultured one'.
(Lidia, Lydie, Lidie)

Lydie See **Lydia**

Lynette [English]
'Idol'.
(Lyn, Lynn, Lynne, Linnet)

Lynn [Celtic]
'A waterfall'. Also dim. of
Carolyn, Evelyn, etc.
(Lynne)

Lynne See **Jocelyn**

Lyonelle [Old French]
'Young lion'.

Lyra See **Lyris**

Lyris [Greek]
'She who plays the harp'.
(Lyra)

Lysandra [Greek]
'The Liberator'. The
prototype of Women's
Lib!

Laban [Hebrew]
'White'.

Labhras See **Lawrence**

Labhruinn See **Lawrence**

Lach [Celtic]
'Dweller by the water'.
(Lache)

Lachlan [Celtic]
'The warlike'.

Lacy [Latin]
'From the Roman manor
house'.

Ladd [Anglo-Saxon]
'Attendant; page'.
(Laddie)

Laddie See **Ladd**

Ladislas [Slavic]
'A glory of power'.

Laibrook [Anglo-Saxon]
'Path by the brook'.

Laidley [Anglo-Saxon]
'From the water
meadow'.

Laird [Celtic]
'The land owner'. The
lord of the manor.

Lamar [Teutonic]
'Famous throughout the
land'.

Lambert [Teutonic]
'Rich in land'. An owner
of vast estates.

Lamech [Hebrew]
'Strong young man'.

Lamond See **Lamont**

Lamont [Norse]
'A lawyer'.
*(Lamond, Lammond,
Lammont)*

Lance See **Lancelot**

Lancelot [French]
'Spear attendant'.
*(Launcelot, Launce, Lancey,
Lance)*

Lancey See **Lancelot**

Lander [Anglo-Saxon]
'Owner of a grassy plain'.
(Launder, Landor, Landers)

Landers See **Lander**

Landon [Anglo-Saxon]
'Dweller on the long hill'.
(Langdon, Langston)

Landor See **Lander**

Landric [Old German]
'Land ruler'.

Lane [Anglo-Saxon]
'From the narrow road'.

Lang [Teutonic]
'Tall or long limbed
man'.

Langdon See **Landon**

Langford [Anglo-Saxon]
'Dweller by the long
ford'.

Langley [Anglo-Saxon]
'Dweller by the long
meadow'.

Langston [Anglo-Saxon]
'The farm belonging to
the tall man'.

Langston See **Landon**

Langworth [Anglo-Saxon]
'From the long
enclosure'.

Larrance See **Lawrence**

Larry See **Lawrence**

Lars See **Lawrence**

Larson [Norse]
'Son of Lars'.

Latham [Norse]
'From the barns'.

Lathrop [Anglo-Saxon]
'From the barn
farmstead'.

Latimer [Anglo-Saxon]
'The interpreter; the
language teacher'.

Launce See **Lancelot**

Lauren See **Lawrence**

Laurent See **Lawrence**

Lauric See **Lawrence**

Lauritz See **Lawrence**

Lawford [Anglo-Saxon]
'Dweller at the ford by
the hill'.

Lawler [Gaelic]
'The mumbler'.

Lawley [Anglo-Saxon]
'From the meadow on the
hill'.

Lawrence [Latin]
'Crowned with laurels'.
The victor's crown of bay
leaves.
*(Laurence, Larrance,
Lawrance, Lorenz, Laurent,
Lars, Larry, Lauren, Lauric,
Lawry, Loren, Lorne, Lorin,
Lon, Lonnie, Lorenzo, Lori,
Lorrie, Lorry, Lauritz,
Labhras, Labhruinn)*

Lawson [Anglo-Saxon]
'Son of Lawrence'.

Lawton [Anglo-Saxon]
'From the town on the
hill'.

Lazar See **Eleazar**

Lazarus See **Eleazar**

Leal [Anglo-Saxon]
'Loyal, true and faithful'.

Leander [Greek]
'The lion man'.

Lee [Anglo-Saxon/Gaelic]
'From the meadow'
(Anglo-Saxon) or
'Poetic' (Gaelic).
(Leigh)

Lee See **Ashley**

Leggett [French]
'Envoy or ambassador'.
(Leggitt, Liggett)

Leicester See **Lester**

Leif [Norse]
'The beloved one'.

Leigh See **Lee**

Leighton [Anglo-Saxon]
'Dweller at the farm by
the meadow'.
(Layton)

Leith [Celtic]
'Broad, wide river'.

Leland [Anglo-Saxon]
'Dweller by the meadow
land'.
(Leyland, Lealand)

Lem See **Lemuel**

Lemmie See **Lemuel**

Lemuel [Hebrew]
'Consecrated to God'.
(Lem, Lemmie)

Lenard See **Leonard**

Lennie See **Leonard**

Lennon [Gaelic]
'Little cloak'.

Lennox [Celtic]
'Grove of elm trees'.

Leo [Latin]
'Lion'.

Leo See **Leopold**

Leon [French]
'Lion-like'.

Leonard [Latin]
'Lion brave'. One with all
the courage and tenacity
of the king of beasts.
*(Leoner, Lennard, Lenard,
Leonhard, Len, Lennie,
Lenny)*

Leoner See **Leonard**

Leonidas [Greek]
'Son of the lion'.

Leopold [Teutonic]
'Brave for the people'.
One who fights for his
countrymen.
(Leo, Lepp)

Lepp See **Leopold**

Leroy [French]
'The king'.
(Lee, Roy)

Leslie [Celtic]
'From the grey fort'.
(Lesley, Les)

Lester [Anglo-Saxon]
'From the army camp'.
(Leicester)

Leverett [French]
'The young hare'.

Leverton [Anglo-Saxon]
'From the rush farm'.

Levi [Hebrew]
'United'.

Lewis [Teutonic]
'Famous battle warrior'.
*(Louis, Ludwig, Lewes,
Ludovic, Ludovick, Lugaidh,
Luthais, Lou, Lew, Ludo)*

Liam See **William**

Lincoln [Celtic]
'From the place by the
pool'.

Lind [Anglo-Saxon]
'From the lime tree'.
(Linden, Lyndon)

Lindberg [Teutonic]
'Lime tree hill'.

Lindell [Anglo-Saxon]
'Dweller by the lime tree
in the valley'.

Linden See **Lind**

Lindley [Anglo-Saxon]
'By the lime tree in the
meadow'.

Lindon See **Lind**

Lindsey [Anglo-Saxon]
'Pool island'.
(Lindsay, Linsay, Linsey)

Linford [Anglo-Saxon]
'From the lime tree ford'.

Link [Anglo-Saxon]
'From the bank or edge'.

Linley [Anglo-Saxon]
'From the flax field'.

Linn See **Lynn**

Linton [Anglo-Saxon]
'From the flax farm'.

Linus [Greek]
'Flax coloured hair'.

Lion See **Lionel**

Lionel [French]
'The young lion'.
(Lion)

Lisle See **Lyle**

Litton [Anglo-Saxon]
'Farm on the hillside'.

Livingston [Old English]
'From Leif's town'.

Lleufer [Welsh]
'Splendid'.

Llewellyn [Welsh]
'Lion like' or 'Like a
ruler'.

Lloyd [Welsh]
'Grey-haired'.
(Floyd)

Locke [Anglo-Saxon]
'Dweller in the
stronghold'.

Logan [Celtic]
'Little hollow'.

Lombard [Latin]
'Long bearded one'.

Lon [Gaelic]
'Strong, fierce'. Also dim.
of Lawrence.

Lon See **Lawrence**

Lonnie See **Lawrence**

Lonny See **Zebulon**

Loren See **Lawrence**

Lorenze See **Lawrence**

Lorenzo See **Lawrence**

Lori See **Lawrence**

Lorimer [Latin]
'Harness maker'.

Loring [Teutonic]
'Man from Lorraine'.

Lorrie See **Lawrence**

Lothaire See **Luther**

Lothar See **Luther**

Lothario See **Luther**

Lou See **Lewis**

Louis See **Lewis**

Lovel See **Lowell**

Lowell [Anglo-Saxon]
'The beloved one'.
(Lovel, Lovell)

Loyal See **Leal**

Lubin [Old English]
'Dear friend'.

Lucas See **Lucius**

Luce See **Lucius**

Lucian See **Lucius**

Lucius [Latin]
'Light'.
*(Lucas, Luke, Lucian, Luck,
Luc, Lukas, Lucais, Luce,
Lukey)*

Luck See **Lucius**

Ludlow [Anglo-Saxon]
'From the hill of the
prince'.

Ludo See **Lewis**

Ludolf [Old Germans]
'Famous wolf'.

Ludovic See **Lewis**

Ludwig See **Aloysius** or
Lewis

Luke See **Lucius**

Lukey See **Lucius**

Lundy [French]
'Born on Monday'.

Lunn [Gaelic]
'From the grove'.

Lunt [Norse]
'Strong and fierce'.

Lute See **Luther**

Luthais See **Lewis**

Luther [Teutonic]
'Famous warrior'.
*(Lothar, Lothaire, Lothario,
Lute)*

Lyall See **Lyle**

Lycidas [Greek]
'Wolf son'.

Lyle [French]
'From the island'.
(Lyall, Lyell, Lisle, Liall)

Lyman [Anglo-Saxon]
'Man from the meadow'.
(Leyman)

Lyndon See **Lind**

Lynfa [Welsh]
'From the lake'.

Lynn [Welsh]
'From the pool or
waterfall'.
(Lyn, Lin, Linn)

Lysander [Greek]
'The liberator'.
(Sandy)

Girls

Mab [Gaelic]
'Mirthful joy'.
(*Mave, Meave, Mavis*)

Mabel [Latin]
'Amiable and loving'. An
endearing companion.
(*Mable, Maybelle, Maible,
Moibeal*)

Mada See **Madeline**

Maddy See **Madeline**

Madel See **Madeline**

Madelia See **Madeline**

Madeline [Greek]
'Tower of strength'. A
woman of great physical
and moral courage, on
whom many could lean in
difficult times.

*(Madeleine, Madelaine,
Madaline, Madaleine,
Madalaine, Madalena,
Maddalena, Maddalene,
Madelon, Madlin, Madel,
Madelia, Madella, Madelle,
Magdala, Magdaa,
Magdalen, Magdalene,
Magdalyn, Magdalane,
Malena, Marleen, Marlene,
Marline, Marlena, Malina,
Mada, Madelle, Maddy,
Maighdlin, Mala)*

Madella See **Madeline**

Madelle See **Madeline**

Madelon See **Madeline**

Madge See **Margaret**

Madlin See **Madeline**

Madora See **Medea**

Madra [Spanish]
'The matriarch'.

Mae See **May**

Maeve [Irish]
The warrior queen of
Connaught
(Mave, Meave)

Magdaa See **Madeline**

Magdala See **Madeline**

Magdalen See **Madeline**

Magdalene See
Madeleine

Magdalyn See **Madeline**

Magena [North American
Indian]
'The coming moon'.

Maggie See **Magnilda** or
Margaret

Magnilda [Teutonic]
'Great battle maid'.
*(Magnilde, Magnhilda,
Magnhilde, Mag, Maggie,
Nilda, Nillie)*

Magnilde See **Magnilda**

Magnolia [Latin]
'Magnolia flower'.
(Mag, Maggie, Nola, Nolie)

Mahala [Hebrew]
'Tenderness'.
(Mahalah, Mahalia)

Mahalia See **Mahala**

Maia See **May**

Maida [Anglo-Saxon]
  'The maiden'.
  (Maidie, Mady, Maidel,
  Mayda, Mayde, Maydena)

Maidel See **Maida**

Maidie See **Maida**

Maigrghread See
  Margaret

Maisie See **Margaret**

Majesta [Latin]
  'Majestic One'.

Mala See **Madeline**

Malan See **Melanie**

Malena See **Madeline**

Malise [Gaelic]
  'Servant of God'.

Malva [Greek]
  'Soft and tender'.
  (Melva, Melba)

Malva See **Malvina** or
  Mauve

Malvie See **Malvina**

Malvina [Gaelic]
  'Polished chieftain'.

(Malva, Melva, Melvina,
Malvie, Melvine)

Mamie See **Mary**

Manette See **Mary**

Manon See **Mary**

Manuela [Spanish]
  'God with us'.
  (Manuella)

Mara See **Damara** or **Mary**

Marcelia See **Marcella**

Marcella [Latin]
  'Belonging to Mars'.
  (Marcie, Marcia, Marcy,
  Marcelle, Marcelline,
  Marcelline, Marcile,
  Marcille, Marcela,
  Marcelia, Marchella,
  Marchelle, Marchelline,
  Marchita, Marquita,
  Marsha, Marilda)

Marcelle See **Marcella**

Marcelline See **Marcella**

Marchelle See **Marcella**

Marchelline See **Marcella**

Marchita See **Marcella**

Marcia See **Marcella**

Marcie See **Marcella**

Marcile See **Marcella**

Marelda [Teutonic]
'Famous battle maiden'.

Maretta See **Mary**

Marfot See **Margaret**

Margalo See **Margaret**

Margaret [Latin]
'A pearl'.
*(Margareta, Margaretta,
Margarita, Margery,
Margory, Marjery,
Marjorie, Margorie,
Margerie, Margharita,
Marget, Margette,
Margetta, Margalo,
Marguerite, Margerita,
Margueritta, Marguerita,
Marfot, Margarethe,
Margethe, Margaretha,
Maigrghread, Margo,
Margao, Marge, Maggie,
Meta, Meg, Maisie, Grete,
Greta, Grethe, Gretchen,
Peggy, Rita, Daisy)*

Margareta See **Margaret**

Margaretta See **Margaret**

Marge See **Margaret**

Margerita See **Margaret**

Margery See **Margaret**

Marget See **Margaret**

Margo See **Margaret**

Maria See **Mary**

Mariam See **Marian**

Marian [Hebrew]
'Bitter and graceful'.
*(Marion, Marianne,
Mariana, Marianna,
Maryanne, Mariam,
Mariom)*

Mariana See **Marian**

Marie See **Mary**

Mariel See **Mary**

Marietta See **Mary**

Marigold [English]
'Golden flower girl'.
(Marygold)

Marilda See **Marcella**

Marilla See **Amaryllis** or
Mary

Marilyn See **Mary**

Marina [Latin]
'Lady of the sea'.
(*Marnie*)

Marion See **Marian**

Mariposa [Spanish]
'Butterfly'.

Maris [Latin]
'Of the sea'.
(*Marisa, Marris*)

Maris See **Damara**

Marisa See **Maris**

Marla See **Mary**

Marleen See **Madeline**

Marlena See **Madeline**

Marlene See **Madeleine**

Marnie See **Marina**

Marquita See **Marcella**

Marsha See **Marcella**

Marta See **Martha**

Martella See **Martha**

Martha [Arabic]
'The mistress'.
(*Marta, Marthe, Martie,
Marty, Mattie, Matty,
Martella*)

Martie See **Martha**

Martina [Latin]
'Warlike one'. Fem. of
Martin.
(*Martine, Marta, Tina*)

Martine See **Martina**

Marva See **Marvel**

Marvel [Latin]
'A wondrous miracle'.
(*Marva, Marvella, Marvela,
Marvelle*)

Marvella See **Marvel**

Mary [Hebrew]
'Bitterness'. Although
Hebrew in origin has
become one of the most
consistently popular
names for girls, since the
Christian era.
(*Mara, Maria, Marie,
Maretta, Marette, Marilyn,
Marylyn, Marylin, Marilla,
Marla, Marya, Miriam,
Mamie, Manette, Manon,*

Maryse, Maire, Maureen,
Mearr, Moya, Mairi,
Mariel, Molly, May,
Marietta, Polly, Mitzi,
Mimi, Mariette)

Marya See **Mary**

Marylou [Combination
Mary/Louise]

Maryse See **Mary**

Mathilda [Teutonic]
'Brave little maid'. One
as courageous as a lion.
(Matilda, Matilde,
Mathilde, Maud, Maude,
Mattie, Tilda, Tilly,
Matelda, Maitilde)

Matilde See **Mathilda**

Mattea [Hebrew]
'Gift of God'. Fem. of
Matthew.
(Matthea, Matthia, Mathea,
Mathia)

Mattie See **Mathilda** or
Martha

Maud See **Mathilda**

Mauralia See **Maurilla**

Maureen See **Mary**

Maurilla [Latin]
'Sympathetic woman'.
(Maurilia, Mauralia)

Mauve [Latin]
'Lilac coloured bird'.
(Malva)

Mave See **Mab**

Mavis [French]
'Song thrush'.

Mavis See **Mab**

Maxie See **Maxine**

Maxima See **Maxine**

Maxine [French]
'The greatest'. Fem. of
Maximilian.
(Maxima, Maxene, Maxie)

May [Latin]
'Born in May'. Also dim.
of Mary.
(Maia)

May See **Mary**

Maybelle See **Mabel**

Mayda See **Maida**

Mayde See **Maida**

Maydena See **Maida**

Mead [Greek]
'Honey wine'.
(Meade)

Meara [Gaelic]
'Mirth'.

Mearr See **Mary**

Meave See **Mab**

Meda See **Halimeda**

Medea [Greek]
'The middle child' or
'Enchantress'.
(Media, Madora, Medora)

Medwenna [Welsh]
'Maiden, princess'.
(Modwen, Modwenna)

Megan [Celtic]
'The strong'. Popular
name for Welsh girls.
(Meghan)

Mehetabie See **Mehitabel**

Mehitabel [Hebrew]
'Favoured of God'. One
of the Chosen.
*(Mehetabel, Mehetabie,
Mehetabelle, Mehitable,
Mehitabelle, Metabel, Hetty,
Hitty)*

Melania See **Melanie**

Melanie [Greek]
'Clad in darkness'. Lady
of the night.
*(Melania, Malan, Melan,
Mel, Mellie, Melly,
Melany)*

Melantha [Greek]
'Dark flower'.
(Melanthe)

Melba See **Malva**

Melda See **Imelda**

Melina [Latin]
'Yellow canary'. Also der.
of Madeline.

Melina See **Carmel**

Melinda [Greek]
'Mild and gentle'. A quiet
home loving girl.
(Malinda)

Melisanda See **Millicent**

Melisande See **Millicent**

Melissa [Greek]
'Honey bee'.
(Melisa, Lisa, Mel)

Melita [Greek]
'Little honey flower'.
(Elita, Malita, Melitta)

Mell See **Amelia**

Mellie See **Amelia**

Melly See **Melanie**

Melodia See **Melody**

Melody [Greek]
'Like a song'.
(Melodie, Melodia, Lodie)

Melva See **Malva**

Melvina See **Malvina**

Melvine See **Malvina**

Mercedes [Spanish]
'Compassionate,
merciful'. One who
forgives, not condemns.
(Mercy, Merci)

Mercia [Anglo-Saxon]
'Lady of Mercia'. One
from the old Saxon
kingdom in the centre of
England.

Mercy See **Mercedes**

Merdyce See **Mertice**

Meredith [Celtic]
'Protector from the sea'.
A popular name in Wales
for boys and girls.

*(Meridith, Meredyth,
Meridyth, Merideth,
Meredeth, Meredydd,
Merrie, Merry)*

Meredydd See **Meredyth**

Meriel See **Muriel**

Meritta See **Merritt**

Merla See **Merle**

Merle [Latin]
'The blackbird'.
*(Merl, Merlina, Merline,
Meryl, Myrlene, Merola,
Merla)*

Merlina See **Merle**

Merline See **Merle**

Merna See **Myrna**

Merola See **Merle**

Merrie [Anglo-Saxon]
'Mirthful, joyous'. Also
dim. of Meredith.
(Meri, Merri, Merry)

Merrilees [Old English]
'St. Mary's field'.
(Merrilie)

Merrilie See **Merrilees**

Merritt [Anglo-Saxon]
'Worthy; of merit'.
*(Meritt, Merrit, Meritta,
Merritta)*

Merry See **Meredyth**

Mertice [Anglo-Saxon]
'Famous and pleasant'.
One who has not been
spoiled by adulation.
(Merdyce, Mertyce)

Mertice See **Myrtle**

Meryl See **Merle**

Messina [Latin]
'The middle child'.

Meta [Latin]
'Ambition achieved'.

Meta See **Margaret**

Metabel See **Mehitabel**

Metis [Greek]
'Wisdom and skill'.
(Metys)

Mia [Latin]
'Mine'.

Michaela [Hebrew]
'Likeness to God'. Fem.
of Michael.
(Michaelina, Michaeline,

*Micheline, Michelline,
Micaela, Mikaela, Michel,
Michelle, Michella,
Michaella)*

Michaelina See **Michaela**

Michaeline See **Michaela**

Michal [Hebrew]
'God is perfect.'

Michel See **Michaela**

Michella See **Michaela**

Mignon [French]
'Little, dainty darling'. A
kitten-like creature of
charm and grace.
(Mignonette)

Mignonette See **Mignon**

Mildred [Anglo-Saxon]
'Gentle counsellor'. The
diplomat power behind
the throne.
*(Mildrid, Milli, Millie,
Milly)*

Milicia See **Amelia**

Mill See **Amelia**

Millicent [Teutonic]
'Strong and industrious'.
The hard working
chatelaine.
(Melicent, Melisande,
Mellicent, Melisende,
Melisanda, Melisenda,
Milicent, Milissent,
Milisent, Milli, Millie,
Milly)

Millie See **Amelia** or
Mildred

Mimi See **Mary**

Mimosa [Latin]
'Imitative'.

Mina See **Adamina**, **Minta**
or **Wilhelmina**

Minda See **Minta**

Mindy See **Minta**

Minerva [Latin]
'Wise, purposeful one'.
The Goddess of Wisdom.

Minetta See **Minette**

Minette [French]
'Little kitten'.
(Minetta)

Minette See **Henrietta**

Minna [Old German]
'Tender affection'.

Minnie See **Minta**

Minta [Teutonic]
'Remembered with love'.
(Mina, Minda, Mindy,
Minetta, Minnie)

Minta [Greek]
'The mint plant'. Also
dim. of Araminta.
(Minthe, Mintha)

Minthe See **Minta**

Mira [Latin]
'Wonderful one'.
(Mirella, Mirilla, Myra,
Myrilla, Mireille)

Mirabel [Latin]
'Admired for her beauty'.
(Mirabella, Mirabelle)

Mirabella See **Mirabel**

Miranda [Latin]
'Greatly admired'.
(Randa)

Mireilla See **Mira**

Mirella See **Mira**

Miriam See **Mary**

Mirle See **Myrtle**

Misty [Old English]
'Covered with mist'.

Mitzi See **Mary**

Modesta See **Modesty**

Modeste See **Modesty**

Modestia See **Modesty**

Modestine See **Modesty**

Modesty [Latin]
'Shy, modest'. The
retiring and bashful
maiden.
*(Modesta, Modeste,
Modestia, Modestine, Desta)*

Modwen See **Medwenna**

Moibeal See **Mabel**

Moina [Celtic]
'Soft'.

Moina See **Myrna**

Moira See **Morag**

Molly See **Mary**

Mona See **Monica**

Monca See **Monica**

Monica [Latin]
'Advice giver'.
(Monique, Mona, Monca)

Morag [Celtic]
'Great'.
(Moira, Moyra)

Morette See **Amorette**

Morgana [Welsh]
'From the sea shore'.
(Morgan)

Morgen See **Morgana**

Morna See **Myrna**

Mosella See **Moselle**

Moselle [Hebrew]
'Taken from the water'.
Fem. of Moses.
*(Mosella, Mozel, Mozelle,
Mozella)*

Mosera [Hebrew]
'Bound to men'.

Moya See **Mary**

Moyra See **Morag**

Muire See **Muriel**

Muriel [Celtic]
'Sea bright'.
(Meriel, Muire)

Musetta [French]
'Child of the Muses'.
(Musette)

Musette See **Musetta**

Musidora [Greek]
'Gift of the Muses'.

Mwynen [Welsh]
'Gentle'.

Myfanwy [Welsh]
'My rare one'.
(Myvanwy)

Myrlene See **Merle**

Myrna [Gaelic]
'Beloved'.
*(Merna, Mirna, Moina,
Morna, Moyna)*

Myrta See **Myrtle**

Myrtis See **Myrtle**

Myrtle [Greek]
'Victorious crown'. The
hero's laurel wreath.
*(Myrta, Myrtia, Myrtis,
Mirle, Mertle, Mertice)*

Mabon [Welsh]
'Youth'.

Mac [Celtic]
Used in many Scots and
Irish names and meaning
Son of. Also used in the
form 'Mc'. For instance
Macadam (Son of
Adam), McDonald (Son
of Donald) and so on.

Macarius [Latin]
'Blessed'.

Macy [French]
'From Matthew's estate'.

Maddock [Welsh]
'Beneficent'.
*(Madoc, Madock, Madog,
Maddox)*

Maddox See **Maddock**

Madison [Anglo-Saxon]
'Mighty in battle'.
(Maddison)

Madog See **Maddock**

Maelgwyn [Welsh]
'Metal chief'.

Magee [Gaelic]
'Son of the fiery one'.

Magnus [Latin]
'The great one'. One who
excels all others.

Maitland [Anglo-Saxon]
'Dweller in the meadow
land'.

Major [Latin]
'Greater'. Anything you
can do, he can do better!

Malachi [Hebrew]
'Angel'.

Malcolm [Celtic]
'The dove' or 'Follower of
St. Columba'.

Malik [Muslim]
'Master'.

Malin [Anglo-Saxon]
'Little warrior'.

Malise [Gaelic]
'Servant of Jesus'.

Mallory [Anglo-Saxon/
Latin]
'Army counsellor'
(Anglo-Saxon) or
'Luckless' (Celtic).

Maloney [Gaelic]
'Believer in the Sabbath'.

Malory [Old French]
'Unfortunate'.
(Mallory)

Malvin [Celtic]
'Polished chief'.
(Melvin, Mal, Mel)

Manasseh [Hebrew]
'Making one forget'.

Mandel [Teutonic]
'Almond'.

Mander [Old French]
'Stable lad'.

Manfred [Anglo-Saxon]
'Peaceful hero'.
(Manfried)

Manfried See **Manfred**

Manleich See **Manley**

Manley [Anglo-Saxon]
'The hero's meadow'.
(Manleich)

Manning [Anglo-Saxon]
'Hero's son'.

Manny See **Emmanuel**

Mansfield [Anglo-Saxon]
'Hero's field'.

Manton [Anglo-Saxon]
'Hero's farm'.

Manuel See **Emmanuel**

Manville [French]
'From the great estate'.
(Manvil)

Marcel [Latin]
'Little follower of Mars'.
A warlike person.
(Marcellus, Marcello)

Marcello See **Marcel**

Marcellus See **Marcel**

Marco See **Mark**

Marcus See **Mark**

Marden [Anglo-Saxon]
'From the pool in the
valley'.

Mario See **Marius**

Marion [French]
'Bitter'. A French form of
Mary, often given as a
boy's name in
compliment to the
Virgin.

Marius [Latin]
'The martial one'.
(Mario)

Mark [Latin]
'Follower of Mars; the
warrior'.
(Marcus, Marco, Marc)

Marl See **Merlin**

Marland [Anglo-Saxon]
'Dweller in the lake land'.

Marley [Anglo-Saxon]
'From the lake in the
meadow'.
(Marly)

Marlin See **Merlin**

Marlon See **Merlin**

Marlow [Anglo-Saxon]
'From the lake on the
hill'.
(Marlowe)

Marmaduke [Celtic]
'Sea leader'.
(Duke)

Marmion [French]
'Very small one'.

Marsden [Anglo-Saxon]
'From the marshy valley'.
(Marsdon)

Marsh [Anglo-Saxon]
'From the marsh'.

Marshall [Anglo-Saxon]
'The steward'. The man
who looked after the
estate of a nobleman.

Marston [Anglo-Saxon]
'From the farm by the
lake'.

Marten See **Martin**

Martie See **Martin**

Martin [Latin]
'Warlike person'. A
follower of Mars.
*(Marten, Marton, Mart,
Martie, Marty)*

Marvin [Anglo-Saxon]
'Famous friend'.
(Mervin, Merwin, Merwyn)

Marwood [Anglo-Saxon]
'From the lake in the
forest'.

Maslin [French]
'Small Thomas'.
(Maslen, Maslon)

Maslon See **Maslin**

Mason [Latin]
'Worker in stone'. One
who built castles,
churches, houses, etc.
from stone.

Massey See **Thomas**

Mata See **Matthew**

Math [Welsh]
'Treasure'.

Mather [Anglo-Saxon]
'Powerful army'.

Mathias See **Matthew**

Matt See **Matthew**

Matthew [Hebrew]
'Gift of God'. One of the
12 Apostles.
*(Mathew, Mathias,
Mattias, Mata, Matthias,
Mat, Matt, Mattie, Matty)*

Mattias See **Matthew**

Mattie See **Matthew**

Maurey See **Maurice**

Maurice [Latin]
'Moorish looking; dark
complexioned'.
*(Morris, Morrell, Morel,
Morice, Maurey, Morry,
Morrie, Maury, Mo)*

Maxey See **Maximilian**

Maxi See **Maxwell**

Maxim See **Maximilian**

Maximilian [Latin]
'The greatest; the most
excellent'. One without
equal.
*(Max, Maxey, Maxie,
Maxim, Maxy, Maximilien)*

Maximilien See
Maximilian

Maxwell [Anglo-Saxon]
'Large spring'.
(Max, Maxie, Maxi)

Mayer [Latin]
'Greater'. The major
character.
(Myer)

Mayfield [Anglo-Saxon]
'From the field of the
warrior'.

Mayhew [French]
'Gift of God'. Another
form of Matthew.

Maynard [Teutonic]
'Powerfully strong;
brave'.
(Menard)

Mayo [Gaelic]
'From the plain of the
yew trees'.

Mead [Anglo-Saxon]
'From the meadow'.

Medwin [Teutonic]
'Strong and powerful
friend'.

Meilyr [Welsh]
'Man of iron'.

Melbourne [Anglo-Saxon]
'From the mill stream'.
*(Melburn, Melburne,
Milbourn, Milbourne,
Milburne, Milburn)*

Melburn See **Melbourne**

Melchior [Persian]
'King of light'.

Meldon [Anglo-Saxon]
'From the mill on the
hill'.

Melmoth [Celtic]
'Servant of Math'.

Melville [French]
'From the estate of the
industrious'.
(Melvil, Mel)

Melvin See **Malvin**

Menachin [Hebrew]
'Comforter'.
(Menahem)

Menahem See **Menachin**

Menard See **Maynard**

Mendel [Semitic]
'Wisdom'.

Mercer [Anglo-Saxon]
'Merchant'.

Meredith [Welsh]
'Guardian from the sea'.
*(Meredydd, Meridith,
Merideth, Meredyth,
Meridyth, Merry)*

Meredydd See **Meredith**

Merl See **Merlin**

Merle [Latin]
'The blackbird; the black
haired one'.

Merlin [Anglo-Saxon]
'The falcon'. The
legendary wizard of King
Arthur's court.
*(Marlin, Marlen, Marlon,
Marl, Merl)*

Merrick See **Emery**

Merrill [French]
'Little famous one'.
(Merritt)

Merrill See **Myron**

Merritt See **Merrill**

Merry See **Meredith**

Merton [Anglo-Saxon]
'From the farm by the
sea'.

Mervin See **Marvin**

Merwin See **Marvin**

Methuselah [Hebrew]
'Man of the javelin'.

Meyer [Teutonic]
'Steward'.

Micah See **Michael**

Michael [Hebrew]
'Like unto the Lord'.
(Micah, Mitchell, Michel,

*Mischa, Mitch, Mich, Mike,
Mickie, Micky)*

Mickie See **Michael**

Mike See **Michael**

Milan [Slavic]
'Beloved'.

Milbourn See **Melbourne**

Milburne See **Melbourne**

Miles [Greek/Latin]
'The millstone' (Greek)
or 'The soldier' (Latin).

Milford [Anglo-Saxon]
'From the mill ford'.
(Millford)

Millard [French]
'Strong and victorious'.

Miller [Anglo-Saxon]
'Grain grinder'.

Milo [Latin]
'The miller'.

Milton [Anglo-Saxon]
'From the mill town'.

Milward [Anglo-Saxon]
'The mill keeper'.

Miner [French/Latin]
'A miner' (French);
'Young person' (Latin).
(Minor)

Mischa See **Michael**

Mitch See **Michael**

Mitchell See **Michael**

Mithell See **Michael**

Modred [Anglo-Saxon]
'Brave counsellor'. One
who advised honestly
without fear of reprisal.

Moe See **Moses**

Moelwyn [Welsh]
'Fair headed'.

Moise See **Moses**

Monroe [Celtic]
'From the red swamp'.
(Munro, Monro, Munroe)

Montague [French]
'From the pointed
mountain'.
(Monte, Monty, Montagu)

Monte See **Montague**

Montgomery [French]
'The mountain hunter'.
(Monte, Monty)

Moore [French]
'Dark complexioned;
Moor'.
(More)

Mordecai [Hebrew]
'Belonging to Marduk'.

Moreland [Anglo-Saxon]
'From the moors'.

Morfin See **Morven**

Morgan [Welsh]
'White sea'. The foam
flecked waves.
(Morgen)

Moriah [Hebrew]
'Man chosen by
Jehovah'.

Morley [Anglo-Saxon]
'From the moor
meadow'.

Morrell See **Maurice**

Morris See **Maurice**

Morrison [Anglo-Saxon]
'Maurice's son'.
(Morison)

Morse [Anglo-Saxon]
'Maurice's son'.

Mortimer [French]
'From the quiet water'.
*(Mortemer, Mortermer,
Morthermer)*

Morton [Anglo-Saxon]
'From the farm on the
moor'.

Morven [Gaelic]
'Blond giant'.
(Morfin)

Mose See **Moses**

Moses [Hebrew]
'Saved from the water'.
The great prophet of
Israel.
*(Moise, Mose, Mosie, Moe,
Moss)*

Mosie See **Moses**

Moss See **Moses**

Muhammad [Arabic]
'Praised'.

Muir [Celtic]
'From the moor'.

Mungo [Gaelic]
'Lovable'.

Munroe See **Monroe**

Murdoch [Celtic]
'Prosperous from the sea'.
(Murdock, Murtagh)

Murphy [Gaelic]
'Sea warrior'.

Murray [Celtic]
'The mariner; sea
fighter'.

Murtagh See **Murdoch**

Myer See **Mayer**

Myles See **Miles**

Myron [Greek]
'The fragrant oil'.
(Merrill)

Girls

Naashom [Hebrew]
'Enchantress'.
(Nashom, Nashoma)

Nada See **Nadine**

Nadia See **Nadine**

Nadine [French]
'Hope'.
(Nada, Nadia)

Naida [Latin]
'The water nymph'.
From the streams of
Arcadia.
(Naiada)

Nairne [Gaelic]
'From the river'.

Nan See **Anne**

Nana See **Anne**

Nancy See **Anne**

Nanetta See **Anne**

Nanette See **Anne**

Nanine See **Anne**

Nanon See **Anne**

Naomi [Hebrew]
'The pleasant one'.
*(Naoma, Noami, Nomi,
Nomie)*

Napea [Latin]
'Girl of the valley'.
(Napaea, Napia)

Nara [English]
'Nearest and dearest'.
Also dim. of Narda.

Nara See **Narda**

Narda [Latin]
'Fragrant perfume'. The
lingering essence.
(Nara)

Nashoma See **Naashom**

Nastasya See **Natalie**

Nasya [Hebrew]
'Miracle of God'.

Natala See **Natalie**

Natale See **Natalie**

Natalie [Latin]
'Born at Christmas tide'.
*(Natalia, Natala, Natale,
Natasha, Nathalie, Natica,
Natika, Natacha, Natividad,
Nastasya, Nattie, Netta,
Nettie, Netty, Noel, Noelle,
Novella)*

Natasha See **Natalie**

Natene See **Nathania**

Nathania [Hebrew]
'Gift of God'.
(Natene, Nathene, Nathane)

Natica See **Natalie**

Natividad See **Natalie**

Nattie See **Natalie**

Neala [Gaelic]
'The champion'. Fem. of
Neil.

Nebula [Latin]
'A cloud of mist'.

Neda [Slav]
'Born on Sunday'.
(Nedda)

Nela See **Cornelia** or **Nila**

Nelda [Anglo-Saxon]
'Born under the elder
tree'.

Nelie See **Cornelia**

Nell See **Helen**

Nellwyn [Greek]
'Bright friend and
companion'.

Neola [Greek]
'The young one'.

Neoma [Greek]
'The new moon'.

Nerice See **Nerima**

Nerima [Greek]
'From the sea'.
*(Nerissa, Nerine, Nerita,
Nerice)*

Nerine See **Nerima**

Nerissa See **Nerima**

Nerita See **Nerima**

Nerys [Welsh]
'Lordly one'.

Nessa See **Agnes**

Nessie See **Agnes**

Nesta See **Agnes**

Netie See **Henrietta**

Netta See **Antonia**,
Henrietta, **Natalia**, etc.

Nettie See **Antonia**

Neva [Spanish]
'As white as the moon'.
(Nevada)

Nevada See **Neva**

Neysa See **Agnes**

Nicholina See **Nicole**

Nicola See **Nicole**

Nicole [Greek]
'The people's victory'.
*(Nicola, Nichola, Nicholina,
Nicol, Nicolina, Nicoline,
Nikola, Nikki, Nickie,
Nicky)*

Nicoline See **Nicole**

Nikki See **Nicole**

Nila [Latin]
'From the Nile'.
(Nela)

Nilda See **Magnilda**

Nillie See **Magnilda**

Nina [Spanish]
'The daughter'.
(Nineta, Ninetta, Ninette)

Nina See **Anne**

Nineta See **Nina**

Ninette See **Anne** or **Nina**

Ninon See **Anne**

Nirah [Hebrew]
'Light'.

Nissa [Scandinavian]
'Friendly elf'. A fairy who
can be seen only by
lovers.

Nissie See **Nixie**

Nita See **Anne**, **Jane** or
Bonita

Nixie [Teutonic]
'Water sprite'.
(Nissie, Nissy)

Noami See **Naomi**

Noel See **Natalie**

Noelle See **Natalia**

Nokomis [American
Indian]
'The grandmother'. From
the legend of Hiawatha.

Nola [Gaelic]
'Famous one'. See also
Olivia.

Nola See **Magnolia** or
Olive

Noleta [Latin]
'Unwilling'.
(Nolita)

Nolie See **Magnolia**

Nolita See **Noleta**

Nollie See **Olive**

Nomi See **Naomi**

Nona [Latin]
'Ninth born'.

Nonnie See **Anona**

Nora See **Honora**,
Eleanor, **Helen**

Norah See **Helen**

Norberta [Teutonic]
'Bright heroine'.
*(Norberte, Norbertha,
Norberthe)*

Norberte See **Norberta**

Nordica [Teutonic]
'Girl from the North'.
(Nordika)

Noreen See **Honora** or
Norma

Norma [Latin]
'A pattern, or rule'. The
template of the perfect
girl.
(Normi, Normie, Noreen)

Normi See **Norma**

Norna [Norse]
'Destiny'. The goddess of
Fate.

Nova See **Novia**

Novella See **Natalie**

Novia [Latin]
'The newcomer'.
(Nova)

Nuala [Gaelic]
'Fair shouldered one'.

Numidia [Latin]
'The traveller'.

Nunciata [Italian]
'She has good news'.
(Annunciata)

Nydia [Latin]
'A refuge'.

Nyssa [Greek]
'Starting point'.

Nyx [Greek]
'White haired'.

Naaman [Hebrew]
'Pleasant one'.

Nahum [Hebrew]
'Comfort'.

Nairn [Celtic]
'Dweller by the alder
tree'.

Naldo See **Reginald**

Napoleon [Greek]
'Lion of the woodland
dell'.

Nat See **Nathan**

Natal See **Noel**

Nathan [Hebrew]
'Gift of God'.
*(Nathaniel, Nat, Nataniel,
Nate, Nattie)*

Nathaniel See **Nathan**

Neacail See **Nicholas**

Neal [Gaelic]
'The champion'.

*(Niall, Neil, Neill, Neall,
Neale, Neel, Niels, Niles,
Nils)*

Neal See **Cornelius**

Ned See **Edward**,
Edmund or **Edgar**

Neddy See **Edward**

Nehemiah [Hebrew]
'Consolation of the Lord'.

Nelson [Celtic]
'Son of Neal'.

Nemo [Greek]
'From the glen'.

Nero [Latin]
'Dark complexioned,
black haired'.

Nestor [Greek]
'Ancient wisdom'.

Neville [Latin]
'From the new town'.
(Nevil, Nevile, Nev)

Nevin [Anglo-Saxon/
Gaelic]
'The nephew' (Anglo-
Saxon) or 'Worshipper of
Saints' (Gaelic).
(Nevins, Niven, Nivens)

Nevins See **Nevin**

Newbold [Old English]
'From the new building'.

Newel See **Noel**

Newell [Anglo-Saxon]
'From the new hall'.
(Newall)

Newland [Anglo-Saxon]
'From the new lands'.
(Newlands)

Newlands See **Newland**

Newlin [Celtic]
'Dweller by the new
pool'. *(Newlyn)*

Newman [Anglo-Saxon]
'The newcomer; the new
arrival'.

Newton [Anglo-Saxon]
'From the new estate'.

Niall See **Neal**

Nic See **Dominic**

Nicander [Greek]
'Man of victory'.

Nichol See **Nicholas**

Nicholas [Greek]
'Victorious people's
army'. The leader of the
people.
*(Nicolas, Nichol, Nicholl,
Niles, Nicol, Neacail, Nick,
Nickie, Nicky, Nik, Nikki,
Cole, Claus, Klaus, Colin,
Colley)*

Nickie See **Nicholas**

Nicky See **Dominic**

Nico [Greek]
'Victory'.

Nicodemus [Greek]
'Conqueror for the
people'.
*(Nick, Nickie, Nicky, Nik,
Nikki, Nikky)*

Nigel [Latin]
'Black haired one'.

Niles See **Nicholas** or
Neal

Nils See **Neal**

Nimrod [Hebrew]
'Valiant'.

Ninian See **Vivien**

Niven See **Nevin**

Nivens See **Nevin**

Nixon [Anglo-Saxon]
'Nicholas's son'.
(Nickson)

Noah [Hebrew]
'Rest, comfort and
peace'.

Nobel See **Noble**

Noble [Latin]
'Noble and famous'.
(Nobel, Nolan)

Noel [French]
'Born at Christmas'. A
suitable name for a boy
born on Christmas Day.
*(Nowell, Newel, Newell,
Natal, Natale)*

Nolan See **Noble**

Noll See **Oliver**

Nollie See **Oliver**

Norbert [Teutonic]
'Brilliant sea hero'. The

courageous commander
of ships.

Norm See **Norman**

Norman [French]
'Man from the north; a
Northman'. The
venturesome and bold
Viking from Scandinavia.
*(Normand, Norris, Normie,
Norm)*

Normand See **Norman**

Normie See **Norman**

Norris See **Norman**

Northcliffe [Anglo-Saxon]
'Man from the north
cliff'.
(Northcliff)

Northrop [Anglo-Saxon]
'From the northern farm'.
*(Northrup, Nortrop,
Nortrup)*

Northrup See **Northrop**

Norton [Anglo-Saxon]
'From the north farm'.

Nortrop See **Northrop**

Nortrup See **Northrop**

Norval [Old French]
  'Northern valley'.

Norvel See **Norville**

Norvie See **Norville**

Norville [French]
  'From the north town'.
  (Norvil, Norvel, Norvie)

Norvin [Anglo-Saxon]
  'Friend from the north'.
  (Norwyn, Norwin, Norvyn)

Norward [Anglo-Saxon]
  'Guardian from the
  north'.

Norwell [Anglo-Saxon]
  'From the north well'.

Norwood [Anglo-Saxon]
  'From the north forest'.

Norwyn See **Norvin**

Nowell See **Noel**

Nye See **Aneurin**

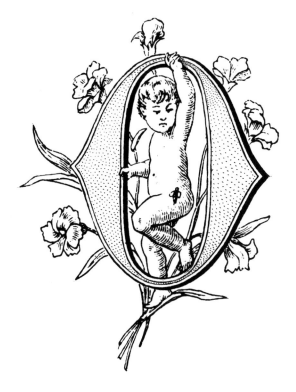

Girls

Obelia [Greek]
'A pointed pillar'.

Octavia [Latin]
'The eighth child'.
*(Octavie, Ottavia, Ottavie,
Tavia, Tavi, Tavie, Tavy)*

Octavie See **Octavia**

Odelette [French]
'A small lyric'.
(Odelet)

Odelia [Teutonic]
'Prosperous one'.
*(Odelie, Odella, Odelinda,
Odilla, Odilia, Otha,
Othilla, Ottilie)*

Odelie See **Odelia**

Odella See **Odelia**

Odessa [Greek]
'A long journey'.

Odette [French]
'Home lover'. One who
makes a house a home.

Odilla See **Odelia**

Ofrah [Hebrew]
'Young hind; lively
maiden'.

Ola [Scandinavia]
'Descendant'. The
daughter of a chief.

Olave [Teutonic]
'Ancestor's relic'.

Oleta See **Olethea**

Olethea [Latin]
'Truth'.
(Alethea, Oleta)

Olga [Teutonic]
'Holy'. One who has
been anointed in the
service of God.
*(Olva, Olivia, Olive, Elga,
Livi, Livie, Livia, Livvi,
Ollie)*

Olga See **Elga**

Olien [Russian]
'Deer'.

Olimpie See **Olympia**

Olinda [Latin]
'Fragrant herb'.

Olive [Latin]
'Symbol of peace'. The
olive branch. Also der. of
Olga.
*(Olivia, Livia, Nollie, Nola,
Olivette, Olva)*

Olive See **Olga**

Olivette See **Olive**

Olivia See **Olga**

Ollie See **Olga**

Olva See **Olga**

Olwyn [Welsh]
'White clover'.
(Olwen)

Olympe See **Olympia**

Olympia [Greek]
'Heavenly one'.
*(Olympe, Olympie, Olimpie,
Pia)*

Ona See **Una**

Onawa [American Indian]
'Maiden who is wide
awake'.

Ondine [Latin]
'Wave'.
(Undine)

Oneida [North American
Indian]
'Expected'.
(Onida)

Oona, Oonagh See **Una**

Opal [Sanskrit]
'Precious jewel'.
(Opalina, Opaline)

Opalina See **Opal**

Opaline See **Opal**

Ophelia [Greek]
'Wise and immortal'.
(Ofelia, Ofilia, Phelia)

Ora [Latin]
'Golden one'.
(Orabel, Orabella, Orabelle)

Ora See **Aurelia**

Orabel See **Ora**

Orabella See **Ora**

Oralia See **Aurelia**

Ordelia [Teutonic]
'Elf's spear'.

Orea [Greek]
'Of the mountain'. The
original maid of the
mountains.

Orel See **Bambi**

Orela [Latin]
'Divine pronouncement'.
The oracle.

Orenda [American
Indian]
'Magic power'.

Oriana [Latin]
'Golden one'.

Oriel See **Aurelia**

Orla [Irish]
'Golden lady'.

Orlanda See **Rolanda**

Orna [Gaelic]
'Pale coloured'.

Orpah [Hebrew]
'A fawn'. From the Song
of Solomon.

Orsa See **Ursula**

Orsola See **Ursula**

Orva [Teutonic]
'Spear friend'.

Osanna [Latin]
'Filled with mercy'.

Osnat [Hebrew]
'Favourite of the deity'.

Otha See **Odelia**

Othilla See **Odelia**

Ottavia See **Octavia**

Ottavie See **Octavia**

Ottilie See **Odelia**

Owena [Welsh]
'Well-born'.

Ozora [Hebrew]
'Strength of the Lord'.

Oakes [Anglo-Saxon]
'Dweller by the oak tree'.

Oakley [Anglo-Saxon]
'From the oak tree meadow'.
(Oakly, Okely, Okeley)

Obadiah [Hebrew]
'Servant of the Lord'.
The obedient one.

Oberon See **Auberon**

Obert [Teutonic]
'Wealthy and brilliant'.

Octave See **Octavius**

Octavian See **Octavius**

Octavius [Latin]
'The eighth born'.
(Octave, Octavian, Octavus, Tavey)

Octavus See **Octavius**

Odell [Teutonic]
'Wealthy one'.
(Odin, Odo)

Odin See **Odell**

Odo See **Odell**

Odolf [Teutonic]
'The wealthy wolf'.

Ogden [Anglo-Saxon]
'From the oak valley'.

Ogilvie [Celtic]
'From the high peak'.

Oglesby [Anglo-Saxon]
'Awe inspiring'.

Okely See **Oakley**

Olaf [Scandinavian]
'Ancestral relic' or
'Peaceful reminder'.
(Olav, Olen, Amhlaoibh)

Olav See **Olaf**

Ole [Scandinavian]
'Squire'.

Olen See **Olaf**

Olin See **Olaf**

Oliver [Latin]
'Symbol of peace'. The olive branch.

(Oliver, Ollie, Noll, Nollie, Nolly)

Ollie See **Oliver**

Olney [Anglo-Saxon]
'Olla's island'.

Oman [Scandinavian]
'High protector'.

Omar [Arabic]
'The first son' or 'Most high follower of the Prophet'.

Onilwyn [Welsh]
'Ash grove'.

Onslow [Anglo-Saxon]
'Hill of the zealous one'.

Oram [Anglo-Saxon]
'From the enclosure by the riverbank'.

Oran [Gaelic]
'Pale skinned man'.
(Oren, Orin, Orran, Orren, Orrin)

Ordway [Anglo-Saxon]
'The spear fighter'.

Oren See **Oran**

Orestes [Greek]
'The mountain climber'.

Orford [Anglo-Saxon]
'Dweller at the cattle ford'.

Orin See **Oran**

Orion [Greek]
'The son of light'.

Orlan [Anglo-Saxon]
'From the pointed land'.

Orlando See **Roland**

Orman See **Ormond**

Ormen See **Ormond**

Ormin See **Ormond**

Ormond [Teutonic]
'Spearman' or 'Shipman'.
(Orman, Ormand, Ormen, Ormin)

Oro [Spanish]
'Golden haired one'.

Orrick [Anglo-Saxon]
'Dweller by the ancient oak tree'.

Orrin See **Oran**

Orson [Latin/Anglo-Saxon]
'Little bear' (Latin) or 'Son of the spearman'.

Orton [Anglo-Saxon]
'From the shore-
farmstead'.

Orval [Anglo-Saxon]
'Spear mighty'.

Orville [French]
'From the golden town'.
(Orvil)

Orvin [Anglo-Saxon]
'Spear friend'.

Osbert [Anglo-Saxon]
'Divinely bright warrior'.
*(Bert, Bertie, Berty, Oz,
Ozzie)*

Osborn [Anglo-Saxon]
'Divine warrior'.
*(Osborne, Osburn, Osburne,
Osbourn, Osbourne)*

Osburn See **Osborn**

Oscar [Anglo-Saxon]
'Divine spearman'. 'A
fighter for God'.
*(Oskar, Oz, Ozzie, Os,
Ossie)*

Osgood [Scandinavian]
'The divine Goth'.

Osmar [Anglo-Saxon]
'Divinely glorious'.

Osmond [Anglo-Saxon]
'Divine protector'.

Osred [Anglo-Saxon]
'Divine counsellor'.

Oswald [Anglo-Saxon]
'Divinely powerful'.

Othman [Teutonic]
'The prosperous one'.

Otho See **Otto**

Otis [Greek]
'Keen of sight and
hearing'.

Otto [Teutonic]
'Wealthy, prosperous
man'.
(Otho)

Owen [Celtic]
'The young, well born
warrior'.
(Owain, Evan)

Oxford [Anglo-Saxon]
'From the ford where
oxen crossed'.

Oxton [Anglo-Saxon]

Ozzie See **Osbert**

Girls

Paige [Anglo-Saxon]
  'Young child'.
  (Page)

Pallas [Greek]
  'Wisdom and
  knowledge'. Another
  name for the Goddess of
  Wisdom.

Palma [Latin]
  'Palm tree'.
  (Palmer, Palmira)

Palmira See **Palma**

Paloma [Spanish]
  'The dove'. A gentle,
  tender girl.
  (Palometa, Palomita)

Palometa See **Paloma**

Pam See **Pamela**

Pamela [Greek]
'All sweetness and
honey'. A loving person
of great kindness.
*(Pamella, Pamelina,
Pammie, Pammy, Pam)*

Pamelina See **Pamela**

Pammie See **Pamela**

Pamphila [Greek]
'All loving'. One who
loves all humanity.

Pandora [Greek]
'Talented, gifted one'.

Pansy [Greek]
'Fragrant, flowerlike'.

Panthea [Greek]
'Of all the Gods'.
(Panthia)

Parnella [French]
'Little rook'.
(Parnelle, Pernella, Pernelle)

Parnelle See **Parnella**

Parthenia [Greek]
'Sweet virgin'.

Paschasia [Latin]
'Born at Easter'.

Patience [Latin]
'Patient one'. A popular
'virtue' name.
(Pattie, Patty, Patienza)

Patienza See **Patience**

Patrice See **Patricia**

Patricia [Latin]
'Well born maiden'. A
girl born to the noblest of
families.
*(Patrice, Patrizia, Pat,
Patti, Patty, Patsy)*

Patsy See **Patricia**

Pattie See **Patience**

Paula [Latin]
'Little'. Fem. of Paul.
*(Paule, Paulette, Paulina,
Pauline, Paulita, Pauletta,
Pauli, Paulie, Paola)*

Paule See **Paula**

Paulena See **Paula**

Pauletta See **Paula**

Paulette See **Paula**

Pauli See **Paula**

Pauline See **Paula**

Paulita See **Paula**

Peace [Latin]
'Tranquillity, calm'.

Pearl [Latin]
'Precious jewel'. One of
unmatched beauty. Also
der. of Margaret.
*(Pearle, Perle, Perl, Perlie,
Perline, Perlina, Pearlie)*

Peggy See **Margaret**

Pelagia [Greek]
'Mermaid'.

Penelope [Greek]
'The weaver'. The
patient wife of Ulysses
who stitched while he
roamed.
(Pen, Penny)

Penny See **Penelope**

Penthea [Greek]
'Fifth child'.
(Penta, Penthia)

Penthia See **Penthea**

Peony [Latin]
'The gift of healing'.

Pepita See **Josephine**

Perdita [Latin]
'The lost one'.

Perfecta [Spanish]
'The most perfect being'.

Perlie See **Pearl**

Perlina See **Pearl**

Perline See **Pearl**

Pernella See **Parnella**

Pernelle See **Parnella**

Peronel [Latin]
'A rock'.
(Peronelle)

Perrine See **Petrina**

Persephone [Greek]
'Goddess of the
underworld'.

Persis [Latin]
'Woman from Persia'.

Peta [Greek]
'A Rock'.

Petica [Latin]
'Noble one'.

Petra See **Petrina**

Petrina [Greek]
'Steadfast as a rock'.
Fem. of Peter.
*(Petra, Petronia, Petula,
Petronella, Petronelle,
Petronilla, Petronille,
Pierette, Pierrette, Perrine)*

Petronella See **Petrina**

Petronelle See **Petrina**

Petronia See **Petrina**

Petronilla See **Petrina**

Petronille See **Petrina**

Petula [Latin]
'Seeker'.

Petula See **Petrina**

Petunia [Indian]
'Reddish flower'.

Phaidra See **Phedra**

Phedra [Greek]
'Bright one'. The
daughter of Minos of
Crete.
(Phaidra, Phedre)

Phelia See **Ophelia**

Phemie See **Euphemia**

Philadelphia [Greek]
'Brotherly love'.

Philana [Greek]
'Friend of humanity'.
(Filana)

Philantha [Greek]
'Lover of flowers'. Child
of the blossoms.
(Philanthe, Filantha)

Philanthe See **Philantha**

Philberta [Teutonic]
'Very brilliant'.
*(Philberthe, Philbertha,
Filberta, Filberte, Filbertha,
Filberthe)*

Philberthe See **Philberta**

Philippa [Greek]
'Lover of horses'. Fem. of
Philip.
*(Phillippa, Phillipa, Pippa,
Phillie, Filippa, Filipa)*

Phillida [Greek]
'Loving woman'.

Phillie See **Philippa**

Philmen See **Filma**

Philomela [Greek]
'Lover of song'.

Philomena [Greek]
'Lover of the moon'. The
nightingale.

Phoebe [Greek]
'Bright, shining sun'.
Fem. of Phoebus
(Apollo).
(Phebe)

Phoenix [Greek]
'The eagle'. The
legendary bird who
renewed its youth in its
own ashes.
(Fenix)

Pholma See **Filma**

Photina [Greek]
'Light'.

Phyllida See **Phyllis**

Phyllis [Greek]
'A green bough'.
*(Phyllida, Phillida, Phillis,
Philis, Phylis, Fillida,
Filida, Filis, Fillis)*

Pia [Latin]
'Pious'.

Pia See **Olympia**

Pierette See **Petrina**

Pilar [Spanish]
'A foundation or pillar'.

Piper [English]
'Player of the pipes'.

Pippa See **Philippa**

Placida [Latin]
'Peaceful one'.
(Placidia)

Placidia See **Placida**

Platona [Greek]
'Broad shouldered'. Fem.
of Plato. A woman of
wisdom.

Polly See **Mary**

Pomona [Latin]
'Fruitful and fertile'.

Poppaea See **Poppy**

Poppy [Latin]
'Red flower'.
(Poppaea)

Portia [Latin]
'An offering to God'.
(Porcia)

Poupée [French]
'Doll'.

Prima [Latin]
'First born'.

Primavera [Spanish]
'Child of the spring'.

Primrose [Latin]
'The first flower'. The
harbinger of spring.
*(Primula, Primmie, Rose,
Rosa)*

Primula See **Primrose**

Priscilla [Latin]
'Of ancient lineage'. The
descendant of princes.
*(Prisilla, Pris, Prissie,
Cilla)*

Prospera [Latin]
'Favourable'.

Prudence [Latin]
'Cautious foresight'.
*(Prudentia, Prud, Prue,
Prudie, Prudy)*

Prudentia See **Prudence**

Prudie See **Prudence**

Prunella [French]
'Plum coloured'.
(Prunelle)

Prunelle See **Prunella**

Psyche [Greek]
'Of the soul or mind'.
The true inner being.

Purity [Middle English]
'Purity'.

Pyrena [Greek]
'Fiery one'. The warmth
of the home.
(Pyrenia)

Pyrenia See **Pyrena**

Pythia [Greek]
'A prophet'. The oracle.
(Pythea)

Pablo See **Paul**

Paco [Italian]
  'To pack'.

Padarn [Welsh]
  'Fatherly'.

Paddy See **Patrick**

Padgett [French]
  'The young attendant; a
  page'.
  (Padget, Paget, Page)

Padraic See **Patrick**

Page See **Padgett**

Paine [Latin]
  'The country rustic; a
  pagan'.
  (Payne)

Paley See **Paul**

Palladin [North American
  Indian]
  'Fighter'.

Palmer [Latin]
  'The palm bearing
  pilgrim'.

Pancras [Greek]
  'All strength'.

Paolo See **Paul**

Park [Anglo-Saxon]
  'From the park'.
  (Parke)

Parker [Anglo-Saxon]
  'The park keeper'. One
  who guarded the park
  lands.

Parkin [Anglo-Saxon]
  'Little Peter'.
  (Perkin, Peterkin)

Parlan See **Bartholomew**

Parnell See **Peter**

Parr [Anglo-Saxon]
  'Dweller by the cattle
  pen'.

Parrish [Anglo-Saxon]
  'From the church parish'.
  (Parish)

Parry [Celtic/French]
'Harry's son (Ap Harry)'
(Celtic) or 'Protector'
(French).

Pascal [Italian]
'Easter born'. The new
born pascal lamb.

Pat See **Patrick**

Patrick [Latin]
'The noble patrician'.
One of noble birth and
from a noble line.
(Patric, Padraic, Peyton,
Padraig, Padruig, Patrice,
Paddy, Pat, Patsy, Rick)

Patsy See **Patrick**

Patton [Anglo-Saxon]
'From the warrior's
farm'.

Paul [Latin]
'Little'.
(Pablo, Paolo, Paley, Paulie,
Pauley)

Pauley See **Paul**

Paxton [Anglo-Saxon]
'From the warrior's
estate'.

Payne See **Paine**

Payton [Anglo-Saxon]
'Dweller on the warrior's
farm'.

Peadar See **Peter**

Pearce See **Peter**

Pedro See **Peter**

Pell [Anglo-Saxon]
'Scarf'.

Pelton [Anglo-Saxon]
'From the farm by the
pool'.

Pembroke [Celtic]
'From the headland'.

Penley [Anglo-Saxon]
'From the enclosed
meadow'.

Penn [Anglo-Saxon]
'Enclosure'.

Penrod [Teutonic]
'Famous commander'.

Penrose [Celtic]
'Mountain promontory'.

Penwyn [Welsh]
'Fair headed'.

Pepin [Teutonic]
'The petitioner' or 'The
persevered'.
(Peppin, Pepi, Peppi)

Peppi See **Pepin**

Percival [French]
'Valley piercer'.
*(Parsefal, Parsifal, Perceval,
Percy, Perc, Perce, Purcell)*

Peregrine [Latin]
'The wanderer'.
(Perry)

Pericles [Greek]
'Far famed'.

Perkin See **Parkin**

Pernell See **Peter**

Perrin See **Peter**

Perry [Anglo-Saxon]
'From the pear tree'. Also
dim. of Peregrine.

Perry See **Peregrine**

Perseus [Greek]
'Destroyer'.

Perth [Celtic]
'Thorn bush thicket'.

Pete See **Peter**

Peter [Latin]
'The stone; the rock'. The
first Pope.
*(Parnell, Pearce, Pedro,
Pernell, Perrin, Petrie,
Pierce, Pierre, Piers, Pietro,
Pete, Peadar, Pierrot, Pierro,
Piero)*

Peterkin See **Parkin**

Petrie See **Peter**

Peverall [French]
'The piper'.
*(Peverell, Peverill, Peveral,
Peverel, Peveril)*

Peverell See **Peverall**

Peverill See **Peverall**

Peyton See **Patrick** or
Payton

Pharamond [German]
'Journey protection'.

Phelan [Gaelic]
'Brave as the wolf'.

Phelips See **Phillips**

Phelps [Anglo-Saxon]
'Son of Philip'.

Phelps See **Philip**

Philemon [Greek]
'Kiss'.

Philip [Greek]
'Lover of horses'.
*(Philipp, Phillip, Phillipp,
Filip, Fillip, Phelps, Pilib,
Filib, Phil, Phillie, Philly)*

Phillie See **Philip**

Phillips [Anglo-Saxon]
'Philip's son'.
*(Phelips, Phellips, Phellipps,
Philips, Phillipps, Felips,
Fellips)*

Philo [Greek]
'Friendly love'.

Phineas [Greek]
'Mouth of brass'.

Pickford [Anglo-Saxon]
'From the ford at the
peak'.

Pickworth [Anglo-Saxon]
'From the estate of the
hewer'.

Pierce See **Peter**

Piero See **Peter**

Pierre See **Peter**

Pierro See **Peter**

Pierrot See **Peter**

Piers See **Peter**

Pietro See **Peter**

Pilib See **Philip**

Pitney [Anglo-Saxon]
'Preserving one's island'.

Pitt [Anglo-Saxon]
'From the hollow'.

Plato [Greek]
'The broad shouldered
one'. The great
philosopher.

Platt [French]
'From the plateau'.

Pollard [Old German]
'Cropped hair'.

Pollock [Anglo-Saxon]
'Little Paul'.

Pollux [Greek]
'Crown'.

Pomeroy [French]
'From the apple orchard'.

Porter [French]
'Gatekeeper'.

Powell [Celtic]
'Alert' or 'Son of Howell'.

Prentice [Anglo-Saxon]
'A learner or apprentice'.

Prescott [Anglo-Saxon]
'From the priest's house'.
(Prescot)

Preston [Anglo-Saxon]
'From the priest's farm'.

Prewitt [French]
'Little valiant warrior'.
*(Prewit, Prewett, Prewet,
Pruitt)*

Price [Celtic]
'Son of a loving man'.

Primo [Latin]
'The first born son'.

Prince [Latin]
'Chief'.

Prior [Latin]
'The Father Superior, the
Head of the Monastery'.
(Pryor)

Probus [Latin]
'Honest'.

Proctor [Latin]
'The administrator'.

Purcell See **Percival**

Purvis [English]
'To provide food'.

Putnam [Anglo-Saxon]
'From the pit dweller's
estate'.

Pwyll [Welsh]
'Prudence'.

Girls

Queena [Teutonic]
'The queen'. The
supreme woman.
(Queenie)

Queenie See **Queena**

Quenberga [Latin]
'Queen pledge'.

Quenby [Scandinavian]
'Womanly; perfect wife'.

Quendrida [Latin]
'Queen threatener'.

Querida [Spanish]
'Beloved one'. *(Cherida)*

Questa [French]
'Searcher'.

Quinta [Latin]
'The fifth child'.
*(Quintilla, Quintella,
Quintina)*

Quintella See **Quinta**

Quintessa [Latin]
'Essence'.

Quintilla See **Quinta**

Quintina See **Quinta**

Quemby See **Quimby**

Quenby See **Quimby**

Quennel [French]
'Dweller by the little oak'.

Quent See **Quentin**

Quentin [Latin]
'The fifth born'.
(Quinton, Quintin, Quent)

Quigley [Gaelic]
'Distaff'.

Quillan [Gaelic]
'Cub'.

Quillon [Latin]
'Sword'.

Quimby [Norse]
'From the woman's
estate'.
(Quinby, Quemby, Quenby)

Quinby See **Quimby**

Quincy [French/Latin]
'From the fifth son's
estate'.

Quinlan [Gaelic]
'The well formed one'.
One with the body of an
Adonis.

Quinn [Gaelic]
'Wise and intelligent'.

Quinton See **Quentin**

Girls

Rabi [Arabic]
'The harvest'.

Rachel [Hebrew]
'Innocent as a lamb'.
One who suffers in
silence.
*(Rachele, Rachelle, Raquel,
Rahel, Raoghnailt, Rochelle,
Rae, Ray, Shelley)*

Rachelle See **Rachel**

Radella [Anglo-Saxon]
'Elf-like adviser'. A fairy-
like creature whose
advice is weighty.

Radinka [Slavic]
'Alive and joyful'.

Radmilla [Slavic]
'Worker for the people'.

Rae [Middle English]
'A doe deer'. Also dim. of
Rachel.

Rae See **Rachel**

Raina See **Regina**

Raissa [French]
'The believer'.
(Raisse)

Raisse See **Raissa**

Rama See **Ramona**

Ramona [Teutonic]
'Wise protector'. Fem. of
Raymond.
*(Ramonda, Raymonde,
Raymonda, Mona, Rama)*

Ramonda See **Ramona**

Ramonde See **Ramona**

Rana [Sanskrit]
'Of royal birth; a queen'.
(Ranee, Rani)

Randa See **Miranda**

Ranee See **Rana**

Raoghnailt See **Rachel**

Raphaela [Hebrew]
'Blessed healer'. One

having the God-given
healing touch.
*(Rafaela, Rafaella,
Raphaella)*

Raquel See **Rachel**

Rashida [African]
'Righteous'.

Rasia See **Rose**

Ray See **Rachel**

Rayna See **Regina**

Reba See **Rebecca**

Rebecca [Hebrew]
'The captivator'.
*(Rebeka, Rebekah, Rebekka,
Rebeca, Reba, Riva, Riba,
Beckie, Becky, Bekky)*

Rechaba [Hebrew]
'Horse woman'.

Regan See **Regina**

Regina [Latin]
'A queen; born to rule'.
*(Regan, Regine, Raina,
Reine, Raine, Rayna, Reina,
Rioghnach, Rina, Gina)*

Regine See **Regina**

Reine See **Regina**

Reini See **Irene**

Rena [Hebrew]
'Song'.

Rena See **Irene**

Renata [Latin]
'Born again'. The spirit of
reincarnation.
*(Rene, Renee, Rennie,
Renate)*

Renata See **Irene**

Rene See **Irene, Renata**

Renita [Latin]
'A rebel'.

Rennie See **Renata**

Reseda [Latin]
'Mignonette flower'.

Reva [Latin]
'Strength regained'.

Rexana [Latin]
'Regally graceful'. One
whose bearing is regal.
(Rexanna)

Rhea [Greek]
'Mother' or 'Poppy'. The
mother of the Grecian
Gods.
(Rea)

Rhedyn [Welsh]
'Fern'.

Rheta [Greek]
'An orator'.

Rhiannon [Welsh]
'Nymph'.

Rhianwen [Welsh]
'Blessed maiden'.

Rhoda [Greek]
'Garland of roses; girl
from Rhodes'.
(Rhodia)

Rhoda See **Rose**

Rhodanthe [Greek]
'The rose of roses'.

Rhodia See **Rhoda** or
Rose

Rhonda [Welsh]
'Grand'.

Rhonwen [Welsh]
'White lance'.

Ria [Spanish]
'The river'.

Riba See **Rebecca**

Rica See **Roderica** or
Ulrica

Ricadonna [Italian]
'Ruling lady'. One who
rules in her own right or
on behalf of her son.

Ricarda [Teutonic]
'Powerful ruler'. Fem. of
Richard.
(Richarda, Richarde, Rickie,
Ricky, Dickie, Dicky)

Richarde See **Ricarda**

Rilla [Teutonic]
'A stream or brook'.
(Rille, Rillette)

Rille See **Rilla**

Rillette See **Rilla**

Rina See **Regina**

Rinah [Hebrew]
'Song; joy'.

Rioghnach See **Regina**

Risa [Latin]
'Laughter'.

Rita See **Margaret**

Riva [French]
'Riverbank'.

Roanna [Latin]
'Sweet and gracious'.
(Rohanna, Rohanne)

Roberta [Anglo-Saxon]
'Of shining fame'. Fem.
of Robert.
(Robina, Roberta, Robinia,
Robinette, Robertha,
Roberthe, Ruberta, Ruperta,
Bobette, Bobina, Bobbie,
Bobby, Bertie)

Robin [Old English]
'Bright or shining with
fame'.
(Robina, Robyn)

Robina See **Robin**

Robinette See **Roberta**

Robinia See **Roberta**

Rochalla See **Rochelle**

Rochelle [French]
'From the small rock'.
(Rochalla, Rochalle,
Rochella, Rochette)

Rochette See **Rochelle**

Roddie See **Roderica**

Roderica [Teutonic]
'Famous ruler'. Fem. of
Roderick.
*(Rodericka, Rica, Roddie,
Roddy, Rickie)*

Rohana [Hindu]
'Sandalwood; sweet
incense'.
(Rohanna, Rohane)

Rohane See **Rohana**

Rohanne See **Roanna**

Rohesia See **Rose**

Rois See **Rose**

Rola See **Rolanda**

Rolanda [Teutonic]
'From the famed land'.
Fem. of Roland.
*(Rolande, Orlanda, Orlande,
Ro, Rola)*

Rolande See **Rolanda**

Roma See **Romola**

Romella See **Romola**

Romelle See **Romola**

Romilda [Teutonic]
'Glorious warrior
maiden'.
*(Romilde, Romhilda,
Romhilde)*

Romilde See **Romilda**

Romola [Latin]
'Lady of Rome'.
*(Roma, Romella, Romelle,
Romula)*

Romula See **Romola**

Ronalda [Teutonic]
'All powerful'. Fem. of
Ronald.
(Ronalde, Ronnie, Ronny)

Ronalde See **Ronalda**

Ronnie See **Ronalda** or
Veronica

Ros See **Rosalind**

Rosa See **Primrose** or
Rose

Rosabel [Latin]
'Beautiful rose'.
(Rosabella, Rosabelle)

Rosabella See **Rosabel**

Rosalee See **Rose**

Rosaleen See **Rose**

Rosalia See **Rose**

Rosalie See **Rose**

Rosalind [Latin]
'Fair and beautiful rose'.
(Rosalinda, Rosaline,
Rosalynd, Rosaline, Roseline,
Roselyn, Rosalyn, Roslyn,
Ros, Roz, Rozalind,
Rozaline, Rozeline)

Rosalinda See **Rosalind**

Rosaline See **Rosalind**

Rosamond [French]
'Rose of the world'.
(Rosemond, Rosemund,
Rosamund, Rosamunda,
Rosamonda, Rosmunda,
Rosemonde, Rozamond)

Rosamunda See
Rosamond

Rosanna [English]
'Graceful rose'.
(Rosanne)

Rosanne See **Rosanna**

Rose [Greek]
'The rose'. The most
beautiful of flowers'.
(Rosa, Rosie, Rosalie,
Rosalia, Rosella, Rohesia,
Roselle, Rosetta, Rosette,
Rosina, Rasia, Rosia,
Rozello, Rhoda, Rhodia,

Rosalee, Rosaleen, Rosena,
Rosene, Rosel, Rozalina,
Rosella, Rosy, Rois)

Rose See **Primrose**

Rosel See **Rose**

Rosella See **Rose**

Roselle See **Rose**

Rosemary [Latin]
'Dew of the sea'.
(Rosemarie)

Rosemond See
Rosamond

Rosemund See
Rosamond

Rosena See **Rose**

Rosene See **Rose**

Rosetta See **Rose**

Rosette See **Rose**

Rosia See **Rose**

Rosie See **Rose**

Rosina See **Rose**

Rosslyn [Welsh]
'Moorland lake'.

Rosy See **Rose**

Roux See **La Roux**

Rowena [Anglo-Saxon]
'Friend with white hair'.
(Rowenna)

Roxana [Persian]
'Brilliant dawn'.
(Roxane, Roxanna, Roxanne,
Roxine, Roxina, Rox, Roxie,
Roxy)

Roxane See **Roxana**

Roxie See **Roxana**

Roxina See **Roxana**

Roxine See **Roxana**

Royale [French]
'Regal being'. Fem. of
Roy.

Rozalina See **Rose**

Rozella See **Rose**

Ruberta See **Roberta**

Rubetta See **Ruby**

Rubette See **Ruby**

Rubia See **Ruby**

Rubina See **Ruby**

Ruby [Latin]
'Precious red jewel'.
(Rubetta, Rubette, Rubia,
Rubina, Rubie)

Rudella See **Rudelle**

Rudelle [Teutonic]
'Famous person'.
(Rudella)

Ruella [Combination
Ruth/Ella]

Rufina [Latin]
'Red-haired one'.

Rugina [Latin]
'Girl with bright red hair'.

Rula [Latin]
'A sovereign'. One who
rules by right.

Ruperta See **Roberta**

Ruth [Hebrew]
'Compassionate and
beautiful'.
(Ruthie)

Ruthie See **Ruth**

Rab See **Robert**

Rabbie See **Robert**

Race See **Horace**

Rad [Anglo-Saxon]
'Counsellor; adviser'.
Also dim. of Radcliffe.

Radbert [Teutonic]
'Brilliant counsellor'.

Radborne [Anglo-Saxon]
'From the red stream'.
*(Radbourne, Redbourne,
Radbourn, Redbourn)*

Radcliffe [Anglo-Saxon]
'From the red cliff'.
*(Radcliff, Redcliff,
Redcliffe)*

Radford [Anglo-Saxon]
'From the red ford'.
(Redford, Radvers, Redvers)

Radley [Anglo-Saxon]
'From the red meadow'.
(Radleigh)

Radmund See **Redmond**

Radnor [Anglo-Saxon]
'From the red shore'.

Radolf [Anglo-Saxon]
'Wolf counsellor'. Wolf is
used in the sense 'brave
man'.

Radvers See **Radford**

Rafael See **Raphael**

Raff See **Ralph**

Rafferty [Gaelic]
'Prosperous and rich'.

Raghnall See **Reginald**

Rainier See **Raynor**

Raleigh [Anglo-Saxon]
'Dweller in the meadow
of the roe deer'.
(Ralegh, Rawley, Rawleigh)

Ralph [Anglo-Saxon]
'Counsel wolf'.
*(Ralf, Raff, Rolf, Rolph,
Raoul)*

Ralston [Anglo-Saxon]
'Dweller on Ralph's
farm'.

Rambert [Teutonic]
'Brilliant and mighty'.

Ramon See **Raymond**

Ramsden [Anglo-Saxon]
'Ram's valley'.

Ramsey [Anglo-Saxon]
'From Ram's island' or
'From the raven's island'.

Rance [African]
'Borrowed all'.

Rand See **Randal**

Randal [Old English]
'Shield wolf'.
*(Randall, Rand, Randolph,
Randolf, Ranulf)*

Randolph See **Randal**

Ranger [French]
'Keeper of the forest'.
The gamekeeper who
looked after the trees and
the wildlife.

Rankin [Anglo-Saxon]
'Little shield'.

Ransford [Anglo-Saxon]
'From the raven's ford'.

Ransley [Anglo-Saxon]
'From the raven's
meadow'.

Ransom [Anglo-Saxon]
'Shield warrior's son'.

Ranulf See **Randal**

Raoul See **Ralph**

Raphael [Hebrew]
'Healed by God'.
*(Rafael, Rafaello, Raffaello,
Raff)*

Ras See **Erasmus**

Rasmus See **Erasmus**

Ravi [Hindu]
'Sun'.

Rawley See **Raleigh**

Rawlins [French]
'Son of the wolf
counsellor'.

Rawson [Anglo-Saxon]
'Son of the little wolf'.

Ray [French]
'The sovereign'. Also
dim. of Raymond.

Rayburn [Old English]
'From the deer brook'.

Raymond [Teutonic]
'Wise protection'.
(Raymon, Raimond,
Reamonn, Raymund, Ray)

Raymund See **Raymond**

Raynold See **Reginald**

Raynor [Scandinavian]
'Mighty army'.
(Rainer, Rainier)

Reade [Anglo-Saxon]
'The red headed one'.
(Read, Reed, Reede).

Reading [Anglo-Saxon]
'Son of the red haired
one'.
(Redding)

Redbourne See
Radbourne

Redcliff See **Radcliffe**

Redford See **Radford**

Redley See **Radley**

Redman [Anglo-Saxon]
'Counsellor; advice
giver'.

Redmond [Anglo-Saxon]
'Counsellor, protector,
advisor'.
(Radmund, Redmund)

Redpath See **Ridpath**

Redvers See **Radford**

Redwald [Anglo-Saxon]
'Mighty counsellor'.

Reece [Celtic]
'The ardent one'. One
who loves living.
(Rhett)

Reed See **Reade**

Reeve [Anglo-Saxon]
'The steward'. One who
looked after a great lord's
affairs.

Regan [Gaelic]
'Royalty, a king'.
(Reagan, Reagen, Regen)

Reggie See **Reginald**

Reginald [Teutonic]
'Mighty and powerful
ruler'.
(Raghnall, Raynold,
Reinhold, Reynold, Ronald,
Reg, Reggie, Reggy, Ron,
Ronnie, Ronny, Naldo)

Rehard See **Reynard**

Reinhold See **Reginald**

Remington [Anglo-Saxon]
'From the farm where the
blackbirds sing'.

Remus [Latin]
'Fast rower'. A speedy
oarsman.

Renaud See **Reynard**

Renault See **Reginald**

Rene See **Reginald**

Renfred [Anglo-Saxon]
'Mighty and peaceful'. A
peaceful warrior who
could fight when
necessary.

Renfrew [Celtic]
'From the still river'.

Rennard See **Reynard**

Renny [Gaelic]
'Little mighty and
powerful'. Also der. of
Rene.

Renshaw [Anglo-Saxon]
'From the forest of the
ravens'.

Renton [Anglo-Saxon]
'From the farm of the roe
buck'.

Reuben [Hebrew]
'Behold a son'.
(Ruben, Rube, Rubey, Ruby)

Rex [Latin]
'The king'. The all
powerful monarch.
(Rey, Roy)

Rexford [Anglo-Saxon]
'From the king's ford'.

Rey See **Rex**

Reynard [Teutonic]
'Mighty courage' or 'The
fox'.
*(Rehard, Rennard, Raynard,
Reinhard, Renaud)*

Reynold See **Reginald**

Rhain [Welsh]
'Lance'.

Rhett See **Reece**

Rhodes [Greek]
'The place of roses'.

Rhun [Welsh]
'Grand'.

Rhydwyn [Welsh]
'Dweller by the white
ford'.

Rhys [Celtic]
'Hero'.
(Reece, Rees)

Rich See **Richard**

Richard [Teutonic]
'Wealthy, powerful one'.
*(Ricard, Richerd, Rickert,
Riocard, Rick, Rickie, Ricky,
Rich, Ritch, Ritchie, Dick,
Dickie, Dicky, Dickon,
Diccon)*

Richie See **Alaric**

Richman See **Richmond**

Richmond [Anglo-Saxon]
'Powerful protector'.
(Richman)

Rick See **Alaric**

Ricker [Teutonic]
'Powerful army'.

Rickert See **Richard**

Rickie See **Alaric**

Rickward [Anglo-Saxon]
'Powerful guardian'.
(Rickwood)

Rickwood See **Rickward**

Ricky See **Richard**

Ricy See **Alaric**

Riddock [Gaelic]
'From the barren field'.

Rider [Anglo-Saxon]
'Knight; horse-rider'.
(Ryder)

Ridge [Anglo-Saxon]
'From the ridge'.

Ridgeway [Anglo-Saxon]
'From the ridge road'.

Ridgley [Anglo-Saxon]
'From the ridge meadow'.

Ridley See **Radley**

Ridpath [Anglo-Saxon]
'From the red path'.
(Redpath)

Rigby [Anglo-Saxon]
'Valley of the ruler'.

Rigg [Anglo-Saxon]
'From the ridge'.

Riley [Gaelic]
'Valiant and warlike'.
(Reilly, Ryley)

Ring [Anglo-Saxon]
'A ring'.

Riocard See **Richard**

Riordan [Gaelic]
'Royal bard'
(Reardon, Rearden)

Ripley [Anglo-Saxon]
'From the valley of the
echo'.

Risley [Anglo-Saxon]
'From the brushwood
meadow'.

Riston [Anglo-Saxon]
'From the brushwood
farm'.

Ritchie See **Richard**

Ritter [Teutonic]
'A knight'.

Roald [Teutonic]
'Famous ruler'.

Roan [Anglo-Saxon]
'From the rowan tree'.
(Rowan)

Roarke [Gaelic]
'Famous ruler'.
(Rorke, Rourke, Ruark)

Robby See **Robert**

Robert [Teutonic]
'Bright, shining fame'. A
man of brilliant
reputation.
*(Roberto, Robin, Rupert,
Ruprecht, Rob, Robbie,
Robby, Rab, Rabbie, Rabby,
Bob, Bobbie, Bobby)*

Roberto See **Robert**

Robinson [Anglo-Saxon]
'Son of Robert'.

Rochester [Anglo-Saxon]
'Camp on the rocks'.

Rock [Anglo-Saxon]
'From the rock'.
(Roc, Rocky)

Rockley [Anglo-Saxon]
'From the rocky
meadow'.
(Rockly)

Rockly See **Rockley**

Rockwell [Anglo-Saxon]
'From the rocky well'.

Rocky See **Rock**

Rod See **Roderick**

Rodd See **Roderick**

Roddie See **Roderick**

Roden [Anglo-Saxon]
'From the valley of the reeds'.

Roderick [Teutonic]
'Famous, wealthy ruler'.
(Rodrick, Rodric, Roderic, Broderic, Broderick, Brodrick, Rod, Roddie, Roddy, Rick, Rickie, Ricky, Rory)

Rodge See **Roger**

Rodger See **Roger**

Rodhlann See **Roland**

Rodi See **Rodney**

Rodman [Teutonic]
'Famous hero'.
(Rodmond, Rodmund)

Rodney [Teutonic]
'Famous and renowned'.
(Rod, Roddie, Roddy, Rodi)

Rodolph See **Rudolph**

Rodwell [Anglo-Saxon]
'From the Christian's well'.

Roe [Anglo-Saxon]
'Roe deer'.

Rogan [Gaelic]
'The red haired one'.

Roger [Teutonic]
'Famous spearman; renowned warrior'.
(Rodger, Rodge, Rog)

Roland [Teutonic]
'From the famed land'.
(Rollo, Rowe, Orlando, Rowland, Rollin, Roley, Rodhlann)

Roley See **Roland**

Rolf See **Ralph, Randolph, Rudolph**

Rolfe See **Rudolph**

Rollin See **Roland**

Rollo See **Roland, Rudolph**

Rolt [Teutonic]
'Power and fame'.

Romeo [Latin]
'Man from Rome'.

Romford See **Rumford**

Romney [Celtic]
'Curving river'.

Ronald See **Reginald**

Ronan [Gaelic]
'Little seal'.

Ronnie See **Reginald**

Ronson [Anglo-Saxon]
'Son of Ronald'.

Rooney [Gaelic]
'The red one'. One with a
ruddy complexion.
(Ruan, Rowney)

Roper [Anglo-Saxon]
'Rope maker'.

Rorke See **Roarke**

Rory [Gaelic]
'Red king'. Also der. of
Roderick.
(Ruaidhri, Rorie, Rorry)

Rory See **Roderick**

Roscoe [Scandinavian]
'From the deer forest'.
(Rosco, Ros, Roz)

Roslin [French]
'Small red haired one'.
(Roslyn, Rosselin, Rosslyn)

Ross [Celtic]
'From the peninsula'.
Alternatively, 'Horse'
(Teutonic).

Roswald [Teutonic]
'Mighty steed'.
(Roswall, Roswell)

Roswall See **Roswald**

Roswell See **Roswald**

Roth [Old German]
'Red hair'.

Rothwell [Norse]
'From the red well'.

Rourke See **Roarke**

Rover [Anglo-Saxon]
'A wanderer'.

Rowan [Gaelic]
'Red haired'.
(Rowen, Rowe)

Rowe See **Roland** or
Rowan

Rowell [Anglo-Saxon]
'From the deer well'.

Rowland See **Roland**

Rowley [Anglo-Saxon]
'From the rough
meadow'.

Rowney See **Rooney**

Rowsan [Anglo-Saxon]
'Rowan's son'. Son of a
red haired man.

Roxbury [Anglo-Saxon]
'From the fortress of the
rock'.

Roy [Celtic]
'Red haired' or 'The
king'. (See Rex.)

Roy See **Leroy** or **Rex**

Royal [French]
'Regal one'.

Royce [Anglo-Saxon]
'Son of the king'.

Royd [Norse]
'From the forest clearing'.

Roydon [Anglo-Saxon]
'Dweller on the rye hill'.

Royston [English]
Place in Yorkshire.

Ruaidhri See **Rory**

Ruan See **Rooney**

Rube See **Reuben**

Ruben See **Reuben**

Rubey See **Reuben**

Ruck [Anglo-Saxon]
'The rock'. One with
black hair.

Rudd [Anglo-Saxon]
'Ruddy complexion'.

Rudolph [Teutonic]
'Famous wolf'.
*(Rudolf, Rodolf, Rolfe,
Rollo, Rolph, Rudy, Dolf,
Dolph)*

Rudy See **Rudolph**

Rudyard [Anglo-Saxon]
'From the red enclosure'.

Ruelle See **Rule**

Rufe See **Rufus**

Ruff [French]
'The red haired one'.

Ruff See **Rufus**

Rufford [Anglo-Saxon]
'From the rough ford'.

Rufus [Latin]
'Red haired'.
*(Rufe, Ruff, Griffin,
Griffith, Griff)*

Rufus See **Griffith**

Rugby [Anglo-Saxon]
'From the rook estate'.

Rule [Latin]
'The ruler'.
(Ruelle)

Rumford [Anglo-Saxon]
'From the wide ford'.
(Romford)

Rupert See **Robert**

Ruprecht See **Robert**

Rurik See **Roderick**

Rush [French]
'Red haired'.

Rushford [Anglo-Saxon]
'From the rush ford'.

Ruskin [Teutonic]
'Small red haired one'.

Russ See **Russell**

Russel See **Russell**

Russell [Anglo-Saxon]
'Red as a fox'.
(Rus, Russ, Rusty, Russel)

Russet See **Rust**

Rust [Anglo-Saxon]
'Red haired'.
(Russet, Rusty)

Rusty See **Rust**

Rutherford [Anglo-Saxon]
'From the cattle ford'.

Rutland [Norse]
'From the stump land'.

Rutledge [Anglo-Saxon]
'From the red pool'.
(Routledge)

Rutley [Anglo-Saxon]
'From the stump meadow'.

Ryan [Gaelic]
'Small king'.

Rycroft [Anglo-Saxon]
'From the rye field'.

Ryder See **Rider**

Rye [French]
'From the riverbank'.

Rylan [Anglo-Saxon]
'From the rye land'.
(Ryland)

Ryland See **Rylan**

Ryle [Anglo-Saxon]
'From the rye hill'.

Ryley See **Riley**

Ryman [Anglo-Saxon]
'The rye-seller'.

Ryton [Anglo-Saxon]
'From the rye farm'.

Girls

Saba [Greek]
'Woman of Sheba'.

Sabella [Latin]
'The wise'.
(Sabelle)

Sabelle See **Sabella**

Sabina [Latin]
'Woman of Sabine'.
(Sabine, Savina, Bina, Saidhbhain, Binnie)

Sabine See **Sabina**

Sabra [Hebrew]
'The restful one'.

Sabrina [Latin]
'A princess'.
(Brina, Sabrine)

Sabrine See **Sabrina**

Sacha [Greek]
'Helpmate'.
(Sasha)

Sacharissa [Greek]
'Sweet'.

Sadella See **Sarah**

Sadhth See **Sophia**

Sadie See **Sarah**

Sadira [Persian]
'The lotus eater'.

Saffron [English]
From the plant.

Saidhbhain See **Sabina**

Salaidh See **Sarah**

Salema [Hebrew]
'Girl of peace'.
(Selemas, Selima)

Salina [Greek]
'From the salty place'.

Sallie See **Sarah**

Sally See **Sarah**

Saloma See **Salome**

Salome [Hebrew]
'Peace'. 'Shalom' the
traditional Hebrew
greeting — Peace.
(Saloma, Salomi)

Salomi See **Salome**

Salvia [Latin]
'Sage herb'.
(Salvina)

Salvina See **Salvia**

Samala [Hebrew]
'Asked of God'.

Samantha [Aramaic]
'A listener'.

Samara [Hebrew]
'Watchful, cautious;
guarded by God'.

Samella See **Samuela**

Samelle See **Samuela**

Samuela [Hebrew]
'His name is God'. Fem.
of Samuel.
*(Samella, Samelle, Samuella,
Samuelle)*

Samuelle See **Samuela**

Sancha See **Sancia**

Sancia [Latin]
'Sacred'.
(Sancha, Sanchia)

Sandra See **Alexandra**

Sandy See **Alexandra**

Sapphira [Greek]
'Eyes of sapphire colour'.

Sarah [Hebrew]
'Princess'. One of royal status.
(Sara, Sari, Sarene, Sarine, Sarette, Sadella, Sadie, Sorcha, Salaidh, Sadye, Sal, Sallie, Sally, Sharie, Sarita, Sorcha, Salaidh, Morag, Zara, Zarah, Zaria)

Saree [Arabic]
'Most noble'.

Sarene See **Sarah**

Sarette See **Sarah**

Sari See **Sarah**

Sarita See **Sarah**

Savanna [Spanish]
'An open plain'.

Savina See **Sabina**

Saxona [Teutonic]
'A sword bearer'.

Scarlett [Middle English]
'Scarlet coloured'.
(Scarlet, Scarletta)

Scarletta See **Scarlett**

Scholastica [Latin]
'Scholar'.

Sebestianan See **Sebastiane**

Sebastiane [Latin]
'Revered one'.
(Sebastianan, Sebastianne, Sebastianna, Sebastienna, Sebastienne)

Sebastianna See **Sebastiane**

Sebila [Latin]
'Wise old woman'.

Secunda [Latin]
'Second born'.

Seirian [Welsh]
'Sparkling'.

Seiriol [Welsh]
'Bright'.
(Siriol)

Sela See **Selena**

Selda See **Griselda**

Selena [Greek]
'The Moon'.
(Selina, Selene, Selinda, Salene, Sela, Selie, Sena, Selia, Celene, Celina, Celinda, Celie, Lena)

Selene See **Selena**

Selia See **Selena**

Selie See **Selena**

Selima [Hebrew]
'Peaceful'.

Selinda See **Selena**

Selma [Celtic]
'The fair'. Also der. of
Anselma.

Selma See **Anselma**

Semele [Latin]
'The single one'.
(Semelia)

Semelia See **Semele**

Semira [Hebrew]
'Height of the heavens'.

Sena See **Selena**

Seonaid See **Jane**

Septima [Latin]
'Seventh born'.

Sera See **Seraphina**

Seraphina [Hebrew]
'The ardent believer'.
One with a burning
faith'.

*(Serafina, Seraphine,
Serafine, Sera)*

Seraphine See **Seraphina**

Serena [Latin]
'Bright tranquil one'.

Serica [Latin]
'Silken'.

Serilda [Teutonic]
'Armoured battle maid'.
(Serilde, Serhilda, Serhilde)

Serilde See **Serilda**

Shaina [Hebrew]
'Beautiful'.

Shani [African]
'Marvellous'.

Shanley [Gaelic]
'Child of the old hero'.

Shannon [Gaelic]
'Small, wise'.

Shari See **Sharon**

Sharleen See **Charlotte/
Caroline**

Sharon [Hebrew]
'A princess of exotic
beauty'.
*(Sherry, Shari, Sharri,
Sharry)*

Sharry See **Sharon**

Shea [Gaelic]
'From the fairy fort'.

Shea See **Shelah**

Sheba See **Saba**

Sheela See **Sheena**

Sheena [Gaelic]
'Dim-sighted'.
(Sheela, Sheelah, Sheilah)

Sheila [Celtic]
'Musical'. Var. of Cecilia.
*(Sheela, Sheelah, Sheilah,
Selia)*

Shelah [Hebrew]
'Asked for'.
(Shela, Shaya, Sheya, Shea)

Shelby [Old English]
'From the ledge estate'.

Shelley [English]
'From the edge of the
meadow'.

Shelly See **Rachel**

Shena See **Jane**

Sheri See **Shirley**

Sherrie See **Cherie**

Sherry See **Charlotte**,
Sharon or **Cherie**

Sheryl See **Charlotte**,
Shirley or **Cherie**

Sheya See **Shelah**

Shifra [Hebrew]
'Beautiful'.

Shirleen See **Shirley**

Shirley [Anglo-Saxon]
'From the white
meadow'.
*(Shirlee, Shirlie, Shirleen,
Shirlene, Sheryl, Sherry,
Sheri)*

Shoshana [Hebrew]
'Rose'.

Shulamith [Hebrew]
'Peace'.

Sibella See **Sybil**

Sibie See **Sybil**

Sibilla See **Sybil**

Sibyl See **Sybil**

Sidney/Sidonia See
Sydney

Sidonie See **Sydney**

Sidra [Latin]
'Glittering lady of the
stars'.
(Sidria)

Sidria See **Sidra**

Sierna [Greek]
'A sweetly singing
mermaid'.

Sigfreda [Teutonic]
'Victorious and peaceful'.
(Sigfrieda, Sigfriede)

Sigfriede See **Sigfreda**

Signa [Latin]
'Signed on the heart'.

Sigrath See **Sigrid**

Sigrid [Norse]
'Victorious counsellor'.
(Sigrath, Sigrud, Sigurd)

Sigrud See **Sigrid**

Sigurd See **Sigrid**

Sile See **Julia**

Sileas See **Cecilia** or **Julia**

Silva See **Sylvia**

Silvana [Latin]
'Wood dweller'.

Silvana See **Sylvia**

Silvie See **Sylvia**

Simona See **Simone**

Simone [Hebrew]
'Heard by the Lord'.
Fem. of Simon/Simeon.
*(Simona, Simonette,
Simonetta)*

Simonetta See **Simone**

Simonette See **Simone**

Sine See **Jane**

Sinead [Welsh] See **Jane**

Siobhan [Irish] See **Jane**
or **Judith**

Sirena [Greek]
'Sweet singing mermaid'.
Originally from the sirens
who lured men to their
deaths. Used sometimes
during World War II for
babies born during an air
raid.
(Sirene, Sireen)

Sirene See **Sirena**

Sisle See **Cecilia**

Sissie See **Cecilia**

Skye See **Skylar**

Skylar [Dutch]
'Sheltering'.
(Skye)

Solana [Spanish]
'Sunshine'.

Solange [Latin]
'Good shepherdess'.

Solita [Latin]
'Solitary one'.

Solvig [Teutonic]
'Victorious battle maid'.

Sonia See **Sophia**

Sonja See **Sophia**

Sophia [Greek]
'Wisdom'.
(Sophie, Sophy, Sofia, Sonia,
Sonja, Sonya, Sofie, Sadhbh,
Sadhbha, Beathag)

Sophie See **Sophia**

Sophronia [Greek]
'Sensible one'.

Sorcha [Gaelic]
'Bright one'.

Sorcha See **Sarah**

Sperata [Latin]
'Hoped for'.

Spring [English]
'Joyous season'.

Stacy/Stacia See
Anastasia/Eustacia

Starr [English]
'A star'.
(Star)

Stefa See **Stephanie**

Steffie See **Stephanie**

Stella See **Estelle**

Stelle See **Estelle**

Stephania See **Stephanie**

Stephanie [Greek]
'A crown; garland'. Fem.
of Stephen.
(Stephania, Stephena,
Stevana, Stevania, Stevena,
Stevenia, Stephenie,
Stephenia, Stephena, Stefa,
Stepha, Steffie, Stevie)

Stephena See **Stephanie**

Stevie See **Stephanie**

Storm [Anglo-Saxon]
'A tempest'. One of
turbulent nature.

Sue See **Susan**

Suki See **Susan**

Sunny [Anglo-Saxon]
'Bright and cheerful'.
The brightness of the sun
after the storm.

Susan [Hebrew]
'Graceful lily'.
(Susana, Susanna, Susanne,
Susannah, Suzanna,
Suzanne, Suzette, Susette,
Suzetta, Sue, Susi, Susie,
Susy, Suzie, Suzy, Suki,
Sukey, Suky, Zsa-Zsa)

Susana See **Susan**

Susi See **Susan**

Suzetta See **Susan**

Suzette See **Susan**

Swetlana [German]
'A star'.

Sybil [Greek]
'Prophetess'. The female
soothsayer of ancient
Greece.
(Cybil, Sibyl, Sibil, Sibel,

Sibell, Sybyl, Sibilla,
Sibella, Sybella, Sibille,
Sibylle, Sybille, Sib, Sibie,
Sibbie, Sibby)

Syd See **Sydney**

Sydel [Hebrew]
'That enchantress'.
(Sydelle)

Sydney [French/Hebrew]
'From St. Denis'
(French); 'The enticer'
(Hebrew). Fem. of
Sidney.
(Sidney, Sidonia, Sidonie,
Sid, Syd)

Syl See **Sylvia**

Sylgwyn [Welsh]
'Born on Whitsunday'.

Sylvia [Latin]
'From the forest'.
(Silvia, Silva, Sylva,
Silvana, Slyvana, Zilvia,
Zilva, Sil, Syl, Silvie)

Syna [Greek]
'Together'.
(Syne)

Syne See **Syna**

Syntyche [Greek]
'With good fortune'.

Saber [French]
'A sword'.

Sabin [Latin]
'Man from the Sabines'.

Safford [Anglo-Saxon]
'From the willow ford'.

Saladin [Arabic]
'Goodness of the faith'.

Salomon [Hebrew]
'Peaceful'.

Salton [Anglo-Saxon]
'From the willow farm'.

Salvador [Latin]
'The saviour'.
*(Salvadore, Salvator,
Salvatore)*

Salvator See **Salvador**

Sam See **Sampson**

Sammy See **Sampson**

Sampson [Hebrew]
'Sun's man'.
*(Samson, Simpson, Simson,
Sam, Sammy, Sim)*

Samson See **Sampson**

Samuel [Hebrew]
'His name is God'.
(Sam, Sammie, Sammy)

Sanborn [Anglo-Saxon]
'From the sandy brook'.
(Samborn)

Sancho [Spanish]
'Sincere and truthful'.

Sander See **Alexander**

Sanders [Anglo-Saxon]
'Son of Alexander'.
*(Sanderson, Saunderson,
Saunders, Sandie, Sandy)*

Sanderson See **Sanders**

Sandie See **Alexander**

Sandy See **Lysander**

Sanford [Anglo-Saxon]
'From the sandy ford'.

Sansom See **Sampson**

Santo [Italian]
'Saint like'.

Santon [Anglo-Saxon]
'From the sandy farm'.

Sarge See **Sargent**

Sargent [Latin]
'A military attendant'.
(Sergeant, Sergent, Sarge, Sargie)

Sargie See **Sargent**

Sasha See **Alexander**

Saul [Hebrew]
'Called by God'.

Saunders See **Alexander**

Saunderson See **Sanders**

Saville [French]
'The willow estate'.
(Savile)

Sawyer [Anglo-Saxon]
'A sawer of wood'.

Saxe See **Saxon**

Saxon [Anglo-Saxon]
'People of the swords'.
(Saxe)

Sayer [Celtic]
'Carpenter'.
(Sayre, Sayers, Sayres)

Sayers See **Sayer**

Scanlon [Gaelic]
'A snarer of hearts'.

Schuyler [Dutch]
'A scholar; a wise man' or
'To shield'.

Scipio [Latin]
'Walking stick'.

Scott [Latin/Celtic]
'From Scotland' (Latin)
or 'Tattoed warrior'
(Celtic).
(Scot, Scottie, Scotty)

Scottie See **Scott**

Scoville [French]
'From the Scottish
estate'.

Scully [Gaelic]
'Town crier'. The bringer
of news in the days before
mass media.

Seabert [Anglo-Saxon]
'Sea glorious'.
(Seabright, Sebert)

Seabright See **Seabert**

Seabrook [Anglo-Saxon]
'From a brook by the
sea'.
(Sebrook)

Seamus See **Jacob** or
James

Sean See **John**

Searle [Teutonic]
'Armed warrior'.
(Searl)

Seaton [French]
'From Say's farm'.
(Seton, Seeton, Seetin)

Sebald [Old English]
'Bold in victory'.

Sebastian [Latin]
'Reverenced one'. An
august person.
(Sebastien, Seb)

Sebert [Old English]
'Famous for victory'.

Sebert See **Seabert**

Secundus [Latin]
'Second'.

Sedgley [Anglo-Saxon]
'From the swordsman's

meadow'.
(Sedgeley)

Sedgwick [Anglo-Saxon]
'From the sword grass
place'.
(Sedgewick)

Seeley [Anglo-Saxon]
'Happy and blessed'.
(Seely, Sealey)

Seetin See **Seaton**

Seger [Anglo-Saxon]
'Sea warrior'.
(Seager, Segar)

Selby [Teutonic]
'From the manor farm'.

Selden [Anglo-Saxon]
'From the valley of the
willow tree'.

Selig [Teutonic]
'Blessed happy one'.

Selwyn [Teutonic]
'Friend at the manor
house'.
(Selwin)

Senior [French]
'Lord of the manor'.
(Seigneur)

Sennett [French]
'Old and wise'. The all
knowing seer.

Seosaidh See **Joseph**

Septimus [Latin]
'Seventh born son'.

Sergent See **Sargent**

Serge/Sergeant See
Sargeant

Serle [Teutonic]
'Bearer of arms and
weapons'.

Seth [Hebrew]
'The appointed by God'.

Seton [Anglo-Saxon]
'From the farm by the
sea'.

Seumas [Gaelic] See
James

Severn [Anglo-Saxon]
'The boundary'.

Sewald See **Sewell**

Sewall See **Sewell**

Seward [Anglo-Saxon]
'The sea defender'.

Sewell [Anglo-Saxon]
'Sea powerful'.
(Sewald, Sewall, Siwald)

Sexton [Anglo-Saxon]
'Sacristan'. A church
official.

Sextus [Latin]
'Sixth born son'.

Seymour [French/Anglo-
Saxon]
'From St. Maur'
(French) or 'From the sea
moor' (Anglo-Saxon).

Shadwell [Anglo-Saxon]
'From the well in the
arbour'.

Shamus See **Jacob** or
James

Shanahan [Gaelic]
'The wise one'.

Shandy [Anglo-Saxon]
'Little boisterous one'.

Shane See **John**

Shanley [Gaelic]
'The venerable hero'.

Shannon [Gaelic]
'Old wise one'.

Shattuck [Anglo-Saxon]
'Little shad-fish'.

Shaw [Anglo-Saxon]
'From the grove'.

Shay See **Shea**

Shea [Gaelic]
'Stately, courteous, and
inventive person'. A man
of many parts.
(Shay)

Sheehan [Gaelic]
'Peaceful one'.

Sheffield [Anglo-Saxon]
'From the crooked field'.

Shelby [Anglo-Saxon]
'From the estate on the
cliff edge'.

Sheldon [Anglo-Saxon]
'From the hill ledge'.

Shelley [Anglo-Saxon]
'From the meadow on the
hill ledge'.

Shelton [Anglo-Saxon]
'From the farm on the hill
ledge'.

Shem [Hebrew]
'Renown'.

Shepard [Anglo-Saxon]
'The sheep tender; the
shepherd'.
*(Shepherd, Sheppard,
Shepperd, Shep, Shepp,
Sheppy)*

Shepley [Anglo-Saxon]
'From the sheep
meadow'.

Shepp See **Shepard**

Sheppy See **Shepard**

Sherborne [Anglo-Saxon]
'From the clear stream'.
*(Sherbourn, Sherbourne,
Sherburne, Sherburn)*

Sherburn See **Sherborne**

Sheridan [Gaelic]
'Wild savage'.

Sherlock [Anglo-Saxon]
'White haired man'.

Sherman [Anglo-Saxon]
'Wool shearer; sheep
shearer'.

Sherwin [Anglo-Saxon]
'Loyal friend' or 'Swift
footed'.

Sherwood [Anglo-Saxon]
'Bright forest'.

Shipley [Anglo-Saxon]
'From the sheep
meadow'.

Shipton [Anglo-Saxon]
'From the sheep farm'.

Sholto [Gaelic]
'The wild duck'.

Sian See **John**

Sid See **Sidney**

Siddell [Anglo-Saxon]
'From a wide valley'.

Sidney [French]
'A follower of St. Denis'
or 'Man from Sidon'.
(Sid, Syd, Sydney)

Sigfrid [Teutonic]
'Peace after victory'.
*(Sigfried, Siegfrid,
Siegfried)*

Sigismund See **Sigmund**

Sigmund [Teutonic]
'Victorious protector'.
*(Sigismund, Sigismond,
Sigmond)*

Sigurd [Scandinavian]
'Victorious guardian'.
(Sigerd)

Sigwald [Teutonic]
'Victorious ruler'.

Silas [Latin]
'From the forest'.
*(Silvan, Silvanus, Silvester,
Sylvan, Sylvester, Si)*

Silvan See **Silas**

Silvanus See **Silas**

Silvester See **Silas**

Sim See **Sampson**

Simeon See **Simon**

Simon [Hebrew]
'One who hears'.
*(Simeon, Siomonn, Sim,
Ximenes)*

Simpson See **Sampson**

Sinclair [French]
'From St. Clair' or
'Shining light'.
(St. Clair)

Siward [Teutonic]
'Conquering guardian'.

Skeat See **Skeets**

Skeeter See **Skeets**

Skeets [Anglo-Saxon]
'The swift'.
(Skeat, Skeet, Skeeter)

Skelly [Gaelic]
'Historian'.

Skelton [Anglo-Saxon]
'From the farm on the hill ledge'.

Skerry [Scandinavian]
'From the rocky island'.

Skip [Scandinavian]
'Owner of the ship'.
(Skipp, Skippy)

Skippy See **Skip**

Skipton [Anglo-Saxon]
'From the sheep farm'.

Slade [Anglo-Saxon]
'Valley dweller'.

Slaven See **Slevin**

Slavin See **Slevin**

Sleven See **Slevin**

Slevin [Gaelic]
'The mountain climber'.
(Slaven, Slavin, Sleven)

Sloan [Gaelic]
'Warrior'.
(Sloane)

Smedley [Anglo-Saxon]
'From the flat meadow'.
(Smedly)

Smith [Anglo-Saxon]
'The blacksmith'.

Snowden [Anglo-Saxon]
'From the snowy hill'.
Man from the snowcapped mountains.

Socrates [Greek]
'Self-restrained'.

Sol [Latin]
'The sun'. Also dim. of Solomon.

Solly See **Solomon**

Solomon [Hebrew]
'Wise and peaceful'. The wisdom of Solomon.
(Solamon, Soloman, Salomon, Sol, Sollie, Solly)

Solon [Greek]
'Wise man'. Greek form of Solomon.'

Somerled [Teutonic]
'Summer wanderer'.

Somerset [Anglo-Saxon]
'From the summer place'.
The place where the
wanderers rested for the
summer.

Somerton [Anglo-Saxon]
'From the summer farm'.

Somerville [Anglo-Saxon]
'From the summer
estate'.
(Sommerville)

Sonny See **Tyson**

Sophocles [Greek]
'Glory of wisdom'.

Sorrel [French]
'With brownish hair'.

Southwell [Anglo-Saxon]
'From the south well'.

Spalding [Anglo-Saxon]
'From the split meadow'.
(Spaulding)

Spangler [Teutonic]
'The tinsmith'.

Spark [Anglo-Saxon]
'Gay gallant'. The man
about town.

Speed [Anglo-Saxon]
'Success, prosperity'.

Spence See **Spencer**

Spencer [French]
'Shopkeeper; dispenser of
provisions'.
(Spenser, Spence)

Spiro [Greek]
'Breath of the gods'.

Sproule [Anglo-Saxon]
'Energetic, active
person'.
(Sprowle)

Squire [Anglo-Saxon]
'Knight's shield bearer'.

St Clair See **Sinclair**

St John [English]
A contraction of Saint
John.

Stacey [Latin]
'Prosperous and stable'.
(Stacy)

Stafford [Anglo-Saxon]
'From the ford by the
landing place'.

Stamford [Anglo-Saxon]
'From the stony crossing'.
(Stanford)

Stan See **Stanislaus**

Stanbury [Anglo-Saxon]
'From a stone fortress'.
(Stanberry)

Stancliffe [Anglo-Saxon]
'From the rocky cliff'.
*(Stancliff, Standcliff,
Standcliffe)*

Standcliff See **Stancliffe**

Standish [Anglo-Saxon]
'From the stony park'.

Stanfield [Anglo-Saxon]
'From the stony field'.

Stanford See **Stamford**

Stanhope [Anglo-Saxon]
'From the stony hollow'.

Stanislas See **Stanislaus**

Stanislaus [Slavic]
'Stand of glory'.
*(Stanislas, Stanislav,
Aineislis, Stan)*

Stanislav See **Stanislaus**

Stanley [Slavic/Anglo-
Saxon]
'Pride of the camp'
(Slavic) or 'From the
stony meadow' (Anglo-
Saxon).

*(Stanley, Stanleigh, Stanly,
Stan)*

Stanton [Anglo-Saxon]
'From the rocky lake' or
'From the stony farm'.

Stanway [Anglo-Saxon]
'From the stony road'.

Stanwick [Anglo-Saxon]
'From the stony village'.

Stanwood [Anglo-Saxon]
'From the stony forest'.

Starling [Anglo-Saxon]
'The starling'.

Starr [Anglo-Saxon]
'A star'.

Stavros [Greek]
'Cross'.

Stedman [Anglo-Saxon]
'Farm owner'. One who
owns the land he tills.

Stefan See **Stephen**

Stein [Teutonic]
'The stone'.

Stephen [Greek]
'The crowned one'. A
man who wears the
victor's laurel wreath.

(Steven, Stephenson, Stevenson, Stefan, Steffen, Steve, Stevie)

Stephenson See **Stephen**

Sterling [Teutonic/Celtic] 'Good, honest, worthy' (Teutonic) or 'From the yellow house' (Celtic). *(Stirling)*

Sterne [Anglo-Saxon] 'The austere one; an ascetic'. *(Stern, Stearne, Stearn)*

Steve See **Stephen**

Steven See **Stephen**

Stevie See **Stephen**

Stew See **Stewart**

Steward See **Stewart**

Stewart [Anglo-Saxon] 'The steward'. Name of the Royal House of Scotland. *(Steward, Stuart, Stew, Stu)*

Stillman [Anglo-Saxon] 'Quiet and gentle man'. *(Stilman)*

Stinson [Anglo-Saxon] 'Son of stone'.

Stirling See **Sterling**

Stockley [Anglo-Saxon] 'From the cleared meadow'.

Stockton [Anglo-Saxon] 'From the farm in the clearing'.

Stockwell [Anglo-Saxon] 'From the well in the clearing'.

Stoddard [Anglo-Saxon] 'The horse keeper'.

Stoke [Anglo-Saxon] 'A village'.

Storm [Anglo-Saxon] 'The tempest'.

Storr [Scandinavian] 'Great man'.

Stowe [Anglo-Saxon] 'From the place'.

Strahan [Gaelic] 'The poet'.

Stratford [Anglo-Saxon] 'The street crossing the ford'.

Stroud [Anglo-Saxon]
'From the thicket'.

Struthers [Gaelic]
'From the rivulet'.
(Strothers)

Stuart See **Stewart**

Styles [Anglo-Saxon]
'From the dwelling by the
stile'.
(Stiles)

Suffield [Anglo-Saxon]
'From the south field'.

Sulien [Welsh]
'Sun-born'.

Sullie See **Sullivan**

Sullivan [Gaelic]
'Man with black eyes'.
(Sullie, Sully)

Sully [Anglo-Saxon]
'From the south
meadow'. Also dim. of
Sullivan.

Sumner [Latin]
'One who summons'. The
church official who
summoned the
congregation to prayer.

Sutcliffe [Anglo-Saxon]
'From the south cliff'.
(Sutcliff)

Sutherland [Scandinavian]
'From a southern land'.

Sutton [Anglo-Saxon]
'From the south town'.

Sven [Scandinavian]
'Youth'.

Swain [Anglo-Saxon]
'Herdsman' or 'Knight's
attendant'.
(Sweyn, Swayne)

Sweeney [Gaelic]
'Little hero'.

Swinton [Anglo-Saxon]
'From the pig farm'.

Swithin [Old English]
'Strong'.
(Swithun)

Swithun See **Swithin**

Sydney See **Sidney**

Sylvester See **Silas**

Symington [Anglo-Saxon]
'From Simon's farm'.

Girls

Tabbie See **Tabitha**

Tabina [Arabic]
'Muhammed's follower'.

Tabitha [Aramaic]
'The gazelle'. One of
gentle grace.
(Tabithe, Tabbie, Tabby)

Tabithe See **Tabitha**

Tacita See **Tacitah**

Tacitah [Latin]
'Silence'.
(Tacita)

Tacy [Latin]
'Peace'.

Talitha [Aramaic]
'The maiden'.

Tallie See **Tallulah**

Tallu See **Tallulah**

Tallulah [American Indian]
'Laughing water'. One
who bubbles like a
spring.
(Tallula, Tallu, Tally, Tallie)

Tamar See **Tamara**

Tamara [Hebrew]
'Palm tree'.
(Tamar, Tammie, Tammy)

Tammy [Hebrew]
'Perfection'. Also dim. of
Tamara.

Tammy See **Tamara**

Tamsin See **Thomasina**

Tangerine [Anglo-Saxon]
'Girl from Tangiers'.

Tangwystl [Welsh]
'Peace pledge'.

Tania [Russian]
'The fairy queen'. Also
dim. of Titania.
(Tanya)

Tania See **Titania**

Tansy [Latin]
'Tenacious'. A woman of
determination.

Tara [Gaelic]
'Towering rock'. The
home of the ancient kings
of Ireland.

Tate [Old English]
'To be cheerful'.
(Tatum)

Tatiana [Latin]
'Silver-haired'.

Tatum See **Tate**

Tavia See **Octavia**

Tavie See **Octavia**

Tecla See **Thecla**

Teddie See **Theodora**

Tegan [Welsh]
'Beautiful'.

Tegwen [Welsh]
'Beautiful-blessed'.

Tempest [French]
'Stormy one'.
(Tempesta, Tempeste)

Tempesta See **Tempest**

Teodora See **Theodora**

Teodore See **Theodora**

Terentia [Greek]
'Guardian'. Fem. of
Terence.
*(Terencia, Teri, Terri,
Terrie, Terry)*

Teresa [Greek]
'The harvester'.
*(Theresa, Therese, Terese,
Teressa, Teresita, Toireasa,
Terri, Terrie, Terry, Tessa,
Tessie, Tessy, Tess, Tracie,
Tracy, Zita)*

Teresita See **Teresa**

Terri See **Terentia**

Terry See **Terentia/
Teresa**

Tertia [Latin]
'Third child'.

Terza [Greek]
'Girl from the farm'.

Tess See **Teresa**

Tessa [Greek]
'Fourth child'. Also var.
of Teresa.

Tessa See **Teresa**

Tessy See **Teresa**

Tewdews [Welsh]
'Divinely given'.

Thaddea [Greek]
'Courageous being'. A
girl of great bravery and
endurance.
(Thada, Thadda)

Thalassa [Greek]
'From the sea'.

Thalia [Greek]
'Luxurious blossom'.

Thea [Greek]
'Goddess'. Also dim. of
Dorothea, Theadora,
Anthea, etc.

Thea See **Theodora**

Theadosia See **Theodora**

Theana See **Theano**

Theano [Greek]
'Divine name'.
(Theana)

Theaphania See
Theophila

Thecla [Greek]
'Divine follower'. A
disciple of St. Paul.
(Tecla, Thekla)

Theda See **Theodora**

Thelma [Greek]
'The nursling'.

Theo See **Theodora**

Theodora [Greek]
'Gift of God'. Another
version of Dorothy.
*(Theda, Theadora,
Theadosia, Theodosia,
Teodora, Teodore, Dora,
Fedora, Fedore, Feodora,
Feodore, Feadore, Feadora,
Teddie, Theo, Thea* and all
forms of *Dorothy)*

Theodora See **Dorothy**

Theodosia See **Theodora**

Theofila See **Theophania**

Theofilia See **Theophania**

Theola [Greek]
'Sent from God'.
(Theo, Lola)

Theone [Greek]
'In the name of God'.
(Theona)

Theophania [Greek]
'Beloved of God'.
*(Theofilia, Theofila,
Theophilia)*

Theophanie See
Theophila

Theophila [Greek]
'Appearance of God'.
*(Theaphania, Theafania,
Theophanie, Theofanie,
Tiffanie, Tiffy)*

Theophilia See
Theophania

Theora [Greek]
'Watcher for God'.

Thera [Greek]
'Wild, untamed one'.

Therese See **Teresa**

Thetis [Greek]
'Positive one'. One who
knows her own mind.
(Thetys)

Thia See **Anthea**

Thirza [Hebrew]
'Pleasantness'.
(Thyrza, Tirza)

Thomasa See **Thomasina**

Thomase See **Thomasina**

Thomasina [Hebrew]
'The twin'. Fem. of
Thomas.
*(Thomasine, Tomasine,
Thomase, Thomasa, Tomase,
Tomasa, Tomasina, Tamsin)*

Thomasine See
Thomasina

Thora [Norse]
'Thunder'. From the God
of Thunder — Thor.

Thorberta [Norse]
'Brilliance of Thor'.
*(Thorberte, Thorbertha,
Thorberte)*

Thorberte See **Thorberta**

Thordia See **Thordis**

Thordie See **Thordis**

Thordis [Norse]
'Spirit of Thor'. The
sound of thunder.
(Thordia, Thordie)

Thyra [Greek]
'Shield bearer'.

Tibelda [Teutonic]
'Boldest person'.

Tiberia [Latin]
'From the Tiber'. The
river of ancient Rome.

Tierney [Gaelic]
'Grandchild of the
lordly'.

Tiffanie See **Theophila**

Tiffany [Greek]
'Manifestation of God'.

Tiffy See **Theophila**

Tilda See **Mathilda**

Tilly See **Mathilda**

Tim See **Timothea**

Timmy See **Timothea**

Timothea [Greek]
'Honouring God'.
(Tim, Timmie, Timmy)

Tina See **Christine**,
Martina, **Augusta** etc.

Tish See **Letitia**

Tita [Latin]
'Honoured title'.

Titania [Greek]
'Giantess'. Also the name
of the queen of fairies.
(Tania, Tanya)

Tizane [Hungarian]
'A gypsy'. See also
Gitana.

Tobe See **Tobey**

Tobey [Hebrew]
'God is good'.
(Toby, Tobe, Tobi)

Toinette See **Antonia**

Toni See **Antonia**

Tonia See **Antonia**

Topaz [Latin]
'The topaz gem'.

Tourmalina See
Tourmaline

Tourmaline [Srilangarese]
'A carnelian'.
(Tourmalina)

Tracie See **Teresa**

Tracy [Gaelic]
'Battler'. Also der. of
Teresa.
(Tracey)

Traviata [Italian]
'The frail one'.
Traditionally a
courtesan.

Triantafilia [Greek]
'Rose'.

Trilby [Italian]
'A singer who trills'.

Trina [Greek]
'Girl of purity'.

Triphenia See **Tryphena**

Trista [Latin]
'Melancholia; sorrow'.

Trix See **Beatrice**

Trixie See **Beatrice**

Trudie See **Gertrude**

Trudy [Teutonic]
'Loved one'. Also dim. of
Gertrude.
(Trudi, Trudie, Trudey)

Tryphena [Latin]
'The delicate one'.
*(Triphena, Triphenia,
Tryphenia)*

Tuesday [Anglo-Saxon]
'Born on Tuesday'.

Tullia [Gaelic]
'Peaceful one'.

Twyla [Middle English]
'Woven of double
thread'.

Tyne [Old English]
'River'.

Tab [Teutonic]
'The drummer'.
(Tabb, Tabby)

Tabby See **Tab**

Tad See **Thaddeus**

Tadd [Celtic]
'Father'. Also dim. for
Thaddeus and Theodore.
(Tad)

Taddy See **Thaddeus**

Taffy [Celtic]
Welsh form of David.

Taggart [Gaelic]
'Son of the prelate'.

Taillefer See **Telford**

Talbot [French]
'The looter'. One who
lived by his spoils and
pillages.

Talfryn [Welsh]
'Brow of the hill'.

Taliesin [Welsh]
'Radiant brow'.

Tamar [Hebrew]
'Palm tree'.

Tammany See **Thomas**

Tammy See **Thomas**

Tancred [Old German]
'Thoughtful adviser'.

Tangwyn [Welsh]
'Blessed peace'.

Tanner [Anglo-Saxon]
'Leather worker'.

Tanton [Anglo-Saxon]
'From the quiet river
farm'.

Tarleton [Anglo-Saxon]
'Thor's farm'.

Tarrant [Old Welsh]
'Thunder'.

Tate [Anglo-Saxon]
'Cheerful'.
(Tait, Teyte)

Tavey See **Octavius**

Tavis [Celtic]
'Son of David'. Also der.
(Scottish) of Thomas.
(Tavish, Tevis)

Tavish See **Tavis**

Taylor [Anglo-Saxon]
'The Tailor'.
(Tailor)

Teague [Celtic]
'The poet'.

Tearlach See **Charles**

Tearle [Anglo-Saxon]
'Stern, severe one'.

Tecwyn [Welsh]
'Fair and white'.

Ted See **Theodore**

Teddie See **Theodore**

Teddy See **Edward**

Tedmond [Anglo-Saxon]
'King's protector'.

Tedric See **Theodoric**

Telfer See **Telford**

Telfor See **Telford**

Telford [French]
'Iron hewer'.
*(Telfer, Telfor, Telfour,
Taillefer)*

Templeton [Anglo-Saxon]
'Town of the temple'.

Tennyson [Anglo-Saxon]
'Son of Dennis'.
(Tenison, Tennison)

Terence [Latin]
'Smooth, polished and
tender'.
(Terrene, Torrance, Terry)

Terrell See **Terrill**

Terrene See **Terence**

Terrill [Teutonic]
'Follower of Thor'.
*(Terrell, Tirrell, Tyrrell,
Terell, Tirell, Tyrell, Terrel,
Tirrel, Tyrrel)*

Terry See **Terence**

Tevis See **Tavis**

Thad See **Thaddeus**

Thaddeus [Hebrew/Greek]
'Praise to God' (Hebrew)
or 'Courageous and stout
hearted' (Greek).
(Tad, Thad, Taddy)

Thaine [Anglo-Saxon]
'Warrior attendant'. A
military attendant on a
king or ruler.
(Thane, Thayne)

Thatch See **Thatcher**

Thatcher [Anglo-Saxon]
'A thatcher of roofs'.
(Thatch)

Thaw [Anglo-Saxon]
'Ice breaker'. The perfect
party guest.

Thayer [Anglo-Saxon]
'The nation's army'.

Themistocles [Greek]
'Law and right'.

Theobald [Teutonic]
'Bold leader of the people'.
*(Tybalt, Tibbald, Thibaud,
Thibaut, Tioboid)*

Theodore [Greek]
'Gift of God'.
*(Feodor, Feodore, Tudor,
Dore, Ted, Teddie, Teddy)*

Theodoric [Teutonic]
'Ruler of the people'. The
elected leader.
*(Theodorick, Derek, Derrick,
Tedric, Derk, Dirk, Ted,
Teddie, Teddy)*

Theodosius [Greek]
'God given'.

Theon [Greek]
'Godly man'.

Theophilus [Greek]
'Divinely loved'.

Theron [Greek]
'The hunter'.

Thibaud See **Theobald**

Thibaut See **Theobald**

Thomas [Hebrew]
'The twin'. The devoted
brother.
*(Tomas, Tammany, Tam,
Tammy, Thom, Tom,
Tommy, Massey)*

Thor [Scandinavian]
'God of Thunder'. The
ancient Norse God.
(Tor)

Thorald [Scandinavian]
'Thor's ruler'. One who
ruled in the name of the
thunder-god.
*(Torald, Thorold, Terrell,
Tyrell)*

Thorbert [Scandinavian]
'Brilliance of Thor'.
(Torbert)

Thorburn [Scandinavian]
'Thor's bear'.
(Torburn)

Thorfinn See **Torin**

Thorley [Anglo-Saxon]
'From Thor's meadow'.
(Torley)

Thormund [Anglo-Saxon]
'Protected by Thor'.
(Thormond, Thurmond, Tormond, Tormund)

Thorndyke [Anglo-Saxon]
'From the thorny ditch'.

Thorne [Anglo-Saxon]
'From the thorn tree'.

Thornley [Anglo-Saxon]
'From the thorny meadow'.
(Thornly, Thorneley, Thornely)

Thornton [Anglo-Saxon]
'From the thorny place'.

Thorpe [Anglo-Saxon]
'From the small village'.
(Thorp)

Thorstein See **Thurston**

Thurlow [Anglo-Saxon]
'From Thor's hill'.

Thurmond See
Thormund

Thurston [Anglo-Saxon]
'Thor's jewel'.
(Thorstein, Thurstan)

Tibbald See **Theobald**

Tierman [Gaelic]
'Lord and master'. The overlord or lord of the manor.
(Tierney)

Tierney See **Tierman**

Tiffany [French]
'The divine appearance of God'.

Tilden [Anglo-Saxon]
'From the fertile valley'.

Tilford [Anglo-Saxon]
'From the good man's farm'.

Tim See **Timothy**

Timmie See **Timothy**

Timon [Greek]
'Honour, reward, value'.

Timothy [Greek]
'Honouring God'.
(Tim, Timmie, Timmy, Tiomoid)

Tioboid See **Theobald**

Tioboid See **Tobias**

Tiomoid See **Timothy**

Tirell See **Terrill**

Tirrell See **Terrill**

Tito See **Titus**

Titus [Greek/Latin]
'Of the giants' (Greek)
or 'Saved' (Latin).
(Tito)

Tobias [Hebrew]
'God is good'.
*(Tobe, Toby, Tioboid,
Tobit)*

Tobit See **Tobias**

Todd [Latin]
'The fox'.

Toft [Anglo-Saxon]
'A small farm'.

Toland [Anglo-Saxon]
'Owner of taxed land'.

Tom See **Thomas**

Tomkin [Anglo-Saxon]
'Small Thomas'.
(Tomlin)

Tomlin See **Tomkin**

Tommy See **Thomas**

Tony See **Anthony**

Torbert See **Thorbert**

Torburn See **Thorburn**

Torin [Gaelic]
'Chief'.
(Thorfinn)

Torley See **Thorley**

Tormey [Gaelic]
'Thunder spirit'.
(Tormy)

Tormond See **Thormund**

Tormund See **Thormund**

Torquil [Teutonic]
'Thor's pledge'.

Torr [Anglo-Saxon]
'From the tower'.

Torrance [Gaelic]
'From the little hills'.
Also der. of Terence.

Torrance See **Terence**

Tostig [Welsh]
'Sharp'.

Townley [Anglo-Saxon]
'From the town meadow'.
(Townly)

Townsend [Anglo-Saxon]
'From the end of the
town'.

Tracy [Latin]
'Bold and courageous'.

Trahern [Celtic]
'Iron strength'. One who
could bend an iron bar in
his bare hands.
*(Trehern, Trehearn,
Trehearne, Traheam,
Trahearne)*

Travers [Latin]
'From the crossroads'.
(Travis)

Travis See **Travers**

Tredway [Anglo-Saxon]
'Mighty warrior'.

Trefor See **Trevor**

Trelawny [Cornish]
'From the church town'.
(Trelawney)

Tremayne [Celtic]
'From the house in the
rock'.
(Tremaine)

Trent [Latin]
'The torrent'.

Trevelyan [Celtic]
'From Elian's farm'. An
old Cornish name.

Trevor [Gaelic]
'Prudent, wise and
discreet'. One who can be
trusted to keep secrets.
(Trefor)

Trey [Middle English]
'The third'.

Trigg [Scandinavian]
'True and faithful'.

Tripp [Anglo-Saxon]
'The traveller'.

Tristan [Celtic]
'The noisy one'.
(Tristin, Tristen, Drostan)

Tristin See **Tristan**

Tristram [Celtic]
'The sorrowful one'. Do
not confuse with Tristan.

Trowbridge [Anglo-Saxon]
'From the tree bridge'.

Troy [French]
'From the land of the
people with curly hair'.

True [Anglo-Saxon]
'Faithful and loyal'.

Truesdale [Anglo-Saxon]
'The home of the beloved one'.
(Trusdale)

Truman [Anglo-Saxon]
'A faithful follower'. A loyal servant.
(Trueman, Trumane)

Trumane See **Truman**

Trumble [Anglo-Saxon]
'Bold and strong'.

Trusdale See **Truesdale**

Tucker [Anglo-Saxon]
'Cloth thickener'. A var. of Fuller.

Tudor See **Theodore**

Tully [Gaelic]
'Obedient to the will of God'.

Tupper [Anglo-Saxon]
'A sheep raiser'. One who reared and tended sheep.

Turner [Latin]
'Lathe worker'.

Turpin [Scandinavian]
'Thunder like'. Finnish form of Thor.

Tuxford [Scandinavian]
'From the ford of the champion spear thrower'.

Twain [Anglo-Saxon]
'Divided in two'. A co-heir.

Twitchell [Anglo-Saxon]
'From a narrow passageway'.

Twyford [Anglo-Saxon]
'From the twin river'.

Tybalt See **Theobald**

Tye [Anglo-Saxon]
'From the enclosure'.

Tyler [Anglo-Saxon]
'Maker of tiles or bricks'.
(Tiler, Ty)

Tynam [Gaelic]
'Dark; grey'.

Tyrone [Greek]
'The sovereign'.

Tyson [Teutonic]
'Son of the German'.
(Sonny, Ty)

Girls

Uda [Teutonic]
'Prosperous'. A child of
fortune.
(Udella, Udelle)

Udella See **Uda**

Udelle See **Uda**

Ula [Celtic/Teutonic]
'Jewel of the sea' (Celtic);
'The inheritor'

(Teutonic).
(Oola)

Ulima [Arabic]
'The learned'. A woman
wise in counsel.

Ulrica [Teutonic]
'Ruler of all'.
(Ulrika, Rica)

Ultima [Latin]
'The most distant'.

Ulva [Teutonic]
'The she-wolf'. A symbol
of bravery.

Una [Latin]
'One'. The one and only
girl.
(Ona, Oona, Oonagh)

Undine [Latin]
'A wave'. The wave of
water.
(Ondine)

Undine See **Ondine**

Unity [Middle English]
'Unity'.

Urania [Greek]
'Heavenly'. The Muse of
Astronomy.

Urith [Old German]
'Deserving'.

Ursa See **Ursula**

Ursel See **Ursula**

Ursie See **Ursula**

Ursola See **Ursula**

Ursula [Latin]
'The she-bear'.
*(Ursa, Ursel, Ursie, Ursy,
Ursulette, Ursola, Ursule,
Ursuline, Orsa, Orsola)*

Ursule See **Ursula**

Ursulette See **Ursula**

Ursuline See **Ursula**

Udale See **Udell**

Udall See **Udell**

Udell [Anglo-Saxon]
'From the yew tree
valley'.
(Udale, Udall)

Udolf [Anglo-Saxon]
'Prosperous wolf'.

Uilleam See **William**

Uillioc See **Ulysses**

Ulfred [Anglo-Saxon]
'Peace of the wolf'.

Ulger [Anglo-Saxon]
'Courageous wolf
(spearman)'.

Ullock [Anglo-Saxon]
'Sport of the wolf'.

Ulmar See **Ulmer**

Ulmer [Anglo-Saxon]
'Famous wolf'.
(Ulmar)

Ulric [Teutonic]
'Ruler of all'.
(Alric, Ulrich)

Ulysses [Greek]
'The angry one; the
hater'.
(Ulises, Uillioc)

Umberto See **Humbert**

Unwin [Anglo-Saxon]
'The enemy'.

Upton [Anglo-Saxon]
'From the hill farm'.

Upwood [Anglo-Saxon]
'From the hill forest'.

Urban [Latin]
'From the city'. A
townsman.

Uri [Hebrew]
'Light'.

Uriah [Hebrew]
'The Lord is my light; the
Lord's light'.
(Urias, Uriel)

Urias See **Uriah**

Uriel See **Uriah**

Urien [Welsh]
'Town-born'.

Urson See **Orson**

Uzziah [Hebrew]
'Might of the Lord'.

Girls

Vala [Teutonic]
'The chosen one'. Ideal
name for the adopted
daughter.

Valborga [Teutonic]
'Protecting ruler'.
*(Walburga, Walborga,
Valburga)*

Valburga See **Valborga**

Valda [Teutonic]
'Ruler'.
(Walda, Welda)

Valeda See **Valentina**

Valencia See **Valentina**

Valentina [Latin]
'Strong and vigorous'.
(Valentine, Valencia,

Valentia, Valeda, Valida,
Val, Vallie)

Valentine See **Valentina**

Valeria See **Valerie**

Valerie [French]
'Strong'.
(Valeria, Valery, Valory,
Valorie, Valorey, Valora,
Val, Vallie)

Valeska [Slavic]
'Glorious ruler'.
(Waleska)

Valida See **Velda**

Valma [Welsh]
'Mayflower'.
(Valmai)

Valmai See **Valma**

Valona See **Valonia**

Valonia [Latin]
'From the vale'.
(Valona)

Valora See **Valerie**

Valory See **Valerie**

Vancy See **Evangeline**

Vanessa [Greek]
'The butterfly'. A name
also derived by Jonathan
Swift from 'Esther van
Homrigh', one of his
correspondents.
(Van, Vanni, Vannie, Vanny,
Vanna, Vania, Vanya)

Vangie See **Evangeline**

Vania See **Vanessa**

Vannie See **Vanessa**

Vanora See **Genevieve**

Varina [Slavic]
'Stranger'.

Vahsti [Persian]
'Beautiful one'.

Veda [Sanskrit]
'Wisdom and
knowledge'.
(Vedis)

Vedetta See **Vedette**

Vedette [Italian]
'The sentinel'.
(Vedetta)

Vedis See **Veda**

Vega [Arabic]
'The great one'.

Velda [Teutonic]
'Very wise'.
(Valida)

Velika [Slavic]
'The falling one'.
(Velica)

Velma See **Wilhelmina**

Velvet [English]
'Soft as velvet'.

Venetia [Latin]
'Lady of Venice'.

Venita See **Venus**

Ventura [Spanish]
'Happiness and good luck'.

Venus [Latin]
'Loveliness; beauty'. The Goddess of Beauty and Love.
(Venita, Vinita, Vinny, Vinnie)

Vera [Latin]
'Truth'. One who is honest and steadfast.
(Vere, Verena, Verene, Verina, Verine, Verla)

Verbena [Latin]
'The sacred bough'.

Verda [Latin]
'Fresh youth'. The verdant qualities of spring.

Verda See **Verna**

Vere See **Vera**

Verena See **Vera** or **Verna**

Verene See **Vera**

Verity [Latin]
'Truth'.

Verla See **Vera**

Verna [Latin]
'Spring like'.
(Vernice, Vernita, Verneta, Verda, Verena, Vernis, Virna, Virina)

Verna See **Laverne**

Verne See **Laverne**

Vernice See **Verna**

Vernis See **Verna**

Vernita See **Verna**

Verona [Latin]
'Lady of Verona'. Also dim. of Veronica.

Verona See **Veronica**

Veronica [Latin]
'True image'. Also var. of
Bernice.
(Verona, Vonnie, Vonny,
Ronnie, Ronny, and all var.
of *Bernice)*

Veronica See **Bernice**

Vesna [Slavic]
'Spring'.

Vespera [Latin]
'The evening star'.

Vesta [Latin]
'Guardian of the sacred
flame'. A Vestal virgin.
'Melodious one'.

Veta See **Vita**

Vevila [Gaelic]
'Melodious one'.

Vicenta See **Vincentia**

Victoria [Latin]
'The victorious one'.
Attained popularity in
Britain following the long
reign of Queen Victoria.
(Tory, Victorine, Vitoria,
Vittoria, Victorie, Vicki,
Vicky)

Victorie See **Victoria**

Victorine See **Victoria**

Vida [Hebrew]
'Beloved one'. Fem. of
David.

Vidonia [Portuguese]
'Vine branch'.

Vigilia [Latin]
'The alert; vigilant'.

Vignette [French]
'The little vine'.

Villette [French]
'From the village'.

Vina [Spanish]
'From the vineyard'.

Vina See **Alvina** or
Lavinia

Vincentia [Latin]
'The conqueror'. Fem. of
Vincent.
(Vincencia, Vicenta)

Vinia See **Lavinia**

Vinita See **Venus**

Vinnie See **Venus**

Viola See **Violet**

Violante See **Violet**

Violet [Latin]
'Modest flower'. Like the
shy, retiring violet.
*(Viola, Violetta, Violette, Vi,
Iolanthe, Yolanda, Yolande,
Yolanthe, Violante)*

Violetta See **Violet**

Virdis [Latin]
'Fresh, blooming'.

Virgie See **Virginia**

Virgilia [Latin]
'The staff bearer'.

Virginia [Latin]
'The virgin; maidenly
and pure'.
*(Virginie, Virgi, Virgie,
Virgy, Ginger, Ginny,
Ginnie, Jinny)*

Virginie See **Virginia**

Viridis [Latin]
'The green bough'.

Virina See **Verna**

Vita [Latin]
'Life'. One who likes
living.
(Evita, Veta, Vitia)

Vitia See **Vita**

Vitoria See **Victoria**

Vivia See **Vivian**

Vivian [Latin]
'Alive'. Vivid and vibrant
with life.
*(Viviana, Vivien, Vivienne,
Vivienna, Vivyan, Vyvyan,
Viviane, Viviene, Viv, Vivi,
Vivia, Vivie)*

Viviana See **Vivian**

Volante [Latin]
'The flying one'. One
who steps so lightly that
she seems to fly.

Voleta [French]
'A floating veil'
(Voletta)

Von See **Yvonne**

Vonnie See **Veronica**

Vonny See **Veronica**

Vachel [French]
'Little cow'.

Vail [Anglo-Saxon]
'From the valley'.
(Vale, Valle)

Val [Teutonic]
'Mighty power'. Also
dim. for any name
beginning with 'Val'.

Valarian [Latin]
'Healthy'.
(Valarius)

Valarius See **Valarian**

Valdemar [Teutonic]
'Famous ruler'.
(Valdimar, Valdemar)

Valente See **Valentine**

Valentin See **Valentine**

Valentine [Latin]
'Healthy, strong and
valorous'.
*(Valentin, Valentino,
Vailintin, Valente, Valiant)*

Valentino See **Valentine**

Valerian [Latin]
'Strong and powerful' or
'Belonging to Valentine'.

Valiant See **Valentine**

Valle See **Vail**

Vallis [French]
'The Welshman'.

Van [Dutch]
'From' or 'Of'. More
generally used as a prefix
to a surname, but
occasionally found on its
own as a forename.

Vance [Anglo-Saxon]
'From the grain barn'.

Varden [Anglo-Saxon]
'From a green hill'.
(Vardon, Verden, Verdon)

Vardon See **Varden**

Varian [Latin]
'Changeable'.

Vassily [Slavic]
'Unwavering protector'.

Vassily See **Basil**

Vaughan [Celtic]
'The small one'.
(Vaughn, Vawn)

Vere [Latin]
'Faithful and true'. The
loyal one.

Vern See **Vernon**

Verne See **Vernon**

Verner See **Vernon**

Verney [French]
'From the alder grove'.

Vernon [Latin]
'Growing, flourishing'.
As the trees in spring.
(Verne, Verner, Vern)

Verrell [French]
'The honest one'.
(Verrall, Verrill, Verill)

Verrill See **Verrell**

Vick See **Victor**

Victor [Latin]
'The conqueror'.
(Vic, Vick, Victoir)

Vincent See **Victor**

Vinson [Anglo-Saxon]
'Son of Vincent'.

Virge See **Virgil**

Virgil [Latin]
'Staff bearer' or 'Strong
and flourishing'.
(Vergil, Virge, Virgie, Virgy)

Vito [Latin]
'Alive; vital'.

Vivien [Latin]
'Lively one'.
(Vivian, Ninian)

Vladimir [Slavic]
'Royally famous'. A
renowned monarch.

Vladislav [Slavic]
'Glorious ruler'.

Vychan [Welsh]
'Little'.

Girls

Walborga See **Valborga**

Walburga See **Valborga**

Walda See **Valda**

Waleska See **Valeska**

Wallace See **Wallis**

Wallis [Anglo-Saxon]
'The Welshwoman; the stranger'.
(Wallace, Wallie, Wally)

Wally See **Wallis**

Wanda [Teutonic]
'The wanderer'. The restless roamer.
(Wandie, Wandis, Wenda, Wendy, Wendeline)

Wandie See **Wanda**

Wandis See **Wanda**

Wanetta [Anglo-Saxon]
'The pale one'.
(Wanette)

Wanette See **Wanetta**

Warda [Teutonic]
'The guardian'.

Welda See **Valda**

Welma See **Wilhelmina**

Wenda See **Wanda**

Wendeline See **Wanda**

Wendy See **Gwendoline**,
Wanda

Whitney [Old English]
'From the white island'.

Wilf See **Wilfreda**

Wilfreda [Teutonic]
'The peacemaker'. Fem.
of Wilfred.
*(Wilfrieda, Wilfreida,
Freda, Wilf, Freddie)*

Wilhelmina [Teutonic]
'The protectress'. One
who guards resolutely

what is her own.
*(Wilma, Welma, Velma,
Willa, Willie, Willy,
Minnie, Minny, Billie,
Billy, Helma, Mina, Guilla)*

Willa [Anglo-Saxon]
'Desirable'. Also dim. of
Wilhelmina.

Willa See **Billie**,
Wilhelmina

Willie See **Wilhelmina**

Willow [English]
Plant name.

Wilma See **Wilhelmina**

Win See **Edwina**

Wina See **Edwina**

Winifred [Teutonic]
'Peaceful friend'. A
restful person to have
around.
*(Winifrida, Winifreida,
Winifrieda, Winnie, Winny)*

Winifrida See **Winifred**

Winnie See **Edwina** or
Winifred

Winola [Teutonic]
'Gracious friend'.

Winona [American-Indian]
'First born daughter'.
*(Winonah, Wenona,
Wenonah)*

Winsome [English]
'Pleasant, attractive'.

Wren [Old English]
'Wren'.

Wynne [Celtic]
'Fair, white maiden'.
(Win, Wyne)

Wace [Anglo-Saxon]
'A vassal'.

Wade [Anglo-Saxon]
'Mover; wanderer'.

Wadley [Anglo-Saxon]
'From the wanderer's
meadow'.

Wadsworth [Anglo-Saxon]
'From the wanderer's
estate'.

Wagner [Teutonic]
'A waggoner'.

Wainwright [Anglo-Saxon]
'Waggon maker'.

Waite [Anglo-Saxon]
'A guard; a watchman'.

Wake [Anglo-Saxon]
'Alert and watchful'.

Wakefield [Anglo-Saxon]
'From the west field'.

Wakeley [Anglo-Saxon]
'From the wet meadow'.

Wakeman [Anglo-Saxon]
'Watchman'.

Walby [Anglo-Saxon]
'From the ancient walls'.

Walcott [Anglo-Saxon]
'Cottage dweller'.

Waldemar See **Valdemar**

Walden [Anglo-Saxon]
'Dweller in the valley in
the woods'.

Waldo [Teutonic]
'The ruler'.

Waldron [Teutonic]
'Strength of the raven'.

Walker [Anglo-Saxon]
'The walker'.

Wallace [Anglo-Saxon]
'The Welshman; the
stranger'. *(Wallis,
Walsh, Welch, Welsh,
Wallache, Wallie, Wally)*

Wallache See **Wallace**

Walmond [Teutonic]
'Mighty protector'.
(Walmund)

Walsh See **Wallace**

Walter [Teutonic]
'Mighty warrior'.
*(Walther, Walters, Wat,
Wally, Walt)*

Walton [Anglo-Saxon]
'From the forest town'.

Walworth [Anglo-Saxon]
'From the stranger's
farm'.

Walwyn [Anglo-Saxon]
'Friendly stranger'.

Warburton [Anglo-Saxon]
'From the castle town'.

Ward [Anglo-Saxon]
'Watchman; guardian'.

Wardell [Anglo-Saxon]
'From the hill watch'.

Warden [Anglo-Saxon]
'The guardian'.

Wardley [Anglo-Saxon]
'From the watchman's
meadow'.

Ware [Anglo-Saxon]
'Prudent one'. A very
astute person.

Warfield [Anglo-Saxon]
'From the field by the
weir'.

Warford [Anglo-Saxon]
'From the ford by the
weir'.

Waring See **Warren**

Warley [Anglo-Saxon]
'From the meadow by the
weir'.

Warmund [Teutonic]
'Loyal protector'
(Warmond)

Warner [Teutonic]
'Protecting army'.
(Werner, Verner)

Warren [Teutonic]
'The gamekeeper'. One
who looked after the
game preserves.

Warton [Anglo-Saxon]
'From the farm by the
weir'.

Warwick [Anglo-Saxon]
'Strong fortress'.
(Warrick)

Washburn [Anglo-Saxon]
'From the river in spate'.

Washington [Anglo-Saxon]
'From the keen eyed one's farm'.

Watford [Anglo-Saxon]
'From the hurdle by the ford'.

Watkins [Anglo-Saxon]
'Son of Walter'.
(Watson)

Watson See **Watkins**

Waverley [Anglo-Saxon]
'The meadow by the aspen trees'.
(Waverly)

Wayland [Anglo-Saxon]
'From the pathway near the highway'.

Wayne [Teutonic]
'Waggon maker'.
(Waine, Wain)

Webb [Anglo-Saxon]
'A weaver'.
(Webber, Weber, Webster)

Webber See **Webb**

Webley [Anglo-Saxon]
'From the weaver's meadow'.

Webster See **Webb**

Weddell [Anglo-Saxon]
'From the wanderer's hill'.

Welborne [Anglo-Saxon]
'From the spring by the brook'.
(Welbourne)

Welby [Anglo-Saxon]
'From the farm by the spring'.

Welch See **Wallace**

Weldon [Anglo-Saxon]
'From the well on the hill'.

Welford [Anglo-Saxon]
'From the ford by the spring'.

Wellington [Anglo-Saxon]
'From the rich man's farm'.

Wells [Anglo-Saxon]
'From the spring'.

Welsh See **Wallace**

Welton [Anglo-Saxon] 'From the farm by the spring'.

Wenceslaus [Slavic] 'Wreath of glory'. *(Wenceslas)*

Wendell [Teutonic] 'The wanderer'. *(Wendel)*

Wentworth [Anglo-Saxon] 'Estate belonging to the white haired one'.

Werner See **Warner**

Wesley [Anglo-Saxon] 'From the west meadow'. *(Wesleigh, Westleigh)*

Westbrook [Anglo-Saxon] 'From the west brook'.

Westby [Anglo-Saxon] 'From the homestead in the west'.

Westcott [Anglo-Saxon] 'From the west cottage'.

Westleigh See **Wesley**

Weston [Anglo-Saxon] 'From the west farm'.

Wetherell [Anglo-Saxon] 'From the sheep hill'. *(Wetherill, Wetherall)*

Wetherill See **Wetherell**

Wetherley [Anglo-Saxon] 'From the sheep meadow'. *(Wetherly)*

Weylin [Celtic] 'Son of the wolf'.

Wharton [Anglo-Saxon] 'Farm in the hollow'.

Wheatley [Anglo-Saxon] 'From the wheat meadow'.

Wheeler [Anglo-Saxon] 'The wheel maker'.

Whistler [Anglo-Saxon] 'The whistler; the piper'.

Whitby [Anglo-Saxon] 'From the white farmstead'.

Whitcomb [Anglo-Saxon] 'From the white hollow'. *(Whitcombe)*

Whitelaw [Anglo-Saxon] 'From the white hill'.

Whitfield [Anglo-Saxon]
'From the white field'.

Whitford [Anglo-Saxon]
'From the white ford'.

Whitley [Anglo-Saxon]
'From the white
meadow'.

Whitlock [Anglo-Saxon]
'White haired one'.

Whitman [Anglo-Saxon]
'White haired man'.

Whitmore [Anglo-Saxon]
'From the white moor'.

Whitney [Anglo-Saxon]
'From the white island'.
(Whitny, Witney, Witny)

Whittaker [Anglo-Saxon]
'One who dwells in the
white field'.
(Whitaker)

Wiatt See **Guy**

Wickham [Anglo-Saxon]
'From the enclosed field
by the village'.
(Wykeham)

Wickley [Anglo-Saxon]
'From the village
meadow'.

Wilbur [Teutonic]
'Resolute and brilliant'.
A determined and clever
person.

Wildon [Old English]
'From the wooden hill'.

Wiley See **William**

Wilford [Anglo-Saxon]
'From the willow ford'.

Wilfred [Teutonic]
'Firm peace maker'.
Peace, but not at any
price.
*(Wilfrid, Fred, Freddie,
Freddy)*

Wilhelm See **William**

Wilkes See **William**

Wilkie See **William**

Will See **William**

Willard [Anglo-Saxon]
'Resolute and brave'.

Willet See **William**

William [Teutonic]
'Determined protector'.
The strong guardian.
*(Wiley, Wilkie, Wilkes,
Liam, Wilson, Williamson,*

Willis, Wilhelm, Willet,
Will, Willie, Willy, Bill,
Billie, Billy, Gwylim,
Uilleam, Uilliam)

Williamson See **William**

Willis See **William**

Willoughby [Anglo-Saxon]
'From the farmstead by
the willows'.

Wilmer [Teutonic]
'Resolute and famous'.
One renowned for his
firmness.

Wilmot [Teutonic]
'Resolute mind'. One
who knows his own mind.

Wilson See **William**
Also 'Son of William'
(Anglo-Saxon).

Wilton [Anglo-Saxon]
'From the farm by the
well'.

Winchell [Anglo-Saxon]
'The bend in the road'.

Windsor [Anglo-Saxon]
'The boundary bank'.

Winfield [Anglo-Saxon]
'From a friend's field'.

Winfred [Anglo-Saxon]
'Peaceful friend'.
(Winifred)

Wingate [Anglo-Saxon]
'From the winding lane'.

Winifred See **Winfred**

Winslow [Anglo-Saxon]
'From a friend's hill'.

Winston [Anglo-Saxon]
'From a friend's estate'.

Winter [Anglo-Saxon]
'Born during winter
months'.

Winthrop [Teutonic]
'From a friendly village'.

Winton [Anglo-Saxon]
'From a friend's farm'.

Winwald See **Winward**

Winward [Anglo-Saxon]
'From the friendly forest'.
(Winwald)

Wirt See **Wirth**

Wirth [Teutonic]
'The master'.
(Wirt)

Witt See **Witter**

Witter [Teutonic]
'Wise warrior'.
(Witt)

Witton [Teutonic]
'From a wise man's
farm'.

Wolcott [Anglo-Saxon]
'From the cottage of the
wolf'. *(Wulcott)*

Wolfe [Teutonic]
'A wolf'. A man of
courage.

Wolfgang [Teutonic]
'The advancing wolf'. A
warrior in the vanguard
of the army.

Wolfram [Teutonic]
'Respected and feared'.

Woodley [Anglo-Saxon]
'From the forest
meadow'.
(Woodly)

Woodrow [Anglo-Saxon]
'From the hedge in the
wood'.

Woodruff [Anglo-Saxon]
'Forest bailiff'.

Woodward [Anglo-Saxon]
'Forest guardian'.

Woolsey [Anglo-Saxon]
'Victorious wolf'.
(Wolsey, Wolseley)

Wooster See **Worcester**

Worcester [Anglo-Saxon]
'Camp in the forest of the
alder trees'.
(Wooster)

Wordsworth [Anglo-
Saxon]
'From the farm of the
wolf'.

Worrall [Anglo-Saxon]
'From the loyal man's
manor'.
(Worrell, Worrill)

Worrill See **Worrall**

Worth [Anglo-Saxon]
'The farmstead'.

Worton [Anglo-Saxon]
'From the vegetable
farm'.

Wray [Scandinavian]
'Dweller in the house on
the corner'.

Wren [Celtic]
'The chief'.

Wright [Anglo-Saxon]
'Craftsman in woodwork;
a carpenter'.

Wulfstan [Old English]
'Wolf stone'.

Wyatt See **Guy**

Wybert [Old English]
'Battle famous'.

Wyborn [Scandinavian]
'Warrior bear'.
(Wyborne)

Wycliff [Anglo-Saxon]
'From the white cliff'.

Wylie [Anglo-Saxon]
'The enchanter; the
beguiler'.

Wyman [Anglo-Saxon]
'The warrior'.

Wymer [Anglo-Saxon]
'Renowned in battle'.

Wyndham [Anglo-Saxon]
'From the village with the
winding path'.
(Windham)

Wynford [Welsh]
'White torrent'.

Wynn [Celtic]
'The fair one'.

Wystan See **Wystand**

Wystand [Old English]
'Battle stone'.
(Wystan)

Wythe [Anglo-Saxon]
'From the dwelling by the
willow tree'.

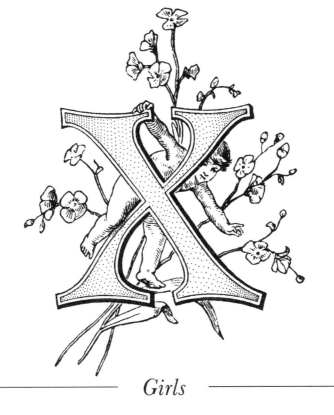

Girls

Xanthe [Greek]
'Golden blonde'.

Xanthippe [Greek]
The wife of Socrates.

Xaverie [Aramaic]
'Bright'.

Xaviera [Spanish]
'Owner of the home'.

Xena [Greek]
'Hospitality'.
(Xenia, Xene, Zenia)

Xene See **Xena**

Xenia See **Xena**

Ximena [Greek]
'Heroine'.

Xylia [Greek]
'From the woods'.
(Xylona)

Xylona See **Xylia**

Xanthus [Latin]
'Golden haired'.

Xavier [Spanish/Arabic]
'New house owner'
(Spanish) or 'Bright'
(Arabic). *(Javier)*

Xenophon [Greek]
'Strong sounding'.

Xenos [Greek]
'The stranger'.

Xerxes [Persian]
'The king'.

Ximenes See **Simon**

Xylon [Greek]
'From the forest'.

Girls

Yasmin See **Jasmin**

Yasmina See **Jasmin**

Yasmine See **Jasmine**

Yedda [Anglo-Saxon]
'The singer'. One with a
melodious voice.

Yerusha See **Jerusha**

Yetta [Anglo-Saxon]
'To give, the giver'. Also
dim. of Henrietta.

Yetta See **Henrietta**

Yevetta See **Yvonne**

Ynes See **Agnes**

Ynez See **Agnes**

Yolanda See **Iolanthe** or **Violet**

Yolande See **Iolanthe** or **Violet**

Yolanthe See **Violet**

Yosepha See **Josephine**

Ysabel See **Isabel**

Yseult See **Isolde**

Yvetta See **Yvonne**

Yvette See **Yvonne**

Yvona See **Yvonne**

Yvonne [French]
'Archer with the yew bow'.
(Yvette, Yvetta, Yvona, Yevetta, Yevette, Ivonne, Von, Vonnie)

Boys

Yale [Teutonic/Anglo-Saxon]
'The one who pays' (Teutonic) — the vanquished; or 'From the corner of the land' (Anglo-Saxon).

Yancy [American Indian]
'The Englishman'. Name given to settlers in New England and subsequently became Yankee.

Yardley [Old English]
'From the enclosed meadow'.

Yates [Anglo-Saxon]
'The dweller at the gates'.

Yehudi [Hebrew]
'Praise be the Lord'.

Yeoman [Anglo-Saxon]
'The tenant farmer'.

Ynyr [Welsh]
'Honour'.

Yorick See **York**

York [Latin/Anglo-Saxon/Celtic]
'Boar estate' (Anglo-Saxon); 'Sacred tree'

(Latin) or 'Yew tree
estate' (Celtic).
(Yorke, Yorick)

Yul [Mongolian]
'Beyond the horizon'.

Yule See **Yules**

Yules [Anglo-Saxon]
'Born at Christmas'.
(Yule)

Yves See **Ives**

Girls

Zabrina [Anglo-Saxon]
'Noble maiden'.

Zada [Arabic]
'Lucky one'. Fortune's
favourite.

Zamira [Hebrew]
'Song'.

Zandra See **Alexandra**

Zaneta See **Jane**

Zara [Hebrew]
'Brightness of dawn'.
Also der. of Sarah.

Zara See **Sarah**

Zaria See **Sarah**

Zea [Latin]
'Ripened grain'.

Zebada [Hebrew]
'Gift of the Lord'.

Zelda See **Grizelda**

Zele See **Zelia**

Zelia [Greek]
'Zealous one'. One with a true devotion to duty.
(Zele, Zelie, Zelina)

Zelie See **Zelia**

Zelina See **Zelia**

Zelma See **Anselma**

Zena [Greek]
'The hospitable one'.

Zena See **Zenobia** or **Zian**

Zenaida See **Zenobia**

Zenda See **Zenobia**

Zenia See **Zenobia**

Zenina See **Zenobia**

Zenna See **Zenobia**

Zennie See **Zenobia**

Zenobia [Greek]
'Zeus gave life'.
(Zena, Zenaida, Zenda, Zenna, Zenia, Zenina, Zennie, Zenorbie)

Zenorbie See **Zenobia**

Zephirah [Hebrew]
'Dawn'.

Zera [Hebrew]
'Seeds'.

Zerelda [Old German]
'Armoured warrior maid'.

Zerla See **Zerlina**

Zerlina [Teutonic]
'Serene beauty'.
(Zerline, Zerla)

Zerlinda [Hebrew]
'Beautiful as the dawn'.

Zerline See **Zerlina**

Zetta [Anglo-Saxon]
'Sixth born'. The sixth letter of the Greek alphabet.
(Zitao)

Zeva [Greek]
'Sword'.

Zia [Latin]
'Kind of grain'.

Zian [Hebrew]
'Abundance'.
(Zinah, Zena)

Zilla [Hebrew]
'Shadow'.
(Zillah)

Zilpah [Hebrew]
'Dropping'.

Zinah See **Zian**

Zinnia [Latin]
'The zinnia flower'.
(Zinia)

Zippora [Hebrew]
'Trumpet' or 'Sparrow'.
(Zipporah)

Zita See **Teresa** or **Zetta**

Zitao See **Zetta**

Zoë [Greek]
'Life'.

Zofeyah [Hebrew]
'God·sees'.

Zohara [Hebrew]
'The bright child'.

Zona [Latin]
'A girdle'. The belt of
Orion.
(Zonie)

Zonie See **Zona**

Zora [Latin]
'The dawn'.
*(Zorina, Zorine, Zorana,
Zorah)*

Zorana See **Zora**

Zorina See **Zora**

Zorine See **Zora**

Zosima [Greek]
'Wealthy woman'.

Zsa See **Susan**

Zsa-Zsa See **Susan**

Zuleika [Arabic]
'Fair'.

Zach See **Zacharias**

Zachaeus [Aramaic]
'Pure'.

Zachariah See **Zacharias**

Zacharias [Hebrew]
'The Lord has
remembered'.
(Zachariah, Zachary, Zach, Zack)

Zachary See **Zacharias**

Zadok [Hebrew]
'The righteous one'.
(Zaloc)

Zaloc See **Zadok**

Zane See **John**

Zared [Hebrew]
'The ambush'.

Zebedee See **Zebediah**

Zebediah [Hebrew]
'Gift of the Lord'.
(Zebedee)

Zebulon [Hebrew]
'The dwelling place'.
(Lonny, Zeb)

Zechariah [Hebrew]
'The Lord is renowned'.

Zedekiah [Hebrew]
'The Lord's justice'.

Zeeman [Dutch]
'The sailor'.

Zeke See **Ezekiel**

Zelig [Teutonic]
'Blessed one'.

Zelotes [Greek]
'The zealous one'.

Zenas [Greek]
'Living being'.

Zeno [Greek]
'Stranger'.

Zeus [Greek]
'Father of the gods'.

Zuriel [Hebrew]
'The Lord is my rock and
foundation'.